CW00546719

HEAD
NORTH

HEAD NORTH

A Rallying Cry for a
More Equal Britain

Andy Burnham &
Steve Rotheram

With Liam Thorp

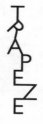

First published in Great Britain in 2024 by Trapeze
an imprint of The Orion Publishing Group Ltd
Carmelite House, 50 Victoria Embankment
London EC4Y 0DZ

An Hachette UK Company

1 3 5 7 9 10 8 6 4 2

ISBN (Hardback) 978 1 3987 1973 6
ISBN (eBook) 978 1 3987 1975 0
ISBN (Audio) 978 1 3987 1976 7

Typeset at The Spartan Press Ltd,
Lymington, Hants

Printed and bound in Great Britain by Clays Ltd,
Elcograf S.p.A.

MIX
Paper from
responsible sources
FSC® C104740

www.orionbooks.co.uk

Dedicated to

Marie-France, Jimmy, Rosie, Annie,
Eileen, Roy, Nick and John

Sandra, Steven, Haylie, Samantha, Mum, David,
Susan, Dorothy, Gail, Paul, Elaine and Robbie

Without you all, none of this
would have been possible.

Contents

Contents

Prologue

It was on a spring evening in March 2016, in a pub on Horseferry Road after a House of Commons vote, when we finally shook hands on something we had been mulling over for months: to leave Westminster together, head north and build something different from the outside.

For us it was a momentous decision. When we were growing up, if someone had told us we would one day become Members of Parliament, we would have struggled to believe it. If they had followed it up by saying we would one day throw it all away and walk out of Parliament, it would have blown our minds.

This is the story of why we did it.

Although we were born just three miles apart on the outskirts of Liverpool, and had similar family backgrounds and formative influences, the paths that took us to Parliament were very different. One ran through the Falklands and the building sites of the North West; the other through the cloisters of Cambridge University and the connected world of London. Two completely different journeys reflecting the two worlds of Britain and the parallel lives people here lead. But they had the same starting point: a sense of injustice about the way our part of the country and its people are treated. Those paths eventually crossed in 2008, when Liverpool celebrated its year as European Capital of Culture. Having never met before, we ended up bumping into each other almost every week at the many events taking place across the city. It was a hushed conversation in Liverpool Anglican Cathedral in early 2009, as we waited for a delayed funeral to start, which was to change everything.

'Just giving you the heads up,' whispered Lord Mayor Steve Rotheram into the ear of Culture Secretary Andy Burnham. 'You're about to get an

invite to the twentieth anniversary memorial service of the Hillsborough disaster at Anfield.'

From then on, two paths were one. We became utterly focused on what had brought us into politics in the first place: securing justice for our people and our place. Perhaps because of our different life journeys, we became quite an effective double act. However, it was the experience of taking our fight into the heart of the establishment, and the lid we lifted on the running of the country, which gave us clarity: the Westminster system was our problem and, in its current form, could never be our solution. It had created the conditions for injustices to go uncovered and the North–South divide to become so entrenched.

Head North *is half-memoir, half-manifesto: the first part very much informs the second. We want to take you on our journey up to that 2016 handshake in the pub and through the eight years beyond, so that you can understand why we think and feel as we do and why, in the second half, we propose our ten changes for the country with the conviction that we do. You really do need to know that, if Peter Hain had not made a mistake with his election expenses, none of this would have happened and this book would never have been written. That is how random Westminster is. It is neither programmed nor structured to deliver the social change the country needs.*

But Head North *is also an invitation to join us. It is a prompt to anyone, in any part of the UK, who feels frustrated about the position the country is in, to do what we did: to move away from the mindset that Westminster is the only show in town and start thinking about what a different political system could look like; one built with the interests of your region or nation at its heart. Westminster remains an antiquated world into which degrees of democracy were introduced as the franchise was extended. But, fundamentally, it remains the same: a system built to concentrate power in the hands of the already-powerful and that much has not changed through the centuries. This over-concentration of political power in one place in too few hands is the main reason why Britain is one of the most politically centralised and economically unbalanced countries in the developed world. In our view, it is also the underlying explanation for more widespread failure.*

As we write this, we can see evidence of a country that doesn't work for most people all around us. Raw sewage in our rivers and on our beaches. Chaos on our railways. Energy bills beyond the means of ordinary people. We watch the dramatisation of the Post Office scandal on our TV screens; we read about the Infected Blood Inquiry – and all we hear are echoes of Hillsborough and a pattern that keeps on repeating.

Infrastructure that doesn't work for anyone.

Injustices left standing for decades.

Inequality between people and places.

These things are no accident. They are the product of a political system that allows itself to be manipulated by powerful vested interests. It begs the question: how has it stood for so long?

One answer is divide and rule. As you will read, the government tried, without success, to separate Liverpool and Manchester in the middle of the Covid-19 pandemic. It is a time-honoured tactic with the establishment prepared to play public opinion against parts of the North of England, Northern Ireland, Wales or Scotland whenever it has suited them. They do it because they fear nothing more than the regions and nations uniting in common cause against a system that doesn't have their interests at heart. So why don't we do that?

Head North is a rallying cry for a more equal Britain. It proposes a ten-point plan to rewire the country, taking power out of the Westminster system and putting it into the hands of people and places across our islands. We hope it provides a platform around which people who vote for all parties, but feel the same as us, can coalesce, campaign and build a unifying movement for change. While we are aligned in our vision for the North and the country as a whole, our individual stories are of course very different. From this point on, the text will be split into two distinct voices. Steve's voice will be set in **bold** *text, while Andy's voice will be set in non-bold text. Where we are speaking together, those sections will appear in italics, like this Prologue.*

1

Our Journey

1
The Day That Changed Everything

I can remember exactly where I was, who I was with and what I was doing on the night of Friday, 14 April 1989. I was in the smoke-filled back room of the Cherry Tree in Culcheth with my brother, Nick, and friends John Hunt and Stephen Turner, drinking pints of Tetley's bitter and Castlemaine XXXX and listening to 'Panic' by The Smiths, which always seemed to be playing on the jukebox. The Cherry is more of a gastropub these days but, back then, it had pool tables, a dartboard and a bloke who came around selling seafood out of a basket. Cockles always seemed like a good idea on a Friday night but never with a spinning head in the early hours of Saturday. On that particular night, I can remember how good it felt to be in the Cherry's warm embrace. I was nineteen years old, home from university and enjoying some brief respite from a severe case of imposter syndrome which had been afflicting me during my first two terms at Cambridge University.

Culcheth is located halfway between Liverpool and Manchester. It became home because, a year after I was born in Old Roan near Aintree, my dad's promotion within the old Post Office took him to Dial House in Manchester city centre. Not wanting to live all the way over there, mum Eileen and dad Roy randomly decided on Culcheth because Roy had once spent the day there working at the little telephone exchange over the road from the Cherry and liked the feel of the place.

Although Culcheth leant more towards Manchester than Liverpool, the back room was full, as usual, of people in Liverpool

7

shirts. John's uncle Roger, hero of the Kop and World Cup winner in 1966, had been born in nearby Glazebury and lived a couple of streets away from the Cherry, as did former Liverpool goalkeeper Tommy Lawrence, whose daughter Jayne I had once taken home to meet the family. To this day, they have never let me live it down. The Burnhams were the only match-going Everton family in an otherwise Liverpool-affiliated village.

On that warm April night, there was only one topic of conversation: the two FA Cup semi-finals to be played the next day with a simultaneous 3 p.m. kick-off. We would be travelling to Villa Park in Birmingham to watch Everton take on Norwich, while my friend Stephen (or Ste, as we all called him) was off to Sheffield to watch Liverpool play Nottingham Forest at Hillsborough, an exact repeat of the same semi-final from 1988. Among the excitement, there was already a note of anxiety.

'I can't believe they've put you in there again,' I remember saying to Ste. 'They' meaning the FA and 'there' meaning the Leppings Lane end. You would often feel unsafe at football matches in the 80s but Hillsborough was the worst and we all knew it. 'I know,' he replied. He was nervous about it.

I had been going to watch Liverpool FC play since the age of eleven. Incredibly, I used to make my own way to Anfield at that age; nothing could stop me. I will never forget the smell as the ground neared. It was a heady blend of fried onions, hotdogs, Higson's ale, cigarette smoke and flatulence. Then came the anticipation of climbing upstairs, and the excitement of walking out into the stadium, leaving behind the greyness of the gritty streets to be met with the vivid green of the hallowed Anfield turf. As a youngster, I would watch matches in the legendary Boys' Pen, a section of the ground where lots of young lads would congregate before they were old enough to transition into other parts of the stadium, although some of them would find clever ways to climb up into the adult sections. The kids in there were tough and the cage had fencing and barbed wire all around it. But it was cheap at about 30p a ticket, with a great atmosphere. This is where I fell in love with the beautiful game.

As I got older, I started to follow the team home and away. I was fortunate enough to witness some of the greatest moments in our rich and storied history. I watched us win our first European Cup and an array of domestic silverware. I saw legends like Kevin Keegan and Kenny Dalglish at their magisterial best. I visited grounds across the country and abroad I'd only ever seen on TV. It was a hell of a ride. By the time I was a young man, going to watch Liverpool home and away was a huge part of my life. Even my meagre weekly income of £16.50 didn't stop me.

At the time, I was working on building sites. I had to make sure I had earned enough money each week to help my mum out, go for a night out with my mates and go to the match at the weekend. If a new Jam record was due for release, then it was essential I had enough to purchase it on the very day it was out. And, of course, I had to be able to buy the right clothes because matchday fashion was a big deal, particularly in Liverpool. Even though me and my friends didn't have a lot of money, we would save up to make sure we had the latest T-shirts made by Fred Perry, Sergio Tacchini, Lacoste and Fila, smart jeans and the obligatory Adidas trainers. You wanted to look good at the match. It was as important as the bands you followed. Because Liverpool were perennially in European competition, those that travelled abroad would return with the latest European fashions. They were the real stand-outs on the terraces.

In April 1988, a year before the disaster, some friends and I went to watch Liverpool play Nottingham Forest in the semi-final of the FA Cup at Hillsborough Stadium, the home of Sheffield Wednesday. The same cup competition, the same stage and the same stadium. It was a horrible experience. We had made our way into the Leppings Lane end of the ground, through the infamous tunnel and into the central pens. It quickly became uncomfortably packed full of Liverpool supporters. With me on the terraces that day was a friend called Donnie. He was a strapping bloke from the Royal Navy who was covered in tattoos. I had been working on building sites for a decade at this point so I was pretty fit and strong myself. Despite that, both of us were regularly lifted off our feet during the match, unable to control our own movements. Occasionally, we pinned our knees painfully against a metal barrier to try to avoid the pressure from the crowd behind us. It was grim and dangerous.

I had been in the central pens of the Leppings Lane end the year before to watch Everton play Sheffield Wednesday in a third round FA Cup game. It was two days after my eighteenth birthday and a surprise second interview at Cambridge, having spectacularly failed the first at St Catharine's College and been scooped up out of 'the pool' by Fitzwilliam College.

The afternoon of 9 January 1988 remains the worst I have ever spent at a football match. I don't remember much of the action. I spent the entirety of the second half with my eyes fixed on the back of my dad's and younger brother John's heads, desperate not to lose sight of them in the crush. I had my chest pressed up against people, struggling to breathe at points, just desperate for it to be over. Peter Reid's eighty-first-minute equaliser only made matters worse. As we walked out of the ground, my dad did something that day that I had never seen him do before and never have since: he sat down on the kerbside to recover his breath.

So, nobody in the Cherry Tree on the evening of Friday, 14 April 1989 could understand why this stadium had again been chosen by the FA, with Liverpool supporters in the same section of the ground where they had experienced problems the year before and which we all knew to be dangerous.

It was a lovely spring morning on the 15th and a group of us met at the Carters Arms pub in Kirkby, not far from where I lived, ready to get on the coach to Sheffield. There were about fifty of us and the atmosphere was great. I was twenty-seven years old. On that day, we were all full of optimism. Everyone was having a beer, playing cards, telling jokes and singing songs. We were buzzing for the match and knew we had a very good chance of beating a strong Nottingham Forest side, with the potential of then meeting Everton in an all-Merseyside FA Cup Final.

Liverpool were frequent visitors to the twin towers of Wembley for finals so travelling to big football matches, surrounded by friends, was about as good as it got. I loved every second of it. The weather continued to improve as we travelled, turning from a bright morning into a balmy afternoon as we arrived in Sheffield. We got off the coach and walked up the road towards the stadium. We had visited just the year before when we'd beaten Nottingham Forest in that year's semi-final, so we knew what to expect. We were in a celebratory mood, contrary to what others would later claim. The previous year we had been stopped by stewards and had our tickets checked. But that didn't happen this time. No one checked anything.

It was bright and breezy as I set off with my dad, Roy, and brothers, Nick and John, for the M6 junction at the Thelwall Viaduct and the straightforward drive down to Villa Park, a ground you can see from the motorway. We had beaten Sheffield Wednesday there three years before and had spent the journey listening to an obscure indie band called The June Brides on the car stereo. When it came to Everton, we were a superstitious lot and insisted on a repeat performance, despite my dad's protestations of not wanting to listen to 'that shite' again.

In the mid-80s, Everton were arguably the best team in Europe and, although we had dropped off a little by 1989, we still had good players like Pat Nevin and Tony Cottee. On the journey down, we were unusually optimistic about our chances. We were facing a weaker team in Norwich and were confident of getting a chance to take our revenge in a second all-Merseyside FA Cup Final.

We met my uncle Roger, who lived in the Midlands, in a pub on the outskirts of Birmingham. We stood outside in the fresh spring air, enjoyed a quick pint of Banks's in a plastic glass and then started our walk to Villa Park – a classic semi-final ground whose playing surface, I reminded everyone, I had invaded with joy three years before when a Graeme Sharp volley hit the net.

As we approached the stadium, things didn't feel right. I had been to a lot of football matches but this was different. Usually, queues formed feeding the turnstiles with a steady flow of fans, but people were just milling about without any recognisable organisation from South Yorkshire Police. We were standing in the area outside the stadium and not moving at all. As other supporters joined behind us, it became crowded, tight and claustrophobic. Occasionally, a police officer on horseback would bark out instructions to try to get people into some sort of order. But it was difficult to hear anything with the huge numbers now congregated and impossible to move freely. It was getting close to kick-off and people were asking what on earth was going on. The few mounted police officers in black coats were forcing us in one direction or another but we couldn't move. The turnstiles weren't coping with the throng and were processing just a trickle of the thousands stuck outside. We were about twenty yards from the turnstiles but pinned into position. People's reactions started to turn from just being annoyed to getting quite anxious.

I struck up a conversation with some lads who were standing near to me about the chaos. I asked them which part of the ground they were in. They had two tickets for the Leppings Lane end and one for the West Stand Upper. My own ticket was for the Leppings Lane and, having experienced that place the year before, I wasn't thrilled about being in there again. I asked the lads if they wanted to swap tickets so they could all be together and they agreed. I took the one ticket for the stand. At least I'll have a seat, I thought.

The intense claustrophobia we were feeling then suddenly

lifted. The concertina gate at the side of the stadium had been opened and people started to flock through it. It was such a relief as I felt fresh air and space. I walked in with a few minutes to go until kick-off and saw the tunnel that took people down to pens three and four. I found my way upstairs to my seat in the West Stand Upper, where I was about sixteen rows back from the front. Everything appeared to be back to normal: fans were finding their seats to get the best possible view, as the noise levels, pre-match atmosphere and anticipation grew. There was a wall at the front of the upper tier and I instantly started to notice a few people being pulled up from the terrace below. I thought nothing of it. This used to happen on occasions at matches as people climbed up to be with their mates. But then I noticed more and more people being helped up. Something was different.

The match at Villa Park was going to plan. Everton were 1–0 up at half-time after a scrappy goal from Pat Nevin. We were comfortably in control and the blue half of the Holte End was in good voice. But within minutes of the second half starting, it fell eerily silent. A message had flashed up suddenly on the old scoreboard: 'Six dead at Hillsborough'. It makes me shiver to think of it now. A chill whipped around the stadium and I felt a sickness in my stomach, instantly recalling our own experiences in the Leppings Lane end the year before. My thoughts turned to the lads I had been with in the Cherry Tree the night before, particularly my close mate Ste. The second half of the match became something of a blur, as rumours circulated of rising casualty numbers. We just wanted to get out and find out if our friends at Hillsborough were still alive.

I could now see people climbing over the fences that caged them into the pens below us but still didn't appreciate the unfolding tragedy just yards away due to our elevated position. The next thing we saw was the referee calling both teams off the pitch. I was still a bit confused as to the extent of the situation. Then a child who had managed to climb onto the pitch suddenly collapsed in front of us. This is when I knew something terrible was happening beneath us. More and more people started to get onto the pitch or were being lifted up into our section from below. We could see Liverpool fans using the advertising hoardings to carry fans who were injured across the pitch, while many of those charged with crowd safety stood idly by.

There was an announcement from the managers of the two teams, Kenny Dalglish and Brian Clough, that the match had been abandoned. By now, the whole pitch was a sea of frantic activity as Liverpool fans fought to assist the injured and the dying. It was so surreal. People started to leave the ground. The next thing I knew, as we made our way down the stairs, was merging with those that had been in the Leppings Lane. I could see their faces were contorted with pain and horror at what they had experienced or witnessed. Some were saying: 'There are people dead in there.' Somebody outside the ground had a transistor radio and there were reports that people inside the ground had in fact died. A cloud of collective gloom overcame us. I was having conversations with people I had never met before about an unimaginable tragedy.

There were no mobile phones in those days so everyone was relying on people with small transistor radios for information. It came in fragments and it was agonising. When the referee blew the final whistle, there were no scenes of jubilation like we had seen at other Everton semi-finals in the 80s. Instead, we silently streamed out of the stadium and headed back to our car. I remember crossing paths on our way out with ITV commentator Jim Rosenthal. He was saying in some distress to a colleague: 'I can't believe it, I can't believe what's happened, it's terrible.' If our mood wasn't sombre enough, it was completely black by that point.

As we exited the Hillsborough Stadium, there was a road full of terraced houses and already they had queues forming outside them. The people of Sheffield had thrown their doors open and were allowing the Liverpool fans to call loved ones back home to let them know they were safe. The fans were leaving a bit of money in their homes to say thank you, but the woman whose phone I used wouldn't take it from me. She just wanted to help. I phoned my mum. 'Mum, I'm fine, but something terrible has happened at the footy.' I also told her that I had just bumped into two brothers, Darryl and Scott, who lived near us. 'Can you tell Doreen [their mum] that I've seen them and that they are safe?' To the day she died, Doreen thanked me every time she saw me for passing on the message that her kids were alive. She said it was the greatest news she had ever received in her life.

We travelled back from Birmingham in silence listening to BBC *Sports Report* as, slowly but surely, the full horror of what had happened became clear. We felt powerless; there was nothing we could do to help. We just sat and listened. I can remember feeling utterly despondent on that journey back to Culcheth and a million miles from the Cambridge I had left weeks before. In those days, after a big win, you would expect to see a lot of fellow supporters on the motorway, hanging out of car windows and sounding their horns. There was none of that on this journey home. There was just a pall of gloom over the car and radio reports getting worse by the minute. I can recall hanging onto every word of broadcasters John Motson and Pat Murphy. They were already reporting some confusion about the circumstances in which a gate had been opened, with police sources claiming it had been forced and supporters saying it had been opened by police. Even at this early stage, the battle for the truth was well underway.

By this point of the 80s, we had become used to people thinking the worst of us. It felt like the city of Liverpool was under siege for most of the decade. When Liverpool played

Everton in the first all-Merseyside FA Cup Final in 1986, and the second in 1989, I can remember the profound emotion I felt when both ends of the old Wembley Stadium joined in a chorus of 'Merseyside, Merseyside'. They were unforgettable acts of defiance towards an establishment, represented by those in the Royal Box, which had viciously turned against the people of one of England's biggest cities.

When we finally got home, the first thing I did was phone the house of my friend Ste. His mum answered in a desperate voice: 'Stephen, Stephen, is that you, are you OK?' I hung up straight away, ashamed that I hadn't thought it through properly and added to her distress. I shuddered as I thought of all the parents sitting by the phone like Ste's mum.

My brothers and I didn't know what to do with ourselves so we headed back to the Cherry Tree and holed up there, waiting for our friends to come back. They arrived in dribs and drabs, like lost souls, dead behind the eyes.

The journey home to Merseyside was the polar opposite of what we had experienced on the way out to Sheffield. We sat quietly on our coach, listening to the radio as reports were coming through about what had happened at the match we had just attended. Every time someone came on the radio with an update, the number of dead had increased and it just kept going up. It started in single figures and grew and grew. We couldn't process it all. Never in our worst nightmares would we have believed that the number would eventually rise to ninety-six, and now ninety-seven.

I kept thinking about the lads I had swapped my tickets with. I didn't know their names and I will probably never know if they got out of that stadium alive. It is a very hard thing to think about. I understand what people mean when they talk about survivor's guilt.

We got back to the Carters Arms and it was one of the first times I ever remember seeing lads hugging each other and showing real emotion. It just wasn't something that Northern men did in those days. That day was an exception. Others who had seen the horrors of the Leppings Lane end up close were recounting what they had witnessed in agonising detail. I remember eventually getting home and seeing my mum for the first time. She just gave me a massive hug. My dad – who was not big on emotional displays – hugged me too when he next saw me. He died shortly after the Hillsborough disaster. It is a day that will always be with me.

For Andy and me, everything leads to and from Hillsborough. It was an event that shaped us both as people and as politicians. The disaster was not just an appalling tragedy. It was entirely man-made and one which the powers-that-be, the establishment, fought tooth and nail to cover up. The treatment of those fans and their families on that day, and in the decades since, represents a pivotal example of how the structures of power in this country do not work for ordinary people. In some cases, like this one, they actively and shamefully work against them.

It was our first taste of an indisputable reality: that not every life in our country is equal and some are worth much more than others. Our experiences on that terrible day and in the years that followed played an enormous role in our lives, our careers, our friendship and our eventual decision to leave Westminster and try to shape something better from the outside. For us both, it all comes back to Hillsborough and it always will.

2

Growing Up in Granadaland

I am one of eight siblings. My mum always used to say I was the middle one because I've got twins older than me, so was the fourth of seven pregnancies. Growing up in Kirkby on Merseyside, I don't think I realised at the time the level of the poverty around us. My family were from Anfield but our house was knocked down as part of the slum clearance programme taking place in Liverpool at the time. We were moved to a new town on the outskirts, which is now part of the Knowsley borough. We were promised some sort of new utopia, with houses that had an inside toilet and front and back gardens. But it wasn't quite the case. We were raised in a bottom maisonette with just three bedrooms. We didn't have a lot and I would never go to bed with a full stomach. I was often hungry, but I wouldn't say I was ever starving. There was usually some bread and jam or bread and dripping to tide me over. Another favourite were sugar butties, although they are not recommended for healthy teeth.

My mother Dorothy was a very intelligent woman. When she was at school, she and her brother both had the opportunity to get a scholarship to continue their education. But, because she was the woman and he was the man, he got to take it and she didn't finish her schooling. That always rankled with her. When she was in her late sixties and early seventies, she went back to college to do A levels. I think she just wanted to prove she could do it.

We didn't have much money but one thing we did have in

our house in abundance was unconditional love. My mother had limitless reserves of love and my siblings and I were brought up in a home where we were always treated as the most important people in the world. Mum dedicated her life to the eight of us and I think it is down to her that we went on in our diverse careers and all did well for ourselves. We are the people we are today because of the values she espoused. Those principles she instilled in all of us were genuine socialist values and they have stayed with us all to this day. All eight siblings have always stayed close-knit and we regularly get together and still get on well. We're really lucky in that respect.

My parents got divorced and I think politics had a significant part to play in the marriage breakdown. My dad, Harry, was a forklift truck driver and a local Labour councillor for the Kirkby area. He was out at the local Labour club every night of the week as he was the master of ceremonies there. If he got paid £10, half would go to my mum and the other half would go over the bar to the club. Obviously, he would end up having a few pints every night he was there. It was one of the reasons I think eventually they didn't stay together, but there were a multitude of other factors.

We have always been a close-knit family. My childhood, while fairly ordinary by the standards of the 70s and 80s, was also wonderful in every way. Our lifestyle was modest, and we never had a family holiday abroad, but we didn't want for anything.

Neither my dad, Roy, nor my mum, Eileen, went to university. But both could have done if they had grown up in a different time and in a different place. Their knowledge of that fact seemed to make them all the more determined that their three sons would go. But that did not make them pushy parents in any way. Their approach was one of quiet encouragement and confidence-building. Our family home in Culcheth was always full of music, life, laughter, love and support. Perhaps you would expect nothing less if your mother was an original early-60s 'Cavern Girl' like ours.

Our home needed to be a fortress given what was going on outside of it. Growing up in the 70s and 80s in 'Granadaland', a nickname given to the North West because of our strangely named ITV region, it was hard not to pick up the subliminal message that we couldn't aspire to be very much. All around us, industry was in decline and jobs were going at an alarming rate.

Alan Bleasdale's television show *Boys from the Blackstuff* caught the mood of the times. I can't tell you what an impact it had on us. We used to watch it every week as a family and my brother, Nick, and I would ask whether things were really like that for people in Liverpool. The rawness of it all, and the injustices it captured, planted the first political seeds in my mind. It was the first TV programme to portray the decline of the North of England under the Thatcher government – a theme that would grow over the decade – and remains one of the most powerful depictions ever made of the desperation and loss of dignity that comes with unemployment. One episode sticks in my mind. 'George's Last Ride' followed an old docker living out his last days and, as he was pushed in his wheelchair around a derelict Albert Dock, he reminisced about the past grandeur of the Liverpool waterfront. I remember turning away from the screen to see the tears streaming down my mum's face. Her dad, Jimmy, had worked on those docks as a lorry driver for Tate & Lyle, as had our Irish ancestors before him. It was painfully close to home.

I left school at sixteen. I wasn't forced to but maybe it was expected. At that stage, with eight mouths to feed, there was just the unwritten understanding that, when you were old enough, you would go out and earn some money to bring home. I wanted to play football for a living but wasn't ever good enough, although I did play a decent standard and formed friendships with teammates that have lasted until this day. I distinctly recall my careers adviser telling me rather plainly that my options at the age of sixteen were to go into the army or onto building sites. My brother had served in the army, so

I didn't fancy following in his footsteps. In any case, I had always been good with my hands, so I opted for the latter.

Being a young man in Liverpool during the late 70s was very difficult. The city's docks and manufacturing industries had gone into a rapid decline and work was scarce. It was a tough time to be on building sites too, with scant regard for health and safety, and bosses who would sack you if you put one foot wrong. At one point, I was working on a huge project in St Helens and there was a dispute with the electricians over pay. They all went on strike. Obviously, no one would cross the picket lines but, as a young apprentice, I was expected to go in and work. I said there was no chance as I would never cross a picket line. The company threatened to sack me. We had a mass meeting on the building site where, unbelievably, management were present. They told me and this other lad that we weren't allowed to vote on the proposed industrial action because we were apprentices. Inevitably I ignored it and put my hand up to vote for strike action right in front of company spies. I knew I would be targeted by the bosses, but I felt I had to do it; it was in my blood from an early age.

It was a terrible time. The decline of the once prosperous docks in Liverpool, partly because they weren't designed for the rise in larger container ships, and the soaring unemployment in the city meant that I had to travel anywhere there was work. I would jump on the train to head off to London and places all over the country because there was literally no work in Liverpool – nothing. On one occasion my mum gave me one pound to put petrol in the car so that I could drive to St Helens, Widnes and other nearby towns asking if any sites were looking for bricklayers. We couldn't find anything. It was all pretty desperate. Andy has already mentioned the seminal television series *Boys from the Blackstuff* about the impact of unemployment on Northern communities. Well, it was very true to life at that time for us. I do, however, hate the Giz-a-job references... In London there was work everywhere. Every building site I would turn up at would be full of Scousers, Mancunians and Geordies. People had to migrate away from their cities just to make a few quid. Just to try and survive. At one point my search for work – and maybe my search for something a bit different – took me as far away as the Falkland Islands. In 1981, I found myself working close to where the riots had taken place in Toxteth on a civil engineering project to widen the arterial road as far as the Albert Dock, which at that time was derelict and being used as a compound to store plant and machinery. One day, in 1982, the foreman came to speak with me while I was down a manhole repointing the brickwork. He said that the company was looking for tradesmen to work in the Falklands and, if I was interested, to let him know. The Argentinians had recently surrendered and there was the need to reconstruct the roads in Port Stanley due to war damage. Despite now being on a full wage as a time-served bricklayer, I thought it could be an opportunity to save some money as I'd always fancied starting my own business. That weekend, I was playing football and was telling some of the lads in the changing rooms that I was thinking of working away in the Falklands. One of my mates, John, said: 'Ask if they are looking for plumbers.' So on the Monday when I was back in work, I spoke with the foreman and he confirmed that they were. Within weeks, we had completed the application process, medicals and all sorts of administrative faff and found ourselves at RAF Brize Norton bound for the Ascension Islands in the middle of the Atlantic Ocean.

We flew on a VC10 with the seats facing backwards. So it was an interesting take-off to say the least. From there, we were transported by helicopter to the SS *Uganda*, which had served as a hospital ship throughout the conflict. It took ten days until we eventually docked in Port William and Port Stanley. Tensions between the UK and Argentina were still heightened so everything had to be blacked out. We lived aboard a freight ship in the bay for a few weeks until our temporary accommodation could be transported by barge close to where we were to construct a workers' village on the outskirts of Stanley. We lived under the threat that there might be an Exocet missile attack on shipping in the harbour, much of which was whipped up by the many friends we were now making in the armed forces who thought it was a good idea to scare the shit out of us.

I was there for eight months in total. I was twenty-one, and thought of it as an adventure, but it turned into a hard slog with little to do for entertainment and constant work demands. A few of us borrowed a Land Rover and visited famous landmarks where fierce battles had taken place, such as Mount Tumbledown and Two Sisters, although we had to be careful where we went as there were fenced-off sections due to landmines. I saw first-hand the Argentinian positions that British forces had taken. There were uniforms, toothbrushes and shaving equipment placed exactly where they had been left by the Argentinian troops who had fled or surrendered. There were lots of bullets, guns and armaments abandoned during the battles that ensued. The weather was extreme, and sometimes it was too cold to lay bricks, so I ended up helping my mate John to unfreeze pipes to get the water running on site. We could experience four seasons in one day. While I was being updated about how sunny things were back home, the long hot summer just passed me by.

There was no television and the only radio stations were the Falkland Islands Broadcasting Station or the British Forces Broadcasting Station. There were three pubs that non-locals could frequent and not much else to do, although they did have a football pitch which we were able to use once. If you wanted to call home, you had to book a telephone slot in advance with a company called Cable & Wireless, who not only charged a fortune for the call but also listened to it as they were all monitored. It was a miserable existence. I couldn't wait to return home to the place and the people I loved.

Looking back, I think it was impossible not to become political then if you lived in the North. In Liverpool, we thought that the Prime Minister, Margaret Thatcher, was the devil incarnate. The city was facing huge economic and social challenges in terms of mass unemployment and social unrest, and the government's policies were a big part of those problems. I would say many of Liverpool's issues could be traced back to the doorstep of 10 Downing Street. It felt contrived. Thatcher knew that the policies she was pursuing, and the decimation of certain industries, would see Northern areas suffer most. She was happy for our city, and places like ours, to be collateral damage in her pursuit of right-wing dogma. In some areas, she wiped out the miners and their communities. Liverpool became a particular target for her and her egregious government.

It later became known that Thatcher's Chancellor, Geoffrey Howe, had urged the Prime Minister to abandon Liverpool to a fate of 'managed decline' after the Toxteth riots in 1981. He said the government shouldn't spend money on the 'stony ground' of Merseyside. Thankfully, Michael Heseltine stepped in and started to champion the city. But those words were incredibly damaging and show how the most senior members of Thatcher's government felt about Liverpool. They weren't just indifferent to its suffering; they'd actively considered a policy that would inflict increased suffering.

By the mid-80s, the North West was in pretty steep decline. In Liverpool, the docks were a diminished force; over in Manchester, once the epicentre of global industry, 207,000 manufacturing jobs were lost between 1972 and 1984. In between the two big cities, close to where I grew up and went to school, lay the old Lancashire coalfield. The Miners' Strike of 1984, and the fears for the long-term prospects of the pits, started to spread the feeling of impending doom down the A580 East Lancashire Road.

It seems hard to believe now but, in this period, *ITV News at Ten* used to put up a weekly job loss counter every Friday night. Trevor McDonald would read out the grim toll of job casualties, mainly in the North and Midlands, and the ticker behind him would keep on racking up the cumulative numbers. Unsurprisingly, hope was in short supply.

And yet, around the same time, those same TV screens began to show images of what appeared to us to be a foreign land. Some of the big privatisations of the 80s always seemed to be greeted by pictures of people in braces popping champagne corks somewhere in the City of London. My dad's job with the old Post Office was privatised with the creation of British Telecom and, although he had the chance to buy a modest number of shares, he didn't agree with it. As I travelled the country watching Everton away games, I began to feel that England was in fact two different countries. Alan Bleasdale's political seeds were beginning to germinate.

I was brought up in a house full of noise. There were ten of us sharing a relatively small space so there was a cacophony of chatter, laughter and music. On a Sunday morning, my mum would get up early to do a roast dinner for the multitude and she would have Roy Orbison, Jim Reeves or Mario Lanza blaring out of the radiogram. I especially liked Roy Orbison's 'In Dreams' but I was obsessed with The Beatles. At every chance, I would play one of their albums bought by my elder siblings. I started listening to the early stuff and was then transfixed when they sang about areas like 'Strawberry Fields' and 'Penny Lane' which were just minutes away from where we lived. I couldn't believe that four lads from the same streets I was from could produce such musical magic. I am still a massive fan today and devour anything by the fab four.

While life as a young man in 70s and 80s Liverpool was tough, I found real joy through music and football. I've written earlier about how important following Liverpool Football Club was for me during this period. They gave me an outlet and provided a city that was in real crisis a source of pride – because they were so successful. I still go to the match religiously and, even after five decades, enjoy everything from the anticipation of the forthcoming fixture to the arrangements of where to meet my mate Fletch and others and whether to grab a quick drink afterwards. Our seats are in the Upper Sir Kenny Dalglish stand

and if anyone deserved a stand named after them then it is the King for everything he did for us.

When I was younger, I had a Kenny Dalglish pillow case that my mum bought for me. So, it's a strange thing that I now know him, his wife Marina and their children so well. At the end of 2023, I was invited to the BBC Sports Personality of the Year awards in Manchester where Kenny was to receive a lifetime achievement award. The evening was televised live so, during the showing of some pre-recorded interviews, his family and friends were ushered on stage. As we proudly lined up awaiting Kenny's induction, one of the producers of the show, with clipboard in hand, asked whether Steve Rotheram and John Bishop were present. We both gingerly raised our hands. 'Sorry,' she said. 'You should be on the other side of the stage with the football legends.' Long overdue recognition and about time, I thought, as I lined up alongside Andy Robertson, Alan Shearer, Tim Sherwood, Ian Rush, John Barnes, Graham Souness and Alan Hansen.

Along with footy, music has always played an essential role in my life. I often say there are two moments when I fell in love and my life changed: meeting my wife Sandra (of course) and seeing The Jam perform for the first time. But it wasn't just the music of Paul Weller, Bruce Foxton and Rick Buckler that I fell in love with. It was their style, their fashion and their approach to life. I became a mod and still am a mod. As the Modfather himself once famously said: 'You can bury me a mod.' Deriving from the word 'modernist', Mod Culture began in London and spread around the country from the 50s, 60s and beyond. It is a subculture with a real focus on music and fashion – not to mention motor scooters. I still have a Vespa 125PX, which was immortalised when the *Liverpool Echo* did a fashion photoshoot of me when I was Lord Mayor with the caption, 'Mod father of the City'. It's still my favourite headline to date.

In 1979, I queued around the block with my friend Phil Jones to watch the classic film *Quadrophenia*. The story revolves around the rivalry between mods and rockers and it just blew my mind. I was fully sold on being a mod. I think what I really connected with was this idea of always wanting to look smart and convey a certain image of yourself. My friends and I were all working class, and didn't have a lot of money, but it meant a lot to us to try and look good. The mod clothes were all very expensive, but there was a shop called 67A in Liverpool that sold second-hand vintage items. We loved it. You could go there and get original mod suits and shirts for very reasonable prices. The music meant everything to us. I devoured as many gigs as I could afford and spent many a night in raptures at the legendary Eric's club in Liverpool.

We didn't have a lot of hope at the time, so to hear bands like The Chords playing songs like 'Maybe Tomorrow' that we could connect with was huge. There is a Jam song called 'Saturday's Kids' with the lyrics: *'Saturday's kids live life with insults, drink lots of beer and wait for half-time results.'* That was us. We were Saturday's kids. The two-tone genre was also on the rise, combining influences from Jamaican ska and reggae music with punk rock and new wave. It was so exciting. The songs and the lyrics opened my eyes to other cultures and some of the political and social challenges faced by people from different backgrounds. When I first heard Bob Marley's 'Redemption Song', I listened closely to the lyrics – and it awoke something in me. The power of music to educate and inform is often underplayed. The Special AKA song 'Free Nelson Mandela' brought the anti-apartheid struggle to millions of people who knew little of what was happening in South Africa at the time.

Perhaps it was all these early influences which would lead me, in later life, to use music as a tool to highlight my own definition of injustice. Following the conclusions of the Hillsborough Independent Panel in September 2012, at their next home game, Everton famously brought out two children onto the pitch: a girl in an Everton kit and a small boy in Liverpool colours. They walked hand in hand towards the centre circle, with numbers '9' and '6' on their backs, to the strains of 'He Ain't Heavy, He's My Brother' by Manchester band

The Hollies. Then Everton Chairman and theatrical impresario Bill Kenwright had personally chosen the tune. I had already been in touch with a loose collection of musicians called The Justice Collective who were supporting our campaigning efforts on Hillsborough. At the time, we had been thinking about whether we could find a piece of music to challenge for the 2012 Christmas No.1, and Mr Kenwright had given us our eureka moment. Working with Guy Chambers, we pulled together a cast of stellar musicians, including Paul McCartney, who did an updated version. It got to the top of the charts in the week before Christmas and brought Hillsborough into the living rooms of millions as they watched *Top of the Pops* after their Christmas dinners. When Bill sadly passed away towards the end of 2023, Andy and I were at his memorial service in Liverpool Anglican Cathedral and we recalled his incredible support for the Hillsborough families as one of the many things he did for the city.

Music was massive in my formative years and a major escape from the difficulties all around us. Whether it was listening to The Specials singing about the bleak realities in 'Ghost Town', The Beat's anti-Thatcher protest song 'Stand Down Margaret' or the upbeat craziness of 'Baggy Trousers' by Madness, there was some recognition that we weren't alone and a sense of escapism from the misery. When following bands to gigs in other parts of the country, the music, the fashion, the culture – and of course the football – gave us something to cling to.

Everything happening around that time, the political atmosphere and the protest songs, helped to crystallise the views that were already developing in me from a young age. Those feelings would only get stronger.

I went to a Catholic comprehensive school in Newton-le-Willows called St Aelred's. Culcheth had its most famous son Roger Hunt and, while I was at school there, Newton found its own called Rick. Rick Astley didn't go to our school but instead went to our fierce local rivals, Selwyn Jones. However, he was the drummer in a band called FBI who mainly hailed from St Aelred's. When he made his way through our school to the music rooms for lunchtime practice, he would draw a few looks from the hard lads. However, when he was discovered a few years later at Earlestown Labour Club by Pete Waterman, we all happily claimed Rick as our own. Rick and Roger, music and football: these have always been the prime sources of North West pride and identity and, same as Steve, they were the twin pillars of my life.

St Aelred's was close to the old Parkside Colliery and, for that reason, the Miners' Strike had a big impact on me. My school bus would pass the main entrance to the colliery every day and we would bang on the windows to show our support for those on the picket line. There were lots of kids at my school who had dads out on strike so tins of food were regularly brought in to help them.

The decade had begun with the Toxteth and Moss Side riots. While we knew where those places were, we didn't know anyone involved. By the middle of the decade, the Miners' Strike brought the problems of the 80s a step closer to our door. At the end of it, Hillsborough brought them right through it. It involved our friends and could so easily have been us.

And yet it would be wrong to leave the impression that the 80s were relentlessly grim up North. In fact, while we were bottom of the jobs league, the North West of England was bossing the world when it came to music and football. Everton were at their peak in the mid-80s and, as I got older, Nick and I would follow them everywhere. Going to the match was a serious business, particularly the away games. Great care was taken over choice of match gear although, to look at some of the photos now, you wouldn't believe it. As we didn't have a great deal of money, I had to start my fashion career with some of the more affordable options available at the market underneath the Arndale Centre, such as a yellow Pierre Sangam jumper and brown bell-bottom cords. In time, my Saturday best would evolve into a combination of Sergio Tacchini trackie bottoms, a Lacoste T-shirt and a Kappa jumper. Adidas trainers – pronounced a-dee-das, never a-di-das

– were compulsory. As 1984 turned into 1985, my outfit was supplemented by a hairstyle popularised by the character Damon Grant on *Brookside* – now known as a mullet – and, worse still, as 85 became 86, it turned into a permed mullet like that of his brother, Barry Grant.

My questionable fashion choices became a matter of public record after we travelled to Highbury, Arsenal's magnificent old ground, to watch Everton beat Southampton in an FA Cup semi-final in 1984. Bear in mind that, at this point, Everton had never featured in an FA Cup Final in my lifetime. When Adrian Heath scored the winner in the last minute of extra time in front of the North Bank, it was like the breaking of the dam. I was straight over the perimeter wall and onto the pitch to celebrate. The jubilant scenes were captured by the *Match of the Day* cameras so, that night, millions caught a glimpse of my nauseating yellow jumper flashing across the screen. This incident would also later bring my first noteworthy reference in print. The 90s literary sensation *Fever Pitch* by Nick Hornby records his annoyance that Highbury lost its status as a venue for FA Cup semi-finals because 'some stupid Everton fans ran on the pitch in 1984'. I can't deny it; I was one. My apologies, Nick.

Music was my other obsession and, during the early 80s, my favourite album was *Signing On* by UB40. The album cover was a copy of the unemployment benefit form from which the band took their name. The song 'One in Ten', about the unemployment figures, was the soundtrack of our times. Later on, as I was getting ready to take my O Levels in 1986, a schoolfriend lent me *Hatful of Hollow* by The Smiths. It changed everything. From that moment, I was a full disciple of Manchester music.

My first few years at St Aelred's had involved me walking something of a tightrope. Because of my mum and dad's insistence that I should aim for university, I would largely try to keep up to date with my work. But, as I grew older and more confident, I realised I could often make the class laugh and that won me credit with the in-crowd. It was hard to be both a good student and one of the lads. I was succeeding more at the latter than the former when the time came for the class to be separated into the O Level set or the lower CSE set. A teacher called Mr Riley, who lived in Culcheth and always looked out for the Burnham brothers, made a point of telling me that I had made the O Level set by the skin of my teeth. I didn't dare admit to him that I had copied from the person next to me in the Maths test. However, it served as a big wake-up call. I went on to do better than expected in my O Levels with five As. When I would later be appointed by Gordon Brown to the Treasury, a rumour went around Westminster that I had failed my Maths O Level. It wasn't true. I am proud to say I got an A. But it is true to say that my interest in Maths went no further than that O Level.

The Smiths and their lead singer Morrissey were very important to me at this point in my life. I saw them perform at Salford University in 1986 on The Queen Is Dead tour and was utterly mesmerised by it. It was a riotous night and remains the best gig I have ever seen. While not in tune with his views now, I can't deny how important Morrissey was to me as I evolved from a mid-80s scally into a late-80s student. Here was a hugely charismatic figure from the North West and he seemed to be saying to us that we could be something. We could dare to aim higher. Yes, we may be hidden by rags, but we have something they'll never have. It was enormously empowering. Contrary to the influences I had felt at school, Morrissey made it cool to be intelligent and well-read and that helped me focus on my English studies as I forged my path to university.

The importance of bands like The Smiths, New Order and many others coming out of the North West at that time cannot be overstated. Our region had been battered through the 80s, with hammer blow after hammer blow, but all of a sudden we had something everyone else wanted. Something at which we were the best. When I arrived at Cambridge University in 1988, people who had been to much posher schools than me were envious of the fact that I had seen The Smiths live. It helped me deal with the imposter syndrome. I had something they'll never have.

I met my wife Sandra in 1980 when I was only eighteen. I was attending the local college to do my bricklaying NVQs and, as part of it, I had to do a night class. Sandra was there at the same time doing a nursing cadet course and her friend suggested she was keen on me. I had been interested in her for a while and, being the gentleman that I am, I invited her for a drink in the Carters Arms in Kirkby – very classy, I know. I think there was a two-for-one deal on Oranjeboom beer at the time, which was a bit of a result to be honest.

We courted for nine years until we were able to save the deposit to buy a house. Sandra's mum was religious, so we only moved in together six months after we bought the house when we got married. When we were courting, I was working away from home on building sites, putting in every hour I could to save up. When I was just twenty-two, I set up my own company, with the savings I had made working for eight months in the Falkland Islands. Sandra also had to work away in Essex for a few years doing nursing. Eventually, we saved enough money and bought the house that we still live in today. It was a bit of a wreck at the time but, being a builder, it was something I knew I could work on to improve. Three decades later, it's nearly finished. When I told Sandra it wouldn't take long to complete the refurbishment, it was only an estimate!

Our firstborn, Steven, came along just before my thirtieth birthday, followed by Haylie and then Samantha a few years after that. I had always worked to better myself at whatever it was that I was doing, and I was on a building site one day and started talking to a guy in a suit. I asked him what he had done to be able to wear a suit on a building site. He explained that he had taken some qualifications at the nearby college in Bootle, which in turn had landed him a promotion. I decided I wanted to change from dirty boots and jeans and do the same. First though, I had to go and get my Maths and English O Levels as I had left school with few qualifications. After completing them, I went on to do an Ordinary National Certificate (ONC).

Having recognisable qualifications led me to getting a job as a training supervisor, teaching people the building skills I had picked up over the years. In another risky move, and after the usual consultation with my wife, I packed this job in to go to university full-time. It was a big decision. It meant giving up a wage at a time when we were raising young children. Sandra was now the only breadwinner and I was effectively a stay-at-home dad for a bit while I was studying. It was amazing to be at home spending that time with the kids at such a developmental stage in their lives. Later in life, I did a part-time Masters degree at Hope University and, later still, participated in a Bloomberg city leadership programme with Harvard University. I suppose I wanted to prove to myself that I wasn't the write-off I had been told I was in school. I thought about that period in higher education a lot when, in 2023, I was awarded an honorary fellowship from Liverpool John Moores University. It was a lovely and proud moment for me and my family and brought things full circle. Back when I was a young lad working on building sites without any real qualifications, I would never have imagined being honoured in that way, or becoming the Mayor of the region. I felt extremely lucky.

During the period when I was looking after the kids and studying, I became more active in politics. A trigger for this occurred when I met Peter Kilfoyle, who was then the Labour MP for Liverpool Walton, at my son Steven's nursery. This was around 1994. The nursery had invited parents to meet Peter to talk about Labour's plans for education if they were to get into power at a future general election. I went along and asked a couple of questions and, after the event finished, Peter invited me to join him in having a chat with the headteacher. Suddenly, I found myself in the middle of this political discussion with a headteacher and a Member of Parliament. It was so stimulating. I loved it.

When we left the school, Peter turned to me and said: 'You can moan as much as you like from the sidelines, but the only way you can change things for the better is by getting actively involved with the party.' He was right, of course, and it was at this point that my journey towards becoming an elected politician started in earnest.

My first interview at Cambridge makes me cringe even now. It was up a winding stone staircase in a wood-panelled and book-lined room in St Catharine's College. I had never seen anyone drink sherry other than my gran on Christmas Day but I was offered a glass of it as I was swallowed up by the biggest sofa I had ever sat on. Not being one to refuse a drink, my head was already spinning by the time the professor asked me whether I saw any parallels between the *Canterbury Tales* and a modern package holiday. I was still pondering what the question meant when the rejection letter dropped onto the doormat a few days later. Cambridge was a completely alien world to my North West habitat and one I thought would never be for me. So it was a complete surprise to get a letter telling me that I had been picked up in the pool of rejected candidates by Fitzwilliam College and they would like to offer me an interview. I told my mum and dad that I had no intention of subjecting myself to the same humiliation again. But they worked on me, saying that Cambridge would open so many doors if I got there. So, on my eighteenth birthday, I made my second trip to Cambridge – this time to Fitz's more modern and less overwhelming surroundings – and I somehow got an offer.

I struggled to feel part of things down there but my growing interest in Manchester music gave me an identity and an advantage. Everyone was fascinated by the Haçienda nightclub and seemed to have the famous poster of The Smiths outside Salford Lads' Club on their wall. I got turned away from the Haçienda more times than I got in by the infamous fashion police on the door. But I did sneak in a few times and, when I casually dropped that into college conversations, it gave me an instant edge.

In the summer of 1989, after my first year at Cambridge, I did a summer job with my dad at BT on Portland Street in Manchester city centre. It was very close to the famous Piccadilly Records, where I spent every lunch hour. As well as racks of records and posters, the shop had a little ticket booth. One day, a fluorescent sign appeared advertising tickets for my new favourite band at the time, The Stone Roses, at the Empress Ballroom in Blackpool on 12 August 1989. That day would be my brother John's fifteenth birthday and I bought three tickets on the spot for the three Burnham brothers. I'm pretty sure it remains the best present I have ever given to him. On the night in question, we travelled up the M6 with what felt like the whole of Manchester and knew we were at the start of something very big.

When I started my second year at Fitz in autumn 1989, the 'Madchester' scene was really getting going and my loose connection to it gave me a new-found confidence. On the first night of the new term, I was trying to impress the newly arrived first-year girls and, after a few failed attempts, found one who was Dutch but lived in Belgium and loved The Smiths. The rest, as they say, is history. Thirty-five years on, Marie-France, Jimmy, Rosie, Annie and I are as tight a five-strong family unit as mine was before us.

Apart from music, football and cricket got me through the bewildering but beautiful experience of Cambridge. Our college football team was mainly made up of Northerners, including a six foot four Geordie called Chris Cathey, who I met at my first training session. He became an instant ally and would go on to become my brother-in-law, marrying Marie-France's sister Claire in 2006. Back then, the Fitz team channelled something of the 'Crazy Gang' spirit of the famous Wimbledon side of that era by taking the mick out of the more refined college sides we would come up against. Having played schoolboy cricket for Lancashire in my youth, I was fascinated to find out that I would be coming up against Michael Atherton in a quarter-final 'Cuppers' match against Downing College. Michael was a year or two older than me but I was well aware of who he was because, for years, his name had been whispered with the greatest respect by everyone in Lancashire cricket circles. He would be a future England captain, they said. From what we saw on a rainy afternoon at Trinity Hall's pitches, nobody was suggesting he would be a future England right back. To the Crazy Gang's great delight, Michael scored an own goal off the top of his head, I added a second and Fitzwilliam went through 2–1.

Days like these helped me to survive and eventually succeed at Cambridge. I graduated with a 2:1 in English and headed back home to start looking for a job in journalism in the North West. When my dad had persuaded me to go for my second interview, he had stressed how many doors it would open for me in later life if I got in. Back home, I started to query the accuracy of his advice. I was sending off CV after CV to local newspapers and getting little response. By contrast, people I had studied alongside at Cambridge were waltzing into placements at *The Times*, *The Guardian* and the BBC. I learnt there and then that it was not the degree that opened the real doors into Britain's powerful professions but the dinner parties people's parents attended.

Finally, a breakthrough did arrive in the form of a role as an unpaid reporter at the *Middleton Guardian*. There was only so long I would be able to make that work and, before long, I came to the same inescapable conclusion of many people of my generation: to get on in life I would have to go south. So, in January 1992, I headed down to London to take up a job with Baltic Publishing in Brentford, working on a number of not particularly glamorous transport magazines. One of the reasons I have never agreed to appear on *Have I Got News for You* is I just know they would make *Tank World* or *Container Management* their guest publication of the week and read out my excruciating articles at great length.

To be fair to my dad, Cambridge did open this door as I found the job via the Cambridge University Careers Service and Baltic Publishing only hired writers who had been to Oxbridge. That said, this was a difficult time for me. I was in London on my own and didn't have many friends. To add insult to injury, Marie-France, who was still in her third year at Cambridge, appeared on the ITV programme *Blind Date*. While I sat alone in my room in London, she disappeared to Gibraltar with Will from Surrey who, believe it or not, would later work for the Conversative Party. I don't think Marie-France will ever recover from the time in 2004 when we were going into the Strangers' Bar in Parliament and bumped into Dr Liam Fox, then Chairman of the Conversative Party, who immediately proceeded to introduce us to his new Chief Marketing Officer. If only Cilla could have seen the faces of 'Our Will from Surrey' and 'Our Frankie from 'Olland' right then!

I coped in the early months of 1992 by becoming absorbed in the general election campaign. When Labour lost, it felt like a bereavement. All I could hear were wails of anguish from home and whoops of joy from the Tories all around me in the office at Baltic Publishing. I had never felt more homesick in all my life. After everything we had been through in the North under Thatcher in the 80s, it was utterly unfathomable to me how the country had voted the Tories back in. As a big fan of Neil Kinnock, I found it crushing to see him lose. It took me weeks to pick myself up but, as I did, I started to think seriously about how I could devote myself to the mission of getting Labour elected.

By then, I had been promoted to a staff writer at *Tank World*. One of my new responsibilities was to conduct the interviews to recruit a new editorial assistant. One highly impressive young woman who had studied at Oxford was head and shoulders above all others and I hired her instantly. We became quite close and used to frequent a pub every lunchtime called the New Inn, which was one of the four famous pubs on the corners of Brentford FC's old Griffin Park. We would sit by the pool table and plot our escape from the world of containers and tanks. She would tell me how she longed to work at *The Guardian* and, increasingly, I would talk about my yearning to find a way into politics. One day she surprised me by saying I should send my CV to her stepmother who was looking for a new Parliamentary assistant.

'Who's your stepmother?' I asked.

'Tessa Jowell,' replied Eleanor Mills, who would go on to edit *The Sunday Times* magazine. From absolutely nowhere, I had my springboard into politics. Today in my job as Mayor of Greater Manchester, I make a point of offering days of work shadowing to as many young people as I can. I tell them all the same thing: when opportunities open up right in front of you, for God's sake make sure you take them. I applied that philosophy to a distinctly average football career as a centre-forward and I have tried my best to apply it to life.

Serving my political apprenticeship at the side of the great Tessa Jowell is one of the most glorious blessings I have ever been given. She was a politician apart. A truly lovely person who would do anything for anyone but someone who knew how to play the game and get on. She was much nicer than 99 per cent of the sharks in Westminster but, when they cut up rough, she could bite back harder than them. I loved that about her. I started working for Tessa in February 1994. Her office was in a building called Norman Shaw North, which was the old Scotland Yard. I had only been in there for a couple of weeks when, around 8 a.m. one morning, the phone rang on the internal system. It was a journalist from the *Evening Standard* ringing from the Parliamentary Press Gallery.

'Can you confirm that the Labour Leader John Smith has died?' barked the unsympathetic hack on the other end of the line.

'No, I can't,' said the stunned, very green Parliamentary researcher. I put the phone down and felt instantly queasy. After Neil, John was my great hope. Now he had gone too. In fact, he was probably the politician who I felt most embodied my own values. John just seemed to talk complete sense every single time he opened his mouth.

As the day wore on, I saw for the first time how quickly Westminster clicks into leadership election mode. It felt unseemly at the time. But, on the corridors of Norman Shaw North, all talk was turning to Tony Blair. He had been shadow home secretary and had coined the famous phrase: 'Tough on crime, tough on the causes of crime.' It was something I strongly agreed with then and still do now. Crime affects the poorest people and communities the most and I have never subscribed to the explain-crime-away-with-excuses approach that you can find in some parts of the Left.

Tessa informed me that day that she was getting involved with Tony's campaign and had volunteered my services. I was happy to help out. It seemed mad that, only a few weeks earlier, I had been writing about containers and was now helping instal the next leader of the Labour Party. Tessa sent me over to 1 Parliament Street and said I should knock on the office door of Mo Mowlam, who I had heard a lot about but never met. I was nervous but, when I peered around her door, I instantly liked her. She was so approachable. Mo asked me where I was from and my Northern roots were met with her approval. She was walking around her office with no shoes on and, before long, let out an almighty belch. 'I hope you don't mind Andy', she said.

'No, not at all,' I replied, 'as long as you don't start farting,' with a confidence I hadn't expected, but which came from being so immediately at ease with someone incredibly down-to-earth.

'Well, be careful, I might,' replied Mo.

When Labour went into government, and Mo got stuck into the Northern Ireland Peace Process, I often had cause to think back to that afternoon. Northern Ireland has big similarities to the North West of England and I understood why they loved her over there. Mo had a warmth and humanity that became all-too-rare in Tony Blair's government, as the technocrats began to take over. I was devastated when Mo died in 2005.

In that summer of 1994, Mo, Tessa and others weaved their magic and Tony Blair comfortably won the leadership election. But, in truth, it wasn't down to them; it was down to him. Tony was like the missing piece in the Labour jigsaw; he gave the party another dimension. In that period, between 1994 and 1997, he was a politician completely at the top of his game. For me, playing just a tiny part in his election as Prime Minister undid some of the damage of 1992. It was a very exciting, hopeful time.

I was lucky to spend the 1997 general election campaign working at Labour's famous Millbank HQ. There were many reasons to be hopeful but a very personal one for me was the pledge in the manifesto to take a fresh look at Hillsborough. That more than anything symbolised to me the difference that a Labour government would make. Only a month after that sweeping victory, I was elated when Jack Straw, the new home secretary, appointed Lord Justice Stuart-Smith to examine the evidence and see if there should be a new inquiry. For the first time in my life, I was feeling the transformative power of a Labour government and I had the extra feeling of pride that I had played a small part in bringing it about.

At the first inquests, which began in November 1990, less than two years after the disaster, the coroner Dr Stefan Popper had refused to hear details of anything that happened after 3.15 p.m. on the day of the match on the grounds that those who lost their lives had already done so by that point. From the time that I first heard about that ruling, it seemed brutal and wrong. How could anyone look at what happened and think a 3.15 p.m. cut-off was in any way acceptable?

I felt confident that the review would deliver a breakthrough for the Hillsborough families. By early 1998, I was working for the new government's Football Task Force and was organising a series of roadshows across the country. As luck would have it, I was driving around Sheffield with BBC Radio 5 Live on in the car when the presenter said they were going live to the House of Commons to hear a statement from the home secretary on Hillsborough. All of a sudden, my heart was in my mouth and I pulled over onto the hard shoulder so I could listen without distraction. When it became clear that there would be no new inquiry, I sat in the car and cried. That was the first time in my life when I felt betrayed by the party I loved.

3

Entering the Bubble

I didn't dare admit it to anyone but, from my early twenties, my ambition was to become a Member of Parliament. It wasn't until I was approaching my thirties that I found the confidence to say it out loud. The person who helped me most to get to that point was my good friend James Purnell, one of the clearest political thinkers I have ever met and someone who would himself go on to serve in the Cabinet. As the 2001 election drew closer, he kept suggesting that I speak with Sally Morgan, the political secretary in 10 Downing Street, about the possibility of running for a seat. Finally, I plucked up the courage and arranged to meet Sally in her office. It was a short meeting but possibly the most consequential of my life.

'We're not going to give you any help, Andy, because we can't help everyone,' she said in her efficient, headteachery manner, 'but Leigh is coming up and I know you're from that area. The best advice I can give you is go all out for that.' It was in fact brilliant advice and exactly what I needed to be told. Many times since, I have had cause to thank Sally for what she did for me. I had gone into Downing Street that day with vague notions of one day getting round to standing for Parliament and I left it with a laser-like focus on returning to my childhood stomping ground to become its next representative. I was going to need it because what lay ahead of me was a political baptism of fire.

I spent much of the next twelve months living back at home with my mum and dad in Culcheth, about four miles from Leigh. The selection contest started unpleasantly, with the hierarchy of Leigh Constituency Labour Party branding me the 'parachute candidate' from London despite my local roots, and ended with echoes of *G.B.H.*, another famous Bleasdale drama. A range of toxic intimidation tactics were deployed by my enemies, including my mum having to answer the door at all hours to unwanted skips and pizzas. At one selection meeting, when asked by a particularly hostile member why he should vote for me, I said: 'Well, for a start, I'm local.'

'Local?' he sneered. 'Culcheth's not local.'

'It's got to be fairly local,' I replied, 'I walked home from Reubens once.'

A light-hearted reference to a legendary Leigh nightclub broke the ice and seemed to get a few people onside. As the contest wore on, despite the hierarchy's opposition, I started to pick up more and more support from the quiet majority of Leigh members and, in the end, won quite easily. That selection contest would in many ways define my political career. In leadership contests to come, I have always found more support among lay members and the wider public than I have ever received from the high-ups in the Labour movement.

By contrast, compared to the selection contest, the delayed general election in June 2001 was a walk in the park. My only wobble came on the night when our deputy leader John Prescott led the evening news for punching a protestor in Rhyl. My fears of a backlash did not materialise – not in Leigh at least. In ex-mining, rugby-league-loving Leigh, the local electorate quickly decided John was well within his rights to throw his left jab. I spent the rest of an uneventful but lovely first campaign approaching shoppers on Bradshawgate, who all laughed and pretended to duck when they saw me approaching in my red rosette. To be elected to represent the great people and town of Leigh was a huge honour which I took deadly seriously and for which I will forever be grateful for.

When I walked into the House of Commons chamber for the first time to take my seat, I remember almost hyperventilating. It was overwhelming. My old imposter syndrome was still lurking in the background but it wasn't enough to ruin the feeling of elation. It was a huge moment in my life. In my maiden speech, I promised to be 'an authentic voice for my home area' and, looking back, I like to think I mostly achieved it.

One thing I refused to do was move my family to London, as everyone was telling me to do. When I first met my wife, Marie-France, at Cambridge, and later when we lived in London in the 90s, I did warn her that staying with me would mean settling in the North West. In the end, it came sooner than we expected. Our son, Jimmy, had been born in March 2000 and we had then got married in the October of that year. By spring 2001, we were ready to leave our two-up, two-down on Regent Road, in the border area between Brixton and Herne Hill, for a new Northern family home. I knew that would exclude me from the London political drinks and dinner party circuit at weekends but I was fine with that. I had reached a stage in my life when I wanted more Goodison and less Groucho.

Tessa remained a great friend and mentor as I found my feet in the House of Commons. But, to my eternal fortune, another one sought me out. Paul Goggins, the MP for Wythenshawe and Sale East, lived near Leigh and saw that we had a lot in common, including a Catholic background, although he was more active on that front and, by my early thirties, I was more of the lapsed variety. Paul was everything a proper MP should be and would pick up the unfashionable causes eschewed by others, such as prisoners' rights. I asked him about this one night over a drink.

'What's the point of coming in here if you use your voice for people who already have power?' he said, looking at me intently. 'You should always use your power for those who have none.' Paul's words would come back to me many times over my sixteen years as an MP. Many people I encountered in Parliament seemed to think that the purpose of being there was so they could cosy up to others with power in the media and business and enter their social networks. Paul stood out to me as a real exception and, as my career progressed, I would increasingly come to follow his advice.

Paul was Parliamentary private secretary to home secretary David Blunkett and, when he was promoted to ministerial office, he recommended to David that I should take over from him. This brought me into direct contact with another exceptional person and politician who would take my political apprenticeship to the next level. David had a habit of surrounding himself with like-minded people. In the early 2000s, his Home Office was something of a Northern enclave in Whitehall. In his ministerial team, alongside Paul, he had two other Greater Manchester MPs, Beverley Hughes and Hazel Blears. When I made it four, we were like a Westminster-based Northerners' support network and would often spend team meetings at the old Home Office on Queen Anne's Gate, laughing together at the London-centric ways of the world around us. Watching David work at close quarters was a complete privilege. Here was someone who was decent with people but clear about what he wanted to achieve and would take no messing from the Whitehall machine. Had I not spent that time with David, and learnt so much at his side, I don't think I would have been ready to fight my own Whitehall battles later in the decade.

Despite the progress I was making in my first term of office, I had a gnawing self-doubt about whether I could ever really fit into this establishment. I would spend much of the week in Westminster way outside my comfort zone and then breathe a sigh of relief when I alighted at Warrington Bank Quay on a Thursday night, the smell of washing powder from the big Unilever factory alongside telling me I was home. By Saturday lunchtime, in a pub near Goodison Park with all the family, my equilibrium would be restored. Then it would be upset again when I returned to Westminster on Monday and found out the gossip from the London set's weekend gatherings where members of both main parties had been hanging out together. It didn't sit well with me.

As with all of the big decisions in my life, the first person with whom I discussed my intentions to become a councillor was my wife, Sandra. As always, she was very supportive. Before the turn of the millennium, I was attending all sorts of Labour meetings and had come into contact with a legendary local councillor and former trade unionist called Jack Spriggs. Jack had known my dad and took me under his wing. The ward I lived in, Fazakerley, was Liberal Democrat-controlled at that point. However, Labour was confident of winning it back at the first available opportunity. So, Jack and the other ward councillor, Dave Hanratty, suggested I put myself forward as the Labour nomination. I told them I would think about it but, in the meantime, I would serve a sort of 'apprenticeship' to understand the role better. For two years, I attended all the council meetings, advice surgeries and other events alongside Jack and Dave to find out what it meant to be a councillor.

I put myself forward to stand for election in the area I lived in then and still live in today. It was great campaigning around there. I enjoyed chatting to everyone about issues affecting the place. If it had been another area, I wouldn't have stood as my heart and soul would not have been in it. I wanted things to improve in the area where I was raising my family.

I knew Labour had a good chance on the election night of 2 May 2002. But I was still nervous. I had never fought an election before and didn't want to let people down. We didn't have sophisticated polling or data back then. All you could do was speak to people and hope that, if they said they were voting for you, they were telling the truth. The count was held at the Picton Leisure Centre in Liverpool. It was a tense atmosphere. The Liberal Democrats were well in control of the council but, as the main opposition party, we needed to make some gains – including the seat where I was challenging them. It was a strange feeling to hear my name read out as being elected for the first time. For most of my life, I had never had any aspirations to be a politician at all. So it did take a while for it to register. It was an amazing night. We went for a few drinks afterwards and I remember someone calling me by the title councillor for the first time. It was surreal and I have to admit that it did make me feel a little bit important at the time.

The warm feeling of winning with a massive swing to Labour on that night has always stayed with me.

As luck would have it, my whole time on the council was spent in opposition to the ruling Liberal Democrat group. I saw my main role as one of scrutinising and holding them to account. I think being a councillor is a good opportunity to cut your teeth in politics and I certainly learnt a lot. At first, I would sit there and listen to other councillors talking at length about issues and just going around the houses. I quickly learnt how to tell when people were filibustering or obfuscating. I appeared to have an inbuilt ability to recognise what was genuine and what was bullshit. These were skills I would draw on regularly when I eventually made it to the House of Commons. I also learnt that persistence is a vital skill in politics. I was naive at first and thought that, now I was a councillor, I would be able to instantly make things happen. But politics rarely works like that and I realised I would have to be dogged if I was to bring about change. That's something that has always stayed with me throughout my career.

Obviously, as a new Member of Parliament, you try to fit in where you can and be a part of things. That was always my approach. I was ambitious and wanted to get on. So it was a moment of huge pride when I got the call from Tony Blair shortly after the 2005 general election offering me the chance to be a minister in the Home Office. I remain hugely grateful to Tony for believing in me at the time and giving me that chance.

Days before that election, our daughter Annie was born. It was a highly eventful time for us. My first outing as a minister at the despatch box came quickly after at Home Office question, and the family came down to see it. If I had been looking for plaudits from the sketch-writers in the papers the next day, I was to be disappointed. Under the headline 'Breastfeeding baby upstages lazy Tory favourite', Simon Hoggart in *The Guardian* described how his attention had been taken away from David Davis MP, who was running at the time to be Tory leader, and towards events in the public gallery. Annie and Marie-France had stolen the show.

As I adjusted to life as a minister, I would soon have to get used to feeling conflicted. On the one hand, I always felt the privilege of the position and came across some incredible, public-spirited people in the civil service. On the other, the more I came to understand the system of government within which they and I had to work, the less I liked it. It simply wasn't set up to advance the kind of changes I wanted to see. It was there to preserve the status quo. On the one occasion in the Home Office when I gently raised the issue of reopening Hillsborough, it was shut down straight away. No chance. Forget it.

At meetings across Whitehall, I would often wince at some of the things I heard. I would find myself wondering what my constituents in Leigh would make of those conversations in the Westminster Bubble, feeling relieved that they couldn't hear them. In 2006, I was moved, becoming a minister in the Department for Health. We were now in Labour's third term and I was conscious of the widening gap between us in government and the people who had put us in power, such as the staff of the NHS. When he appointed me to this position, Tony Blair gave me the specific task of building more support for the government's NHS reforms. We had all felt the growing discontent within the service.

I had the feeling that the then Prime Minister, and Patricia Hewitt, his health secretary, wanted me to tour hospital staffrooms with graphs on a flip-chart telling doctors and nurses: 'No, NHS targets and privatisation are great, really.' Of course, I never intended to do that. Instead, to fulfil my task, I told them I would conduct a major shadowing exercise of staff at all levels of the NHS, listening to them and observing their work, without any cameras or PR. I would then report back on what I found with some recommendations on how we could bring NHS staff back on board. My idea didn't go down very well in the Department of Health. A minister had not done this before and they were not sure what it would reveal. But, to be fair to them, ten shadowing days were set up for the second half of 2006 and I set about my mission.

The visit that sticks most in my mind was when I shadowed a porter at Tameside Hospital. I don't know what I thought the job of a porter involved beforehand but it was definitely nothing like what I observed on that hot July day in the bowels of the hospital. He told me how he had recently unzipped a body bag containing a decaying body that had been brought into the hospital.

'I do all the jobs that no one else will do and I only get the Minimum Wage,' he told me.

'Why do you do it?' I asked.

'Because I believe in the NHS.'

Like this porter, a cleaner I shadowed in a London hospital spoke of her frustration that she was no longer part of the ward team but was instead employed by a private contractor. She told me she used to be proud that she worked for the NHS and it didn't feel the same any more. Her words haunted me.

At the time, 10 Downing Street was pushing hard for more outsourcing of NHS work. They were reading financial spreadsheets but not the feelings of NHS staff whose world was changing. There was minimal understanding of the priceless value of the NHS itself and the fact that staff employed by it give more of themselves to it than they do to a private contractor. At the end of my shadowing journey, I was left feeling deeply uncomfortable that the NHS was being moved further and further away from the people that loved it, and wanted to give everything to it, and that it was happening under a Labour government.

When I handed my report to Patricia Hewitt, it got a mixed reaction. My recommendation of establishing an 'NHS Constitution' to cement its core values was seen as having some merit. My suggestion of encouraging NHS trusts to bring cleaners and porters back in house? Less so. This back-to-the-floor exercise was an early turning point for me in my ministerial career. Up until that point, I had been a loyal foot soldier for the government and hadn't openly questioned anything about its direction. But, with the shadowing exercise, I had broken ranks for the very first time and hadn't produced what was wanted. I was trying in my own way to say that, if we didn't listen, we would lose the next election.

In another minor act of defiance, I had joined a group called Comprehensive Future. I was distinctly uneasy with Labour's drive to remove schools from local authority control and run them through trusts funded directly by the government. One of my early disappointments with the Labour government was when it had proclaimed the end of 'bog standard comprehensives'. I had attended one such school and it had done a great job for me. I didn't think a Labour government should be talking them down like this. It was an attempt to make 'comprehensive' a pejorative term, playing to the prejudices of Middle England. I didn't like it at all. Instead, like the universal NHS, comprehensive education should have been a phrase to celebrate: everyone educated together, seeing life from all sides and a broad curriculum catering for all talents. Sadly, I discovered too many people working in my own party at the time had not been to comprehensive schools and had no real experience nor understanding of this. There was a creeping snobbery about education and an unjustifiable obsession with the university route.

From 2007 onwards, I was looking at things through different eyes. I was still trying to be loyal to the government but had developed enough confidence to speak out and break away from the New Labour consensus where I thought it was wrong. I represented a constituency that needed proper investment in public services and public infrastructure. The idea that the market would magically solve all the problems of a place like Leigh was a non-starter. This was around the time that the Blair era was coming to a close. There was a feeling that he didn't have much time left and it seemed to make those around him double down on policies like outsourcing and privatisation. Tony had taken us into government and won three elections. I won't diminish what he did or what he achieved – he remains the most accomplished politician I have ever seen at close quarters. I am proud of what we achieved as a government and, when contrasted with what has happened to the country since 2010, it stands as a remarkable period of progress for Britain. But, while I was fully in tune with the Tony Blair of 1997, I had begun to find it harder to agree with the Tony Blair of 2007, much as I respect him.

Hardline Blairites had become more sceptical of me and maybe that made Gordon Brown's camp in the Treasury take more notice. I hadn't planned it that way but when the transition from Tony to Gordon took place in 2007, I was ready for it. Gordon's decision to appoint me to his Cabinet as chief secretary to the Treasury would make my Maths O Level work harder than it had ever done before. It would bring me much closer to the centre of government and open my eyes to long-standing Treasury policies which were at the root of the North–South divide.

I arrived in the Treasury with the new Chancellor, Alistair Darling, and our first job was to oversee the Comprehensive Spending Review of 2007. Alistair was another huge talent I had the privilege to see at close quarters. He was fiercely intelligent and hard to get to know but, when you did, you discovered the driest of senses of humour and the warmest of personalities. Even though we weren't close in recent years, my respect for him was colossal and his death in 2023 hit me hard. Alistair played an important part in my political development, particularly when he gave me the specific task of putting the funding package together for what was then called Crossrail and is now known as the Elizabeth Line. My role in bringing about a huge new rail scheme for London and the South East is something of a guilty secret that I must now carry every day across the North West and its broken rail network.

Joking apart, Steve and I have never been anti-London. If we are portrayed as such, it's more than likely a lazy media stereotype. We are both patriotic people and are proud of our capital city and its world-class infrastructure. If we are guilty of anything, it is wanting the same for our part of the country. We both find it frustrating that, in making that case, too many people – including some in our own party – hear it as an attack on London. It isn't.

I would be the first to acknowledge that London made a big

contribution to the cost of Crossrail because that was the nature of the funding package I put together: two-thirds from London businesses and residents and one-third from the Treasury. Even so, it was another huge investment in London and the South East and I said to Treasury civil servants that I couldn't announce it without also committing to a range of regional projects at the same time. I asked for a list of options to be put together.

Weeks passed and nothing came back. As the day of the spending review announcement came closer, I asked my private office to chase it. When it finally arrived, I couldn't believe my eyes. There was only one proposal on it: a feasibility study for the rebuilding of Birmingham New Street. I did manage to get this into the announcement and it did eventually happen. But I asked the civil servants: why could not a single project in the North of England be identified? That was when the scales fell from my eyes.

'No project in the North passed the Green Book, Minister,' said the senior official.

'How is that possible when the railways of the North are falling apart?' I countered.

'Because the Green Book appraises projects on what they will generate for the UK economy within a twenty-five-year period and most projects in the North don't return enough to meet the threshold.'

If anything had brought me into Parliament, it was a mission to close the North–South divide. As I patiently listened to this explanation, sitting in the splendour of the chief secretary's office, with its magnificent view onto Horseguards and St James's Park, I finally realised why it was mission impossible. The North–South divide was no accident. It was the product of permanent UK policy and would continue getting wider for as long as the Green Book remained in place.

While the Treasury was never my natural habitat, I regard my brief time there as critical in my political journey. By seeing how things worked from the inside, I finally understood why England has always felt like two countries. Only the EU funded infrastructure on the basis of social deprivation. The UK government's economic test was a recipe to give more to the places that already had most and widen regional divides. This is what people call 'Treasury orthodoxy'. It is a doctrine based on cold numbers which takes a negative view of our own country. In essence it says: those old industrial communities can't become anything again so why invest in them? Let's just invest in the places that will provide a quicker economic and financial return. Up until this point, I had assumed that the bias against the North was cultural and emotional – a product of the fact that people from the South tended to dominate positions of power across society and made decisions to favour it. While it is partly that, I genuinely hadn't realised that it is supplemented by a bias that is hard-wired into the processes which govern the country. Under this system, the North could cry out for investment for years and would never get it and we have seen that play out ever since.

Shortly after the financial crash of 2008, these short-sighted Treasury doctrines nearly hit my own constituency. I had been working on a scheme to regenerate the area around the former Bickershaw Colliery, which had closed in 1992. It was a depressing wasteland – full of old buildings and slag heaps – and an ongoing reminder of Leigh's decline. Our vision was to replace it with a marina and new housing, funded by a mix of public and private investment. But the scheme had been thrown into doubt as the crash led the private sector to walk away.

Margaret Beckett was the minister with responsibility for it and she wrote to me to say that, because of the exit of the private investors, the rules required the public funding to be withdrawn too. This was devastating for Leigh. I went to see her and told her that the entire area would be blighted for decades if this fell apart. I said that, if we could put the infrastructure in, it would create an attractive place to invest once the recovery came. Margaret's civil servants were advising her to resist but, God bless her, she agreed. If you go to that area today, you will find a part of the North that could easily be mistaken for the South. But, if normal rules had applied, it would never have been built. It only happened to be built because one Cabinet minister was able to speak to another. It shouldn't be like that.

Since the 80s, Britain has been running an economic and political model based on the South East and the City of London. When we came into government, Labour should have made a commitment to end that. Instead, in its early days, the Blair government minimised the significance of the North–South divide and said it didn't exist any more. This seemed to be born out of a theory in parts of the Labour Party which holds that Labour has to stick to certain establishment norms if it is to be trusted with power.

Don't get me wrong: I loved a lot of my time in Whitehall and Westminster and I learnt so much from it. But the biggest of those learnings was that the country is programmed to prioritise some places over others. These are the Whitehall norms within which Labour often feels it has to work. The truth is they are a monumental problem for anyone who wants a more equal country. Our political system has evolved in such a way so as to minimise change to the centuries-old way of doing things. It keeps power in the hands of the powerful. This is nowhere more evident than in the Westminster whip system. It has the effect of transferring power from elected representatives to Whitehall mandarins and makes you vote for things you don't fully believe.

It is why I have always said that the Westminster system can make a fraud out of good people. The longer you stay, the more likely that becomes. I tried to stay true to myself as much as I could. But it is hard. I didn't always manage it. Even from an early stage, I had a feeling that I would eventually run out of patience with Westminster and so it would prove.

One of the first things I did as an elected councillor was to join a working group on Hillsborough. I think that showed my intent from an early stage about what was most important to me. My main scrutiny of the Liberal Democrat leadership of the council primarily focused around preparations for the city's year as European Capital of Culture in 2008. I knew how important this was for Liverpool and that we needed to get it right. The city was badly bruised from the difficulties it had faced during the 80s and 90s. The mass unemployment, poverty and riots that the city had endured had led to mocking, jokes and discrimination elsewhere in the country. So when Tessa Jowell confirmed Liverpool as the European Capital of Culture, it was an enormous opportunity to change the way we were seen. I believed we could alter perceptions and bring about an enormous cultural and economic boost.

I was extremely fortunate that, in that particular year with such an eclectic Capital of Culture programme, I was elected as Lord Mayor of Liverpool. I still can't believe that I got to be first citizen of my city. But to do so, in such a historical moment for us, with so much going on, was truly a dream. I think I still hold the record for the most events attended by any Lord Mayor of Liverpool in a single year – an estimated 2,000 in total – which is quite impressive when you consider that there are only 365 days in a year. It was a crazy year and I loved every minute of it.

Capital of Culture was a definite turning point for Liverpool. People started to look differently at the city and it set the wheels in motion for creating the hugely successful visitor economy we have today. It is not lost on Scousers that it was the European Union which brought all that to our door, supported by a Labour government. People were bursting with civic pride as huge numbers visited. It felt like the moment we had been waiting for and I was honoured to have a front-row seat (quite literally).

When my term as Lord Mayor finished, I went back to being a councillor. I was content to get stuck in to the ruling party on the council and help my party to win seats back from the Lib Dems. My name had begun to be mentioned in discussions about Parliamentary seats, which was very flattering, but it felt like political tittle-tattle with no real substance. One day, however, Peter Kilfoyle asked to see me at my home. He told me that he wasn't planning to stand again in the Liverpool

Walton seat at the 2010 election and wanted me to throw my hat into the ring. I couldn't believe it at first; it felt very surreal to hear those words. But he said he would back me.

As with all big decisions in my life, I had to speak to Sandra. She said I might not ever get an opportunity like that again. So I decided to go for it. I got a large majority of the votes in the Labour selection, which was hugely heartening, and I was subsequently elected as the Member of Parliament for Liverpool Walton at the 2010 general election. It was a crazy few days. We went to the election count on the Thursday night, then spent most of Friday celebrating (with a few too many drinks). On Saturday, I was trying to talk to other MPs to find out what I needed to do and, by Sunday, I was planning to travel down to London but with nowhere to stay. I was completely unprepared for my new life in Westminster.

The year before my election, the Westminster MPs expenses scandal had broken. Reporting of the widespread misuse of the system by MPs had led to a host of resignations and even some prosecutions. The scandal had rocked Westminster and there was a huge amount of understandable anger in the country. The newly-formed Independent Parliamentary Standards Authority (IPSA) was being extremely tough on MPs' expenses by the time I arrived in SW1A 0AA. I had been living on a basic councillor's allowance prior to being elected as an MP and had no family savings to fall back on. This meant I had to take out credit cards to pay for somewhere to live in London. At first, I was just desperately trying to get settled but, slowly, the pieces fell into place.

I had never actually set foot inside the Commons chamber before I became an MP. Talk about a baptism of fire! I didn't know how it all worked. I didn't even know my way around the Palace of Westminster and kept getting lost in its labyrinthine corridors. It was one hell of a learning curve. I felt like a kid who was attending big school on the first day.

As a new MP, you gain valuable Parliamentary experience by joining a select committee. As a former local councillor, I felt my best bet was to join a local government committee given I had some experience in that area. It was another steep learning curve. Many of the other members of that committee were experienced politicians and trained lawyers. The reports we were being given to read were hundreds of pages of complex legalese.

I think it is difficult for people like me, from ordinary backgrounds, to hit the ground running when compared with people who have had the best education money can buy. However, I have always considered myself an autodidact and I pick things up very quickly. But it did feel like different worlds colliding when you saw me, a lad from a building site, working with people who had had every opportunity handed to them on a plate; people who consider it their birthright to be in a position of power like that. I used to tell a joke that it must have been galling for some of these very privileged people to have had unlimited money spent on their education only to end up working in the same place as a brickie from Kirkby.

When I was elected, I was determined to campaign on a number of important issues that meant a lot to the people of my constituency and my city. But I found the machinery of Parliament so frustrating. One campaign I led was to ban dangerously old tyres on coaches and buses. It was brought to me by Frances Molloy, who tragically lost her eighteen-year-old son, Michael when the coach he was travelling on crashed because a nineteen-year-old tyre blew out. You would think that was such an obvious and easy change to make, wouldn't you? In fact, it took years and years to make any progress. The system appeared to be designed to hold things up and make it as hard as possible for people to achieve change rather than facilitate it.

Obviously, we were dealing with a Conservative government and that made things a lot more problematic. They weren't interested in socially led policies. They were focused on forcing through their austerity agenda and spending cuts. David Cameron and George Osborne were spinning the line that the way to improve society was to make poor people poorer and rich people richer and that it would all work out for everyone in the end. I think we can safely say that has not been the case.

It was hard to be in Parliament during this period. I was sitting on the green benches watching Tory MPs cheering brutal spending cuts during the week before heading back to the poorest constituency in the country at the weekend to see first-hand the impacts those cuts were having. My spot in the Commons chamber was directly opposite people like Jacob Rees-Mogg and it used to drive me insane listening to some of the arguments and justifications he and others put forward for tearing billions of pounds out of working-class communities. This act was for the greater good, they claimed. It just made me want to scream. Sometimes I have to admit that I did shout things out in anger because I just couldn't help myself.

It felt like many of these dreadful decisions were being directly aimed at cities like Liverpool, which was brutally battered by the cuts. Most of my Liverpool MP colleagues were not from the city so, as the most recognisable Scouser in the place, I felt an extra responsibility at times to stand up for my home city. I did feel a weight of responsibility and I hope I did a decent job of hitting back at the Tory cuts and highlighting the pain they were inflicting on the people I represented.

As far as I am concerned, the economic policies of a government should be aimed first and foremost at helping the people and places that need it the most, driving those standards up so that places can improve and flourish. That's how you build a decent society and that is one area in which this country fundamentally needs to change. We all know how Ricky Tomlinson would describe levelling up. And he would be right.

4

The Fight for Justice

If 15 April 1989 is the most fundamental day in terms of shaping the people Steve and I are today, then the second most significant day arrived exactly twenty years later on 15 April 2009.

I'm not normally one to believe in fate or divine intervention but could almost be persuaded otherwise when I consider the extraordinary circumstances which brought it about. During the preceding year, 2008, Liverpool had been shining in the spotlight of being the European Capital of Culture. This would prove to be a transformational twelve months for the city. It felt like the hangover from the dark days of the 80s and 90s was finally lifting. Steve had rather fortuitously managed to time his year as Lord Mayor of Liverpool with this big moment for the city. But it was a much bigger twist of fate – you could even say a miraculous one – that would soon make our paths cross for the first time.

I had gone into 2008 as chief secretary and, on Saturday, 12 January, had been invited with Marie-France by my friend James Purnell, the then culture secretary, to the opening night of Liverpool 08 at the newly built Liverpool Echo arena. It was a great night but I spent much of it thinking how lucky James was and wishing I had his job. When Echo & The Bunnymen came on to finish the show with the Liverpool Philharmonic and a beautiful rendition of 'Nothing Lasts Forever', the opening lines of the song caught my feelings perfectly: '*I want it now, I want it now/Not the promises of what tomorrow brings/I need to live in dreams today/I'm tired of the songs that sorrow sings.*'

Precisely twelve days later, the political gods unbelievably answered my call. In the early evening of Thursday, 24 January, as I sat in the chief secretary's office and watched the sky go dark over St James's Park, Maria, my diary secretary, put her head around the door and, to my surprise, said the Number 10 switchboard was on the line and wanted to put me through to the Prime Minister. What followed was a very Gordon call.

'Andy, you probably know Peter has had a problem and he has had to go. I'm putting James in at Work and Pensions.' The Peter in question was Peter Hain, who had resigned as work and pensions secretary over undeclared donations to his campaign for the deputy leadership of the Labour Party. I liked Peter, and felt for him, but politics moves fast in times like these. Then came the moment I will never forget: 'Would you do me a favour and go to Culture?'

'A favour, Gordon? I honestly couldn't think of anything better. I won't let you down.' When I hung up the phone, my feet barely touched the floor. I pretty much flew out of Her Majesty's Treasury and went straight up Whitehall to the Department of Culture, Media and Sport by Trafalgar Square. I stood outside and spoke to reporters, barely able to contain my excitement. When I went inside, I told my private office that I would be doing things differently and not going to Covent Garden and Sadler's Wells, as culture secretaries are expected to do. Instead, I would be spending the year in Liverpool.

Two days later, my first official visit saw me at the building site of the new Museum of Liverpool on the city's famous waterfront. Later that afternoon, I went over to Anfield to see Liverpool take on Havant & Waterlooville in the fourth round of the FA Cup. The minnows actually went 2–0 up and I was doing my best to keep calm in the Director's Box. To my disappointment, Liverpool turned it around and won 5–2. But I was already loving my new job.

From then on, I was a regular at events in the city. At the time, the Liberal Democrats were in control of the city council. Being more tribal in those days, I always tried to avoid the Lord Mayor at official functions when he would come over and try to engage me in conversation. I assumed he was a part of the ruling group. Eventually, at yet another event, Steve's patience ran out: 'You do know I'm Labour, don't you?' It was the cue for the start of a beautiful friendship.

Looking back now, the turn of events that brought us to this moment are mind-boggling. If you go back to that fateful day in 1989, what odds would you have got on Steve becoming Lord Mayor and me culture secretary in the very same year and such an important one for the city? And then, having formed that strong bond, gone forward together into 2009 – another huge year for the city given the impending twentieth anniversary? The answer, surely, is tens of billions to one.

The first thing Steve and I worked on together was the repatriation of an Evertonian who had been tragically murdered in Spain. By February 2009, we had managed to persuade the Spanish authorities to allow Gary Dunne's body to return to Merseyside and we were sitting side by side in the front pew of the Anglican cathedral waiting for his delayed funeral to start. As we waited, Steve leant over and whispered into my ear that I would soon be getting an invitation to address the twentieth anniversary Hillsborough Memorial Service at Anfield. My blood instantly ran cold. I turned to look at him with my eyes wide open and said that nobody would want me or any representative of the government there. He just said: 'You're coming.'

Steve can often have a sixth sense about things. His instincts told him that he needed to build the profile of the twentieth anniversary and he had been working hard with the Hillsborough families to that effect. He was not going to allow me to disrupt his plans. As 'Z-Cars' began to play in the cathedral, and Gary's blue coffin came up the aisle, he finished the brief conversation by stating that, not only would I be going, I would also be speaking. What could I possibly say? On the only previous occasion I had tried to raise Hillsborough in government, it had been shut down quickly. But I was only a very junior minister at that time. Now things were different: I was a Cabinet minister and could certainly do something if I so chose. And yet it would still carry risks. If I raised it but couldn't persuade any of my colleagues to support me, it would make my position untenable.

For weeks after that conversation in the cathedral, I agonised in this way with my family about what to do. Should I go or not? I was worried that it could end up being the worst of all worlds for everyone. I desperately didn't want to upset people or ruin such an important occasion or become the main issue. On the other hand, I had been asked and I knew there was a major wrong that needed to be righted. If I didn't go, I would feel like a coward and it would haunt me for the rest of my life. In the end, it was my younger brother, John, who cut through the confusion with his knack of offering clear and sound advice: 'And, go if you are going to do something for them [the families]. If not, stay away.'

Whenever I have had a big decision to make in my life and career, it has often come back to the collective wisdom of the core group of Eileen, Roy, Nick and John. My younger brother's advice was still going around my head when I came across an article by David Conn in *The Guardian* about a week before the service. David was someone I knew well from my Football Task Force days and is without a doubt one of the finest journalists this country has ever produced. He had been back to some of the police statements that were deposited in the House of Lords Library after the review in 1998, at the instigation of Maria Eagle MP, and had discovered that many of those statements by police officers on duty at Hillsborough had been amended by their superiors. As I sat and read David's article in my kitchen, I could finally see a way forward. I would make a public call for disclosure of all Hillsborough documents using David's article as the trigger. This, of course, was not the government's official position and I was freelancing at this point. For safety in numbers, I called Maria, who was also a minister, and I asked her if she would work with me on it. She said she would. So, a couple of days before the anniversary, David ran a second article reporting the unauthorised disclosure call from two government ministers.

When I woke up on the morning of the anniversary itself, I

could already feel the knot in my stomach and tightness in my chest. I didn't know precisely what would happen later that day but I did know a huge moment was coming. A more diehard Evertonian than my brother John you would struggle to find. He is also a true football man to the core of his being. In 1989, as a teenager, he went to Anfield with my mum to see the sea of flowers and scarves. Since then, he had been to many of the annual memorial services, some of them attended by only a small crowd. In 2009, I was gathered with the Anfield great and good in the boardroom, when I took my phone out of my pocket to turn it off before the service. I found a text from John. It read: 'Don't want to worry you, And, but I'm in the Anfield Road end. The crowd is massive.' That message was the last thing I saw before I joined the official line-up and walked out in front of the Kop.

At the anniversary the year before, in 2008, there were probably fewer than 6,000 people at Anfield. When Andy walked out to do his speech a year on, there were 37,000 people filling all four corners of the ground. I was sitting on the Kop with the Lord Mayor's chain on, next to my wife, Sandra, and she was nervous for Andy. I was too.

We had worked really hard to raise the profile of the anniversary in the hope of having one last concerted attempt at getting some movement towards a new inquiry into what happened at Hillsborough. For so long, the families had been forced to live with the lies and the flawed and unacceptable verdicts from the first inquests.

Before my year as Lord Mayor, I had been to every memorial service for the disaster, apart from the first one. That was too raw for me as someone who had been at the match on that awful day. But here I was, as Liverpool's first citizen, about to address the crowd with my personal thoughts from the day and my frustrations at the failure to recognise such a grave injustice. I was speaking after Andy, so I was hoping everything would go smoothly for him.

Hillsborough was always going to figure heavily in my political life, but when I became Lord Mayor, I finally felt I was in a position to make something happen. There were certain levers I could pull. I invited people into the town hall to discuss what we could collectively do. Even though the role is largely ceremonial, it does command a certain gravitas and an ability to bring different people together.

Phil Hammond, who lost his fourteen-year-old son Philip Junior in the disaster, was the chair of the Hillsborough Families Support Group at the time. He came to see me in the town hall. I told him I wanted to give things another go in terms of focusing attention back onto the fight for justice, for a fresh inquest and, finally, to get the real truth out.

The families certainly hadn't given up, but after twenty years of fighting, they were tired. Phil became unwell and in stepped Margaret Aspinall, whose eighteen-year-old son James was killed, as the new chair. Margaret came to see me at the town hall and we talked about inviting Andy to the upcoming anniversary service, as Phil had previously agreed to my request. Despite the fact she knew there would be resistance from some members of the support group, she just said: 'OK, let's do it.' It's understandable that some group members wouldn't be totally convinced as they had been let down by politicians in the past. But Margaret supported it and we made it happen.

I was determined to get Andy there. He was an ordinary working-class lad and understood our area despite leaving at such an early age. He knew the magnitude of the Hillsborough disaster to a city constantly failed by the establishment. Andy was in a position where he might be able to help us. I wasn't going to take no for an answer from him. I knew if we were going to have a chance to change the course of events then we needed someone in government to take it forward.

There are so many people who had been campaigning for decades and there is not enough space in this book to thank them all. To get the message to as many people as possible, we decided to produce a record to be played during the run-up to the twentieth anniversary. I enlisted the help of people like Peter Hooton from The Farm and we called in a lot of favours to use music as a mechanism to raise the profile of Hillsborough to a new generation of supporters. With artists like John Power of Cast fame giving their time for free, we released a version of 'The Fields of Anfield Road' by the Liverpool Collective in 2009, which charted at No.12 and went to No.1 in the Indie charts. This meant people were again asking questions as to why there had been no truth or justice.

But on the day of the service at Anfield, I was terribly nervous for Andy. I knew it was going to be a difficult gig. Fans wanted action, not more warm words from Westminster politicians. I was worried it could go badly wrong. It was a huge moment for all of us.

As I walked out on that chilly spring afternoon, I just remember this overwhelming feeling of foreboding and a fear of letting people down. I had to be ready for whatever was coming. When my name was finally called to speak, the moment of reckoning had arrived. When I made my way to the podium in front of the Kop, and turned to face it, it felt like I was standing on the edge of the abyss between the government I was in and the people with whom I had grown up. I had written the speech myself and carefully prepared it. Whether I liked it or not, I was there to represent the government at the memorial of one of the cruellest man-made disasters this country has seen. It was the first mention of the words 'Prime Minister' which triggered the avalanche.

'We want justice,' came the first lone cry from about two thirds up the Kop. Within seconds, that first stone was followed by thousands of others as the shouts of 'justice' rolled off the Kop and into living rooms across the land. They then coalesced into the chant of 'Justice for the 96' which rang around all sides of the ground. It feels strange to say this but my main emotion at this point was one of relief. Sometimes, when you are doing a speech and you know there is going to be a reaction from the crowd, the anticipation of that moment is the hardest bit. I knew something had to give on that day and, in Steve's mind, I was there to help it happen. When the dam finally broke, I didn't try to talk through it. Instead, I stepped back and tried to acknowledge what was happening and what they were saying. I knew they were right and the government I was in was wrong. But my feelings were not widely understood. Some people were angry at me for being there. Others were angry at the mention of the government and who could blame them? But, as I finally resumed my speech, the mood changed a little when I talked about being at the other semi-final myself on that same day in 1989. I also talked about Hillsborough being an entirely man-made disaster and, combined with my disclosure call, I was very deliberately going beyond what any member of the Labour government had previously done.

When it was over, I walked back across the front of the Kop towards the Centenary Stand, where the Hillsborough Families Support Group would hold their post-service reception, very conscious of the mixed reactions of those who had come to pay their respects. Inside my suit pocket, I could feel my mobile phone constantly buzzing. Eventually, once inside the stand, I took it out. The screen read: 'GB calling'. At the time, Gordon was facing one crisis after another. I felt guilty that I had caused him another headache. I braced myself as I picked up the call.

'Andy, you've done a great thing by being there and I just wanted you to know that.'

'Really, Gordon? That means so much to me you saying that.'

'If there's something I can do to help, you just ask me.'

'Well, there is something. Do you think I could raise Hillsborough at Cabinet tomorrow?'

'Yes, you do that, I will bring you in at the end of the formal agenda.'

I will never forget that phone call as long as I live, nor what would happen at the Cabinet meeting in Glasgow the following day. It is very rare for items to be added to a Cabinet agenda the day before – but Gordon instantly agreed to it.

As I entered the hospitality suite for the reception, a weight had already been lifted. But I can remember feeling utterly drained. I told Steve I was going to head home. He insisted that I come over to Liverpool Town Hall for the ceremony where the Hillsborough families would be given the freedom of the city. Once again, he had a strong sense of what needed to be done. When I got out of my government car outside the town hall, Joe Anderson, who was the leader of the Labour opposition on Liverpool City Council at the time, was waiting for me. He told me I needed to stop what I was doing. I was raising expectations and creating false hope. That was my first welcoming committee.

A second was assembled on the first floor at the top of the grand staircase. As I trudged up the stairs with the weight of the world on my shoulders, I turned halfway to face a formidable sight for any Evertonian: Kenny Dalglish, Alan Hansen, Jamie Carragher and Steven Gerrard. At the top of this voice, Kenny said: 'Oh no, you've not come here to upset these families all over again, have you?' It would have been wonderful if the ground had swallowed me up, never to be seen again. Although I didn't realise it straight away, this was a prime example of Kenny's famous sledgehammer wit. It was intended to break the ice and, in fact, it did the job perfectly. We all laughed together, and it put me more at ease. Steven and Jamie told me I had done the right thing and that really meant something to me.

Steve was hosting the ceremony as Lord Mayor and had told me he would bring me up to say something more personal. As I sat waiting to be called, my mood was beginning to change. I had gone through the pain barrier and was already emerging on the other side, ready to face up to the opportunity I had created. I told the families that I didn't know what I would be able to achieve for them, but I would give it everything I had, starting with the call for disclosure. It seemed to go down better than my speech earlier that day.

As the event broke up, Anne Williams made a beeline for me. Anne's son Kevin had died at Hillsborough aged just fifteen years old and I knew of her from news reports of her incredible legal fight all the way to the European Court of Human Rights. Anne pinned me up against the wall and fixed me with her piercing stare: 'Kevin was alive at 3.45 p.m. I've got proof.' A day which had started with huge confusion was ending with a growing sense of clarity. That conversation with Anne was the best possible way to end it. She gave me a sense of resolve. I remembered the warning about false hope and was worried about it. But it was too late to step back. I had gone over the line. I was in it 100 per cent.

After that day, there was a spark of hope. I knew getting Andy there was our big chance because he was in the Cabinet and he would understand the situation. He knew what had happened. I knew he would feel the intensity and significance of that day and he did.

After the emotion he had felt at Anfield, Andy definitely wanted to head home. I think he felt a little bruised and drained. I felt that, if he had departed at that point, it would have left a yawning gap between what he had said, on behalf of the government, and what he really felt. I knew that couldn't be the full stop on the day. I had to take him to the town hall to see the families of the victims so that he could understand why things were still so painful and raw.

There was a very strange atmosphere in the town hall. This was supposed to be the commemorative part of the day, a civic service for the families. But after the way things had played out at Anfield, the atmosphere was extremely emotional and intense. When Andy stood up and spoke, without notes and from the heart, I think he convinced a lot of people in that room that there was some hope things could change in the fight for truth and justice. Not everyone was convinced, but there was a beacon of hope that was flickering.

You could actually see the expressions on people's faces change as Andy was speaking. They were starting to believe that he meant what he was saying about being on their side. After his speech, he talked individually with the families and told them he understood their pain and that he was going to take this to the heart of government. The very next day, that is exactly what he did.

By mid-afternoon the following day, I found myself around a table in a nondescript meeting room inside the SECC in Glasgow for a meeting of the Cabinet. When governments become unpopular, they often go out on the road in a desperate attempt to appear in touch with the public. Ours was no different. I could barely focus on the formal business of the meeting. I had caught an early train to get up to Glasgow and the enormity of the day before was taking its toll. As the meeting was coming towards the end, Gordon said: 'You will have seen Andy was at Anfield yesterday for the twentieth anniversary of Hillsborough. We are grateful to him for representing the government. I have asked him to report back and share his perspective on the issues.'

I knew people would think I would be overly emotional following the previous day's events. And they would be right; I was. But I also knew this meant I needed to be as factual and dispassionate as possible. Recalling my conversation with Anne, I told them I knew there was hard evidence to cast serious doubt on the 3.15 p.m. ruling by the original coroner. I made reference to David's *Guardian* article of a few days before. This was why Maria and I had made the call for disclosure, I explained. It may be difficult now to achieve justice for the families. But we did have the power to give them the full truth and that is what we should do. As Gordon opened the floor for contributions, I braced myself. I was about to learn the scale of the fight I would face to open things up. Jack Straw came in early and said he feared it would set a precedent that could make things difficult in other situations. A couple of others agreed with him. But Jacqui Smith, the home secretary, was supportive and so was Alan Johnson, the health secretary. It was hard to gauge the full feeling in the room. It felt more positive than negative but was still tentative. Gordon summed up: 'I've heard what everyone has said and there are some issues which we will have to take into account. But we're going to back Andy on this.' Whenever I recall that moment, it always makes tears spring towards my eyes. It will stay with me for ever.

HEAD NORTH

Two days after that Cabinet meeting, I was due to head to London with Jimmy, my dad, brothers Nick and John, cousin Chris and nephew Joe to see Everton play Manchester United in the FA Cup semi-final at Wembley. We had all stayed at my London flat on the Saturday night and, on the day of the match, I had got up early and waded through the empty cans to go out and get the Sunday papers. I had agreed to give a media interview to Mark Edwardson of BBC North West on the events of the previous few days so needed to know what was in the news. I remember one of the broadsheets carrying a briefing from the Home Office: the home secretary would be asking South Yorkshire Police to open up their Hillsborough files. I referenced it in my discussion with Mark. When the interview was over, he surprised me by telling me he was at Hillsborough and thanked me for being at the twentieth anniversary. It felt like things were beginning to change.

The positive feeling carried on throughout the day with Everton, somewhat unbelievably, winning on penalties. I remember the *Mirror* front page the next day: above the headline 'Justice at Last' was a picture of the entire Everton team running towards our supporters. There will never be a better front page in my life.

From there, a long period of internal wrangling would begin in government over the establishment of the Hillsborough Independent Panel (HIP) to oversee the disclosure of thousands of documents related to the disaster. I was determined that, rather than just throw the documents out into the public domain, the terms of reference needed to require the HIP to produce a report on the extent to which disclosure added to public understanding of the tragedy. It was utterly crucial and, despite attempts by civil servants and politicians to remove it, I succeeded in keeping it in. My mission was to set up the HIP properly in advance of the forthcoming general election so that it would have a chance of completing its job in the 2010 to 2015 Parliament. In early 2010, it emerged that the Bishop of Liverpool, the Right Reverend James Jones, had been asked to chair it. It was met with some criticism from certain quarters in Liverpool. Here was another figure from the establishment that had let the city down, they said. But, from what I knew of Bishop James, I felt he was the right choice – and so it emphatically proved. In September 2012, the HIP produced its earth-shattering report. It found that police failures were the main reason for the disaster. Forty-one of those who died at Hillsborough may have survived with a better emergency response on the day. It revealed the efforts made to cover up the extent of the failure, with 116 of the 164 police statements taken after the tragedy amended to put the police in a better light.

As 2012 came to a close, the High Court ruled, following a referral by then Attorney General Dominic Grieve, that the accidental death verdict of the original inquests should be quashed and new inquests ordered. To cap it all, almost five years to the day after Peter Hain's resignation, Steve Rotheram achieved the highly improbable feat of becoming the first serving MP to achieve a Christmas No.1 in the UK charts. He even appeared on *Top of the Pops* in the video for 'He Ain't Heavy, He's My Brother' – or, more accurately, you can catch a fleeting glimpse of his nose in it. As I said earlier, what odds would you have got on all of that?

There has been the right of 'the people' to present petitions to Parliament since 1669 and, in 2006, Number 10 instigated a system of e-petitions which was separate to the Parliamentary process. In an attempt to look like they cared, the Coalition government promised that, if an online petition got over 100,000 signatures, they would provide Parliamentary time to debate the issue. The new process opened in July 2011 and there was a flurry of applications for a plethora of laudable and controversial subjects.

I had been in London with my wife, Sandra, watching a show, and when we came out there was a missed call on my phone from Kenny Dalglish. I called him back and he said there was a petition calling for the release of documents related to the Hillsborough disaster and asked whether he should support it. It had been prompted by the Cabinet Office turning down a

Freedom of Information request from the BBC for the release of government papers. To be fair to the government, because of the Hillsborough Independent Panel, their position was to wait until it had concluded its work. That said, Andy and I were worried about the level of commitment in the new government to the disclosure process and the e-petition presented an opportunity. I think it had about 20,000 signatures before Kenny got involved. After his endorsement, it just took off – easily hitting the 100,000 mark which, under new government rules, triggered the potential for a debate in Parliament. This was one of the first times the threshold had ever been reached so it was all very new to everyone involved.

There was still some way to go to secure a debate though. It needed someone to steer the application through the Parliamentary process. I was able to get cross-party support to take my case to the Backbench Business Committee in order to argue for the e-petition to get Parliamentary time for debate. Incredibly, I eventually received ninety-six MPs' signatures. It wasn't a contrived number; it just happened to be that many. But I saw it as an omen. The committee initially offered me a Westminster Hall debate, away from the main Commons chamber, but I was never going to accept that. The gravity of what we would be discussing meant that, for me, only the green benches of the House of Commons would suffice.

In the end, we were successful in securing the first ever Commons debate triggered by an e-petition. It was scheduled for October 2011. I would move the motion and that meant I would have an extended time to speak. I would be able to tease out the issues for those hearing them for the first time. But I would also be the first person to tell the Hillsborough truth in Parliament. Just before the debate, Andy asked me if I was going to read out the names of the ninety-six Liverpool fans who, at that point, had died at Hillsborough. The idea was to get their names permanently recorded in Hansard, the report of Parliamentary debates, for the very first time. I was worried that, when I started to read out the names, I would break down or miss someone out. The pressure was enormous.

Many of the Hillsborough families had travelled to London for the debate. As I rose to speak, the public gallery was directly above me so I couldn't see any of their reactions or responses to my words. The only person whose face I vividly remember seeing was that of Theresa May, who was the home secretary at the time. I distinctly remember her expression when I mentioned that the police had tested the blood alcohol levels of every fan who had died, including ten-year-old Jon-Paul Gilhooley, in their attempts to smear Liverpool fans in the wake of the disaster. I could see her wince at the thought – and believed the penny had started to drop for her. She was beginning to understand.

I delivered my speech to an eerie House of Commons in which you could have heard a pin drop. I was determined to be as factual as I could on such an emotional subject because I believed it was important clearly to explain the events of the day and the aftermath. I got through the main body of my speech and then reached the section where I was to list the names and ages of those that had perished on that fateful day.

When I read out the first name, my mouth dried and I stumbled. I felt a huge wave of emotion. For a second, I thought I would be overwhelmed by the enormity of the whole thing. *Pull yourself together man*, I thought. I took a deep breath and got into a rhythm. I was okay after that point. I could just feel the gravity of the moment. It was weighing heavily on me. It was just so important to so many people. At the end of it, I was physically and emotionally drained. I sat down and other Parliamentarians made their speeches. But I remember little of it other than Andy's brilliant contribution.

I didn't agree with Theresa May on virtually any other issue apart from Hillsborough. To her credit, though, she immediately engaged with Andy and me following the Commons debate. She called us and said it was a remarkable thing that had happened in the chamber that night. She would like to try and take things forward.

We kept in contact with her and there was a lot of work

going on behind the scenes. It was then that we started to make real progress and drive things forward. I didn't support what Theresa was doing at the time on issues like the so-called 'hostile environment' for those coming to this country. But I have to say, on Hillsborough, she was true to her word. I grew up never wanting to speak to a Tory in my life and ended up working closely with a future Tory Prime Minister because I realised I had to do that to get the right results for the people I was representing.

This is a rare example of what can be achieved in Westminster when party politics is put to one side so that a crucial issue can be worked on. You don't see that a lot and that is a real problem – it is something that Andy and I will discuss in greater detail later in this book.

I do sometimes wonder, if a similarly appalling tragedy had happened elsewhere in the country, whether the reaction of the establishment of the day would have been as vindictive. I'm not convinced it would have been. There had been a period under Margaret Thatcher when her ministers had called for Liverpool to be left in a state of managed decline and there was a series of vicious battles between the Conservative government and the Militant-led Labour council of Liverpool. In 1985, there was the Heysel Stadium disaster, for which a number of Liverpool fans were jailed. Then, against this difficult backdrop, something catastrophic happened and the establishment decided to close ranks on the city. They knew the truth of what happened at Hillsborough right from the start. But they genuinely believed they would get away with covering it up – and they nearly did.

The system in this country was completely weighted against fans and their families. The government, the police and sections of the media colluded against ordinary working-class people. It was never a fair fight but those families refused to give up. They did an unbelievable job with the odds constantly stacked against them.

5

Heading North

I always say that I took my first steps out of Westminster on 15 April 2009 when I walked out to face the Kop. While it would be another eight years before I finally left, things were never the same after that day. I had experienced the way our political system fails people in a very personal way and, from 2009, the realisation grew that it could only be fixed with wholesale change. The spell was broken and I had fallen out of love with Westminster.

In two campaigns for the Labour leadership – in 2010 and 2015 – I tried to run against the Westminster status quo and make that case for change. Of course, I made plenty of mistakes in both campaigns. But I like to think that the issues I was raising – particularly the way our political system had failed the North – are better understood now than they were then. I hope I have played a part in that.

As the 2010 general election drew close, I pondered what I would do if Labour left government. I was certain David Miliband would stand and become the immediate favourite. I was pretty sure Ed Balls would also stand and initially be seen as his main challenger. However, the problem for them both was that this line-up would create a race that would feel like Tony 2.0 versus Gordon 2.0. Surely there was an opportunity for someone to come through the middle? On the plus side, subsequent events would prove my analysis to be pretty sharp: someone did indeed sneak through. On the downside, that someone would not be me. My failure to spot the eventual winner revealed my limited understanding of the dynamics of political dynasties.

HEAD NORTH

On the Monday after the general election, Westminster was still in limbo. The inconclusive election result meant negotiations were ongoing. The Labour Cabinet met in Number 10 for what would prove to be the final time. The discussion focused on whether we could reach out to the Lib Dems and form an unlikely government. Andrew Adonis was recognised as the best person to lead the approach, but Gordon asked if any others had good relationships with senior Lib Dems. I mentioned how well I had got on with Norman Lamb during our cross-party talks on social care, which the Tories had sabotaged, and it was agreed I should reach out to him.

My memory of that early May evening is not so much the official business, which felt like a long shot, but the unofficial. I was surprised by the extent to which David's leadership campaign was already in full visible flow in the Cabinet room. When I was back at my flat later that night, and a text came back from Norman informing me that the Lib Dems were heading in the opposite direction, I began to think seriously about whether I had it in me to stand. I had an idea. To expose the London-centric nature of the Labour Party, and the other continuity campaigns, I would make a big statement by basing mine in Manchester.

By the Wednesday morning, as David's hat landed in the ring, I was getting closer to doing the same. But that was when my phone rang. It was Ed Miliband telling me he was about to announce his candidacy and was asking for my support. Until that point, I had been working on the basis that one brother would not stand against the other. If the prospect came close, surely a family conclave would be called and a decision reached? Apparently not. In a heartbeat, my space in the race had gone. But I had already gone too far. I kidded myself that I could still do it and that the brothers might cancel each other out. Instead, the fraternal psychodrama would dominate the media for the whole summer. When Ed Miliband narrowly won that contest, I readily agreed to be in his shadow Cabinet, first as shadow education secretary and then as shadow health secretary. I admired what Ed had done in his campaign and that respect and affection for him has only grown since. He is an outstanding politican and wonderful person.

But, at the time, the combination of my ongoing experiences with the Hillsborough justice campaign and the fact that I had spoken freely during the leadership election meant I was a very different politician. I was far less happy to toe the party line. An adviser once briefed a newspaper, not incorrectly, that I had 'left the reservation'.

This more rebellious streak was on show on the eve of the Labour conference in Liverpool in 2012, just a couple of weeks after the Hillsborough Independent Panel had delivered its report. I was shadow health secretary at the time and running a fierce campaign against the government's disastrous new Health and Social Care Bill, which would open the door to more competition and privatisation. On a sunny Saturday evening in the beer garden of the Black Horse on County Road, in the afterglow of a David Moyes-inspired Everton win over Southampton, texts started coming in telling me Ed had given an interview contradicting my firm stance on the Bill. He said that Labour would amend it rather than oppose it outright. 'Would you care to comment?' came the innocent-sounding request from almost every Sunday journalist in the land. I took the route one approach. I put down my pint, typed out 'I'll repeal the Bill. Full stop' and pressed 'Tweet'.

As far as I was concerned, I was simply repeating the position we had agreed. But that was the position before the Bill was passed. We hadn't updated it since. The tweet got a lot of traction that night. I had lost patience with the Westminster habit of nuancing and hedging everything we said. By this point in my political career, I had learnt that winning a leadership election would require a more confident, clear approach than I had previously shown. When we lost again in 2015, I felt much more ready to go again. Steve and I were closer than ever and I asked him to take charge of the Parliamentary side of my campaign. Throughout the 2010 to 2015 Parliament, I had topped the shadow Cabinet poll on LabourList. I was the early frontrunner by a decent margin, up against Yvette Cooper and Liz Kendall, and felt confident that I could get over the line. That was until there was a last-minute addition to the names on the ballot paper.

Andy decided early on in that campaign, against my advice, that he would not take any union funding. He had seen Ed Miliband take a lot of hits from the Tories over that during his leadership of the Labour Party and thought he could avoid attacks if he were to become leader. It meant that we had very little money for the campaign, which made life interesting. We travelled by the cheapest means and stayed at budget hotels.

On many occasions, we would be squeezed into a supporters' car being driven between hustings or from the last event of the day to our luxurious accommodation. Often, we would stop at a service station and buy a few cans of beer and a curled-up sausage roll for the long journey. Early in the campaign, Andy had done a tongue-in-cheek tweet quoting some lyrics from 'Take Over the World' by a band called Courteeners after appearing on the Marr programme one Sunday morning: *'I'm only a paperboy from the North West/But I can scrub up well in my Sunday best'*. Unsurprisingly, this was picked up and retweeted by lots of his followers. It became our unofficial campaign theme tune. On journeys, I would play the song and ramp the sound up to eleven. The irony wasn't lost on us that the chorus included the line: *'I think it's time for me and you, to take over the world'*.

I wouldn't mind but we couldn't even take over the vehicle in front of us with some of the cars we were travelling in!

On one memorable night, we were staying in the North East ahead of an event and all we could afford was one tiny, freezing room in this little budget hotel. Thankfully, we had twin beds. There was a light constantly strobing in the bathroom all night, which fitted quite nicely with the very loud party going on in the next room. The beds were horrific. My pillow was as thin as a Ryvita. I had to fold it over four times just to try and get some comfort. It was not The Ritz.

What made these experiences all the more difficult was the feeling that the contest was already running away from us. That was how it felt from the moment Jeremy Corbyn got the required nominations to get on the ballot paper. After the huge disappointment of the election result in 2015, and the departure of Ed Miliband, it was clear people had an appetite for something very different to what had been on offer. At this point, we were five years into the austerity agenda of the Coalition government, which had seen huge cuts to public services. People were struggling. We knew that, as a very left-wing figure and someone far removed from the Labour team that had lost the previous election, Jeremy could be a popular option for people at that exact moment in time who were desperate for something different.

Andy knew he would be in trouble if Corbyn got on the ballot and he had given me the job of shoring up support to keep Jeremy at bay. We had a big white board with all the names of the Labour MPs who were supporting us and initially we were in great shape. But, once Jeremy started to gain a few signatures, we started to lose some of the promises we had been given by MPs. He was creeping up on us. There were some interesting names nominating Jeremy that you might not have expected, like Sadiq Khan, Margaret Beckett, Frank Field, Emily Thornberry and David Lammy. People wanted to position themselves as the ones opening up the race to a wider field.

I called Andy on the day the nominations closed: 'You know that one job you gave me, to keep Corbyn off the ballot? Well I couldn't do it. He has the required number of backers.' I think he knew straight away he was going to struggle after that. There was this huge tsunami of support behind Jeremy. It swept him into the lead and, as it overwhelmed us, we never caught him.

It was on a Monday lunchtime, just after 12 p.m., when Steve rang me to say Jeremy Corbyn had got the nominations he needed to stand. My heart sank. I knew straight away that all the energy would flow out of my stuttering campaign and into his. From then on, it was gruelling. I kept fighting on, hoping to spark some momentum, and remember belatedly finding my voice in the latter stages of the campaign. By then, I was running hard against an overly London-centric Labour Party and remember giving a stirring speech from the altar of a packed-out church in Sheffield with just a couple of weeks to go. I sat down with my heart beating and a feeling that I was finally coming alive. But then the Chair of the meeting opened up the floor to questions and a gruff Yorkshire voice said from the back: 'Andy, you've given a good account of yourself up there. But do you realise you've been talking for the last twenty minutes under a sign saying "Repent, JC is coming"?' I turned around, looked up above the altar and – sure enough – there it was. People proceeded to fall about laughing in the pews and I knew there and then it was game over. Even the Almighty was backing Jeremy.

Early in the contest, I made the classic mistake of talking too much about how I would handle thorny issues – like the coming EU referendum – rather than giving party members something more hopeful. There is a maxim in politics about 'fighting the election you are in'. I completely forgot about it. I was already preparing for what lay ahead. I felt in my bones that Labour was heading towards a looming crisis and that we needed to anticipate it. Speaking to people on the doorstep in Leigh during the general election had left me in no doubt that Labour was losing its hold on what we now know as the 'Red Wall'. I kept telling my team that I was worried about the level of support for UKIP. I can often come down with a bad dose of 'candidate-itis' towards the end of elections and Kevin Lee, my long-term right-hand man, took the mickey out of my jitters. He was of course right that I was never in danger of losing. But I was also right that something was stirring in Leigh and places like it. That is why I became very worried about the impending EU referendum when David Cameron confirmed it soon into the new Parliament. I was clear from the start that it would be much tougher than people thought and posed big risks for Labour and the country. Unfortunately for me, Labour didn't want to hear it. My negative warnings fell flat while Jeremy's simple but hopeful messages caught fire.

Labour needed to be much less metropolitan and much more focused on the more neglected parts of the Midlands and the North. In retrospect, this was a message the Labour Party clearly needed to take on board. But perhaps I should have delayed the team-talk a little. After all, the vast majority of Labour's members are based in London and this was hardly going to appeal to them. I also talked a lot about the Westminster Bubble – too much – and, as a result, drew some disparaging comments from those MPs and journalists who were very happy with their life inside it. In my defence, I was utterly seized by the fact that we urgently needed a much grittier take on things and maybe events since have borne that out. The referendum was winnable, but we didn't go out and win it. I was not in any way entertaining the idea of leaving the EU. Yet I felt strongly that we needed to meet traditional Labour voters halfway on some of the concerns they had. I had seen first-hand how freedom of movement was having an impact on wages and public services in places like Leigh. I had examples of people's wages being undercut by local firms recruiting whole shifts from Poland or Romania; of school places suddenly becoming unavailable. Difficult issues, yes. But they needed a response. When I raised them at Labour hustings, the only response I got was heckles from the audience.

During the campaign, I went over to Brussels to meet Martin Schulz MEP, then President of the European Parliament, to gauge the appetite of the European left for change. Expecting a difficult meeting, I was hugely encouraged by Martin's similar take as mine on the need for the EU to have better answers for former industrial communities. An engaged Labour Party could have worked with Martin and others like him on a much more left-leaning reform of freedom of movement and measures to prevent the undercutting of skilled wages. Instead, we were trapped between two fixed positions: the Blairite take, represented by Liz in the leadership campaign, and its uncritical defence of the EU status quo; and the radical left's view of the EU as a capitalist conspiracy, represented by Jeremy. Labour was stuck in this simplistic, factional thinking and losing touch with large parts of the country. We had settled into opposition and were in a comfort zone.

By then, social media and particularly Twitter was beginning to play a huge role in internal Labour politics. It had facilitated and accentuated the party's navel-gazing tendency to focus on insular factional debates. During the nomination phase of the leadership contest, Labour MPs were coming under huge online pressure to nominate Jeremy. People who had told Steve to his face that they would nominate me went into the Parliamentary Labour Party office and signed the papers for Jeremy. The deadline for nominations was midday on Monday, 12 June. To get on the ballot paper, Jeremy would need a total of thirty-five MPs to nominate him. When I checked in with Steve earlier on that Monday morning, he told me he was still a few short. Steve was camped outside the PLP office, God bless him, doing everything he could to manage the process. But it was unmanageable. That morning, a number of prominent London MPs, presumably under huge social media pressure from their local members, went into the PLP office to nominate Jeremy with just minutes to go before the deadline. By 12.01, it was clear that he had got thirty-six names – one more than the thirty-five he needed.

All this said, I made many mistakes in that campaign. I will hold my hands up to that. There wasn't enough clarity or control in my messages and I had too many people telling me I had to say certain things to please certain groups. I knew now how David Miliband must have felt in 2010. The curse of the front-runner was a real thing.

The defining moment came in July 2015 and the vote on the Welfare Reform Bill. In the election campaign, the Tories had developed a divisive rhetoric about strivers and skivers and brought forward its proposals on benefits straight after to cause maximum political discomfort for Labour. This was Westminster at its very worst: the huge damage that would be inflicted on people's lives was just an unfortunate by-product of the political game-playing.

When we met in the old shadow Cabinet room on a sunny

July evening, I was stunned when the acting leader of the party Harriet Harman said that we needed to hear what people had said at the election and vote for the Bill or, at very least, abstain on it. I said I couldn't accept that given the damage it would do to people in constituencies like mine. What then ensued were days of wrangling with the chief whip Rosie Winterton over Labour's position. I knew a simple abstention would be deadly for my campaign given that Jeremy had never paid much attention to the Labour whips and would almost certainly oppose it. In the end, I forced the shadow Cabinet to table a reasoned amendment – which meant we would be voting against the Bill but with some caveats. In other words, a more half-hearted form of opposition. It felt like it would be enough – but the black-and-white world of Twitter didn't care much for my nuanced position. On the night of the vote, when Jeremy walked through the No lobby to oppose the Bill outright, the leadership contest was only going to go one way.

Westminster rewards loyalists and mavericks: the former get promoted and the latter get the kudos of looking independent. Anyone in the middle, who tries to change things from the inside, ends up looking a bit lost. People can't see what you are trying to do. The frustration that comes with that was a common feeling for me in my Westminster years and no greater than on that hot July night.

There was another collective failure over the forthcoming EU referendum. It was clear to see that, in his heart of hearts, Jeremy was no believer in the EU. At the hustings, Yvette, Liz and I should have challenged him harder on how he would approach the referendum leading a largely Remain-supporting party. Apart from one Sky hustings when Yvette and I started to open the issue up, we allowed Jeremy to leave the question unanswered. Our failure to ignite this critical issue would come back to haunt Labour in the middle of the following year.

When the leadership result was announced on 12 September, I came a very distant second to Jeremy. It was a tough loss and I feared for what lay ahead. On the Sunday afternoon,

HEAD NORTH

Marie-France had arranged for the five of us to watch the film *Everest* at the IMAX cinema in Waterloo. The bleak nature of the film – and its theme of desolation – certainly matched my mood. The whistling wind was intensified by the immersive cinema and it was a depressing experience. My phone had been off but, when I came out onto the South Bank and turned it back on, there were messages to contact Jeremy's team. It was clear they wanted me to join the shadow Cabinet to show unity. MPs who had been part of my campaign, and were under the same pressure, were also trying to contact me to find out my plans. This was a hard decision to make. I was bruised, down and would rather have gone back in and watched *Everest* all over again than join a meeting of the new shadow Cabinet.

And yet, there was a growing feeling that it was important for the party that I did step forward. That message was being sent to me by senior figures who hadn't supported me in the campaign but could now see the peril it was in. Not for the first time in my career, I felt intense annoyance that a party hierarchy, which had never shown me much support, was again expecting me to put the party first. What I did understand was the way the party members had voted. They wanted a break from the overly-cautious, centrist Labour that had characterised the last decade. So did I. Something different was needed and, between us, Liz, Yvette and I had failed to articulate a more credible alternative. I eventually accepted the job of shadow home secretary because I thought it was the right thing to do. I encouraged others who had been part of my campaign to follow suit. But my feelings about leaving Westminster, rising since 2009, were now very strong. In truth, I felt misunderstood. One version of a London-centric Labour Party had been replaced with another under Jeremy.

As I dragged myself towards Christmas 2015, Steve put the idea in my head of us going together for two newly created positions: Mayor of the Liverpool City Region and Mayor of Greater Manchester. I wasn't sure. Even though I was fed up with Westminster, it had been my life for fourteen years and it would be a wrench to leave. One of the problems with Parliament is that it can institutionalise people. Many stay longer than they should. You can't imagine life away from it. But, not for the first time, Steve's instincts had got me thinking and, periodically, I kept coming back to his idea. In January 2016, I returned to Westminster feeling more recharged after the Christmas break. I had promised Steve to talk about his idea of leaving Westminster and, when we met up, I said I wasn't feeling it and would probably stay where I was. The EU referendum was looming and I felt I had an important role to play as shadow home secretary reaching Labour voters in the North who were thinking of voting Leave. It was a challenge which appealed to me. I knew I had a commitment in March to deliver the prestigious Roscoe Lecture at St George's Hall in Liverpool. I had been thinking a lot over Christmas and New Year about what I would say. I was gearing up to put my tanks on Nigel Farage's lawn and make 'the patriotic case for Remain'.

I reached out to the official Remain campaign, and the Labour campaign led by Alan Johnson, to tell them about my thinking. I said I was keen to get as much media coverage as I could for what I had to say and was wondering if they could help with that. The response was distinctly lukewarm. They said they would be focusing on making a hard-headed economic case for Remain – not an emotional one. They didn't want to detract from that. Undeterred, I arrived in Liverpool on 17 March 2016 to deliver my speech. Some good friends working in rugby league had sought my view about the referendum and had told me they were thinking of voting Leave. I was beginning to realise that their views were probably shared by millions in the North. That's why I thought what I had tell the audience at St George's Hall was important – even if those in London running the Remain campaign didn't. So I went for it:

'You would think that the Leave campaign are the torch-bearers for British patriotism. The only true Brits. If you want to save the country, you must vote Brexit. This is profoundly misleading. They are peddling a fraudulent form of British patriotism that does not offer a return to Britain's past but a decisive break from it. I'm going to say something that I think people don't hear anything like enough from people on the Left of politics. I love this country, our country. I feel proud to be British. I don't subscribe to the current fashion of putting more narrow loyalties first – I am British before I am English. Brits have always been bridge-builders, not isolationists. We have spent centuries painstakingly building unions between countries, not breaking them up. Churchill, the person who most people would look to as the father of our own nation, was a founding father of the European Union. The EU isn't some alien anti-British creation as Boris Johnson claimed this week. It's a British achievement.'

I talked about my great-grandfather, Edmund Burke, a Private in the King's Liverpool Regiment, who died as a prisoner of war in Cologne just before the end of the First World War. I told them about his refrain in his last letter home to his family: 'Don't let them say that Ireland is not doing its share in this war!' I then finished with this:

'If I think about how I honour my great-grandfather's sacrifice, I am in no doubt it is to carry on fighting for a more united, less nationalistic Europe. Now is the time to stand up and be counted. Your country could be about to be taken off you. Don't let them diminish this great country of ours. Don't let them define how we are seen by the rest of the world. Let's fight them on the beaches of what it means to be British and reclaim that ground.'

If you look online for any media reports of that speech, you will find barely any. The London-based Remain campaign, built up from the elites of the three main parties, succeeded in making sure it got blanked. In my view, this was the only appeal to voters in the North that could have cut any ice at that stage of the campaign.

John Moores University kindly hosted my mum and I at a post-lecture dinner that night in Liverpool. I spoke openly about my frustrations with the Remain campaign and Westminster in general. Why didn't I go for the new metro mayor job in the Liverpool City Region and build a new politics in the North, they said one after another. After my experience building up to that day, I was listening to what they were saying. And they persuaded me – but not exactly in the way they hoped. When I got back to Westminster the following week, I told Steve I wanted to meet up again to talk about leaving. I was worried he might have gone cold on the idea after I had effectively dismissed it a few months earlier.

We met in a pub on Horseferry Road after a 7 p.m. vote in the House of Commons. I told him about my experience with the Remain campaign and the speech in Liverpool. I told him about the conversation at the dinner afterwards. Try as we might, we simply couldn't change things from within the London-centric system in which we had to operate. If we left together, and tried to build devolution in the North as a partnership, perhaps we would have half of a chance of making Westminster sit up and take notice? To my great relief, Steve's mind hadn't changed: 'Told ya this was right for us.'

Though I was born in Merseyside, I had looked to Manchester more when I was growing up and had been a Greater Manchester MP for fifteen years at that point. It was never really on the cards for me to be a mayor in Merseyside. It was right for Steve to go for that – and, anyway, he said he wasn't too sure that a Liverpool fan, even a charismatic one like him, could win in Manchester. We laughed and shook hands on it that night. The people who were harder to convince were my mum, dad and brothers. They weren't at all sure about it. They didn't know what the job would entail, whether it was a real job and if I would be happy in it. They were right to make me pause for thought but my mind was made up. Marie-France was positive about it from the start; she knew I needed a change.

In the first week of May, I was going through the motions

doing some local election campaigning when I took a call from Manchester-born journalist Faisal Islam, then working for Sky. He was someone I liked very much and still had impeccable contacts in his home city. He asked me if it was true that I was preparing to leave Parliament and stand to be Mayor of Greater Manchester. I went quiet on the other end of the line. I thought about it for a second, before telling him yes, it was. But I asked if he could hold the news until 10 p.m. on Thursday night after the polls had closed. When Faisal broke the news, shadow chancellor John McDonnell was in the studio and gave the first reaction. It was a gracious response, as was the message I received from Jeremy. On a personal level, I had always got on well with both of them. Some were shocked by the news but not many. I hadn't exactly hidden my frustrations with Westminster. I was ready to come home.

When I decided to run to be the first Mayor of the Liverpool City Region, I felt there was a huge opportunity for Andy and me to do something together. I knew there would be a number of candidates who would go for the new Greater Manchester job and I am sure I could have worked well with whoever was successful. But I wouldn't have worked as well with them as with Andy. Politics is about allegiances. Friendship is about trust. My whole idea was that together we could really work to squeeze more from the synergies between our two city regions. The way I saw it was that, if former Chancellor George Osborne's abstract idea of a Northern Powerhouse hadn't worked, why couldn't Andy and I work together to build a North West Powerhouse instead?

Whoever was going to do these new mayoral roles was going into the unknown. They were completely new positions with new powers and there was going to be a fair amount of learning on the job. I felt that, if Andy and I went for them together, we could really lean on each other as sounding boards, as support systems and as friends.

I wasn't sure that I could convince him to go for it. Things were very fluid at the time. Jeremy Corbyn was Labour leader and there were growing tensions within the Parliamentary Labour Party. We didn't know what was going to happen next. But I just couldn't get away from the thought that, if we stepped out of Westminster together and tried to do something different, it could be truly powerful.

At the time, I had the safest Parliamentary seat in the country in Liverpool Walton. It could easily have been a job for life. But I didn't really take to being in Parliament. I never enjoyed the process of it all. You have to understand how slowly the wheels turn down there. Local government can be ponderous but Westminster is just another level. Some of the legislation you have to deal with is hundreds of pages long. I would be going through all that only to get into the chamber and find that a decision had already been taken on how we were to vote. So what was the point?

I've also always been a very independent person and I like leading. I didn't necessarily accept the idea that, as a Labour MP, you were expected to vote this way or that way, to do this or to do that. With the jobs that Andy and I were looking at in the North West, we would be the ones making decisions. We would be the ones changing things for the people we cared about in an area of the country that desperately needed a change.

Jeremy was brilliant when I told him I was leaving. I had been his Parliamentary private secretary for the previous year or so, acting as his eyes and ears in Westminster. He said he was loath to lose me but very supportive of my decision. I had been offered shadow Cabinet roles but I never wanted to do that. I wanted to spend more time with my family, not less.

I had purposely said when I stood to be the candidate for Labour in the Liverpool Walton selection, prior to my election in 2010, that I had no intention of accepting any other roles during my first term. I wanted to learn the ropes without being encumbered by being a Parliamentary private secretary or working towards a front-bench role. I wanted to serve an apprenticeship. Like all new MPs, I was pulled into the office of Labour's chief whip early on to be told that I had a bright future if I did certain things in a certain way. I was essentially encouraged to play the game. When I said I just wasn't interested in Parliamentary progression, it took them a little by surprise.

Rosie Winterton was the chief whip at the time. I know her very well these days and she would be a great poker player – a very clever politician – but I think she was a bit perplexed when I told her about my lack of front-bench ambition. It reduced the scope for them to work on me. It was strange walking into the whips' office because there is actually a whip hanging on a hatstand, which I think is supposed to be quite intimidating. However, that wasn't the case with Rosie and me. She was just trying to figure me out, asking what I wanted to do and where I saw my future.

I honestly just wanted to get stuck into my constituency work and be a good local MP. Hillsborough was still bubbling away as a key issue and there were other campaigns I wanted to work on that would help people in my constituency. I wasn't bothered about ingratiating myself so that I could get a junior role as a shadow front-bench figure. I think that did free me up a bit down there. Nothing she could have said would have changed my mind on that.

Throughout the seven years I was in Parliament, I formed the opinion that it is not a fit and healthy place for people to be able to do the kind of work they are sent there to do. I truly believe we have a flawed system in this country, with flawed processes. The hours are ridiculous, the lifestyle is unhealthy and the expectations of the public unrealistic. I lived in Pimlico and I walked to Westminster and back every day. I would get to my Parliamentary office at 8.30 a.m. and be on the estate until 10 or 11 p.m. most nights. I could never understand how some MPs had second or third jobs. All I can say is that, other than the odd exception, they couldn't have been doing their first jobs to the best of their ability. I wasn't interested in the dinner party circuit to which some were attracted. It was just all work. I'm in no way trying to garner any sympathy for the relentless nature of the role, as there are many that would jump at the chance to be an MP, but the non-stop nature of Westminster life is not healthy and means people aren't often in the best position to help constituents. I was never comfortable with the lifestyle nor the environment and that contributed to my decision to leave.

Our decision to leave was reinforced within weeks by what unfolded around us. I had already announced my intention to leave after the local elections in May. When the country voted to leave the European Union in June, Westminster went into meltdown.

Early on the Friday morning, I travelled down from Warrington Bank Quay for a shadow Cabinet meeting. I remember the raging bitterness in that room, primarily aimed at Jeremy. People felt he hadn't fought hard enough for the Remain campaign and there was some truth in that. We had begun to show in the leadership campaign the year before that he was half-hearted, at best, on the EU and that was the kindest way you could describe his performances in the referendum campaign. But some of those sounding off at Jeremy needed to look at themselves too. They had been part of a lifeless, London-centric Remain campaign which had been far too aloof – not just in recent months but for years. This failure was on them more than anyone else.

Self-awareness and self-reflection were in short supply that Friday morning. The PLP was entering a collective nervous breakdown. As the shadow Cabinet met, news of the first front-bench resignations began to be announced. This continued throughout the day and into the weekend. There was a coordinated effort within the PLP to make Jeremy the scapegoat. By Sunday lunchtime, I was under pressure to join them with my phone inundated with texts. I decided to distance myself from the hysteria. I tweeted that, among other things, I had never joined a coup against any of the Labour leaders I had served and didn't intend to start now; and that, unlike the rest of the PLP, I had lost to this man less than a year before and had an obligation to respect that result and the members who voted for him over me. It didn't go down well.

The PLP was throwing out vitriol in all directions, including mine. A senior Labour MP, with whom I had a reasonable relationship, was astonishingly rude about my decision not to resign. He clearly thought differently than me about the acceptability of launching a coup against an elected leader, having been part of one against Tony Blair. I remember a phone call with my good friend Karl Turner MP who didn't sound anything like his normal self. People were in a tailspin. This was not something I had seen before in my fifteen years in Parliament. The combination of Corbyn and Brexit had created a form of mass hysteria – most visible at the weekly PLP meetings. Even in the difficult days of Tony, Gordon and Ed, they were always treated with courtesy and respect. Not now. Ian Austin, who was very public in his criticism of Corbyn, would be sat two yards from Jeremy and, when called to speak, scream at him. It was hostility of a kind I had never seen in Westminster. It was becoming a much darker place than the one I had known before and not one I wanted to stay in much longer.

I was in Jeremy's office that same morning. He was supposed to be there at 9 a.m. but was a little bit late. A Labour MP, who I know really well, came to the office door and he was holding an envelope. His hand was shaking because his whole body was trembling. He said: 'Steve, will you give this to Jeremy?'

'OK, what is it?' I asked, quite surprised.

'It's my resignation letter,' he said nervously.

'Are you sure you want me to give this to him?'

This was an MP who had always been generally supportive of Jeremy. He literally broke down in front of me. The pressure being piled on by the Parliamentary Labour Party was unbelievable. I could hear the tension in every word he spoke.

During this period, I had several conversations with people who were trying to convince me to step aside from my role.

Their argument was that if Jeremy didn't have the confidence of his own Parliamentary private secretary, then this would force him out of his position as leader.

When Jeremy Corbyn first asked me to be part of his team, it was just days after I had stood alongside Andy when the Labour leadership result had been announced in the Queen Elizabeth II conference centre in London. We were both devastated by the unequivocal nature of the defeat. Jeremy phoned me the next day and discussed a number of potential roles he thought I might be interested in. I wasn't. He then mentioned he was looking for a Parliamentary private secretary, although he explained that he wasn't asking me directly as he didn't think I would be interested. He thought I might have some suggestions for the role.

I said I'd phone him back when I had had some time for a little think on the matter. I called him the next day: 'Jeremy, you know the role of Parliamentary private secretary you spoke about? Well, I am interested.'

Although he was a little bit surprised, especially as I had firmly nailed my colours to the Burnham leadership mast, he replied: 'OK, let's meet and have a chat.' We arranged to meet and I told him that, despite my friendship with Andy, I would guarantee 100 per cent loyalty to him in all my dealings if I took on the role – and I was as good as my word. So, when I was asked to betray his confidence during the heady days of the attempted coup, I rejected it without a second thought. While I had my own issues with some of the people around him, I remained loyal to the leader of the Labour Party.

When Andy formally announced he wasn't going to buckle and would be staying on as shadow home secretary, the same trembling MP who had tendered his resignation just hours earlier came back to the leader of the opposition's office to see me and asked if he could withdraw his letter. Thankfully, Jeremy hadn't been able to go through his post yet. So the letter was withdrawn without anyone realising. It was a ridiculously difficult and intense period.

As Andy has indicated, things were febrile at the time with David Cameron pandering to his swivel-eyed backbenchers with a referendum, the public voting to leave the EU and Jeremy facing an attempted coup. Politics was in a mess and the public smelt blood. I think the seeds of that Brexit vote were sown as equally in Westminster and Whitehall as much as they were in Brussels and Strasbourg. In many ways, I think people needed something or someone to blame or to protest about, and the European Union was offered up as a patsy in that referendum. People weren't given a referendum on national government or London-centric politics, but I know a lot of people who wanted to use that vote to give our national government and our political system a bloody nose on those very issues. Brexit was a convenient vehicle for a plethora of esoteric debates.

This period definitely highlighted to me the very real disconnect between Westminster and the rest of the country. It felt like there was this big gap between the world down there and what other people were going through. I think a lot of the anger that fuelled the Brexit vote came from this chasm. It certainly cemented our decision to leave.

It is not the case that I didn't appreciate the opportunity of being a Member of Parliament. In fact, I still find it hard to believe that I did end up working in the House of Commons without the need to use my bricklaying skills in its restoration. I know I'm a very lucky person to have been an MP. But what I lived through in that post-referendum period made me certain that, for Andy and me, our efforts could be put to better use by heading back North and using the newly created devolved powers to try and bring people together in the regions we knew and loved.

Unlike first-past-the-post, the Brexit vote created a democratic process that Westminster couldn't control and a result it couldn't ignore. This explains why it went into a meltdown. Over the decades, the political system had allowed the establishment to turn a blind eye to things it found inconvenient, such as the cities of Derry and Liverpool crying injustice and the victims of contaminated blood claiming neglect. This time, they couldn't just brush aside the people who had voted Leave nor the reasons why they had voted in the way that they did. Steve and I had shared vivid lived experience of the disconnect between Westminster and people in the North. When we tried, and failed, to persuade people from our local area to vote Remain, we nevertheless understood why they felt as they did and couldn't blame them. After all, what had the status quo done for them?

For all of our lives, people in the North had been treated by Westminster as second-class citizens. We had become used to both the micro-aggressions and double standards. Sadly, too few others in Parliament seemed to notice or care about the disparities that existed, including the many MPs on both sides with Northern constituencies of convenience. If there was a positive to come out of the referendum, it was that the complacency on the issue of regional inequality – of the main parties, the civil service and the media – was for the first time being directly challenged. I didn't see the Leave vote as a statement confined to the EU or immigration. In my mind, it was a much deeper howl of anger at Westminster and Brussels combined. Millions were saying: 'This system isn't working for us. Give us something better. Something fairer.'

Steve and I felt ready to answer that call. To us, 'Take Back Control' didn't stop with powers brought back to Westminster from Brussels. It also meant neglected places in the North being able to do much more for themselves, such as re-regulate buses and build council houses. If anything, the Brexit result strengthened our resolve to leave Westminster. Our political system had created the conditions that had led to the result and, by definition, couldn't provide all the answers to what the public were saying. It was time to build something new outside of the Westminster Bubble; something that would challenge it more directly, in the way the public had done. The issue wasn't just the London-centricity of our own party and the others. It was also about the culture and practice of politics. In my sixteen years in

Westminster, I noticed a clear trend: as the problems outside were getting bigger, politics was getting smaller. Modern politicians had lost the art of making big arguments and the courage to propose big changes.

As health secretary in 2010, and later as shadow health secretary in 2015, I tried to propose a major reform of social care: in effect, to provide it on NHS terms so that the whole could be integrated as one system. I made the argument that, if people can't be discharged home, broken social care will in the end cause the NHS to collapse. I recall trying to get Ed Balls, the shadow Chancellor, to agree to it only to be told it wasn't a priority in focus groups. I didn't understand it. How could not being able to get the right care for your mum not be a really visceral issue for people? The public didn't see the divide between the NHS and social care in the same way as politicians. In focus groups, they would probably use NHS as a catch-all. Sadly, superficial retail politics was the order of the day. Labour often speaks of its pride in creating the NHS but, if it didn't already exist, there is no way today's generation of politicians would have the wherewithal to create it.

I know times were difficult for Andy. He was a major political figure in the Westminster circus, and I saw at close quarters how some sections of the press manipulated situations to feed a narrative against him: that Andy was shifting positions on an issue. Any nuance was seized upon. I always thought it was unfair but, I suppose, that's the game we were in so it wasn't worth complaining about. This means that, eventually, you tend to err on the side of caution when speaking – not necessarily the masterclass in circumlocution that Rishi Sunak has perfected – but it encourages a tendency to give blander answers.

Unfortunately, I think you inevitably do have to change when you are down in Westminster, even if you don't realise it. In 2012, the Prime Minister at the time, David Cameron, had a pop about my pronunciation and suggested I should read poetry after I had asked him a tricky question at Prime Minister's Questions. It was sneering stuff but it indicated to me what people like that thought of people like me who had come from my sort of background. I wouldn't have minded so much, but I was actually trying to tone down my scouse accent when I asked the question!

The House of Commons is allegedly a place of equals but that is very far from the truth. I made a comment in my maiden speech that Cameron and I were both born on estates – just very different ones. There are plenty of people down there who just believe they are better than others. On my first ever visit to the House of Commons, Jacob Rees-Mogg was discussing Erskine May – as he does – and I thought, who is he talking about? For those that don't know, Erskine May is the eponymous guide to Parliamentary practice and procedure. I didn't know that at the time. I stood up and asked the clerks of the house if they had a translation service so that people on the benches opposite would be able to understand people like me. I've met Tories since who said they picked me out as trouble right away. But I was just being me.

The world of Westminster and the culture of the place was not one I ever felt comfortable within. We used to see people in the voting lobbies on a Wednesday evening dressed in expensive tuxedos, ready to head to their next swanky London event after the last vote at 7 p.m. I always found that so odd. I would be thinking: don't they have work to be doing on behalf of their constituents? That was always where my head was at because you would do such long hours in Parliament that the evenings were often the only chance you would have to take stock, look at casework and catch up with reality. I would go back to the office after a vote and work until about 10 p.m., then head back to the flat and bed. It was certainly never about dinner parties down there for me but for many people it was and still is. Every night, there would be different groups going out for drinks or for meals. It was all extremely centred on the

Westminster bubble and I never thought that was particularly interesting or healthy.

There aren't many regrets from my time in Westminster, but the Welfare Reform Bill vote vote is definitely the big one. It was one that could have torn us apart as a party. I might have my gripes with Labour, but I have been an active supporter since I was eleven years of age, delivering leaflets in Merseyside, and nothing can persuade me that this party isn't the best organ for progressive politics in this country. However, around that time we had lost our way. I remember speaking to a Labour MP who had realised we weren't going to be able to vote against this horrible Bill and he just started crying in front of me. It is a bizarre situation that a politician is literally brought to tears because they are doing something they don't believe in – and for what? It did absolutely nothing for us.

I regretted it massively and I still do. We thought we had to stick together because the Tories were trying to tear us apart. But we had just found ourselves in a bizarre situation with a Labour Party putting down amendments but seemingly failing to vote against brutal cuts to benefits for some of the most vulnerable people in the country. We had just been battered in the election and there was this feeling at the top of the party that the Tories were cutting through with this demonisation of people who needed support, divided into strivers and skivers, workers and shirkers. So, rather than doing something we felt was right or something we believed in, we were taking into account how things might look to an electorate that had overwhelmingly rejected us. We deployed tactical positioning instead of political principles. It was a pretty desperate indication of where Labour was at the time and it just showed how Westminster can chew you up, spit you out and make you do things you just don't believe in. It can make you question your own values.

As an MP, you do have this responsibility to your party. You are effectively a franchise of that party. I am loyal to the Labour Party and always have been. I ruminated on the options in front of us and chose to be loyal to the party because there was the real possibility of implosion.

Straight after losing the election, we had become introspective. The victorious Tories had become even more right wing, so there was this feeling that we needed to follow them and prove how fiscally responsible we were. But we just went straight to panic stations and ended up betraying what we all really believe in, because of how it might have looked to the electorate and how the right-wing press would have reported it. At the end of the day, you can't out-Tory the Tories though.

My vote didn't matter as the Tories were always going to vote it through. But it was the politics and the message we got badly wrong and I will always regret that. Optics are important. These experiences all added to a feeling growing inside me that this just wasn't the place for me.

By late 2016, Steve and I were like fish out of water in Westminster – and one incident illustrates it more than any other. We had got into the habit of avoiding the Strangers' Bar and just going out for a drink together after late votes. But, given we were about to say our goodbyes to colleagues in the Commons, we thought we should show willing and attend the annual PLP 'works do'. As was common on these occasions, a move soon formed to continue the festivities in Soho. When we arrived at a popular late-night watering hole for MPs, we found to our surprise that our names were down on the door as VVIPs. Then, when the waiter brought us in, it was straight to a table in a prime spot. Before long, a chocolate fountain of all things arrived on the table, a bucket of champagne and four flutes. Being a trusting soul, I was thinking how nice of them all this was and started chatting to the two young women who had also unexpectedly sat down with us. It was at this point that I felt a sharp pain under my right kneecap. Steve had planted his winklepicker there. He looked at me and said: 'We are leaving – now.' As we made our excuses, he gestured upwards and I saw the unmistakable circular outline of a camera lens.

HEAD NORTH

There is a saying in Liverpool that people born there learn to read between the lines before they learn to read. That is certainly true of Mr Rotheram. I had a bruise under my knee for weeks after but I was grateful for it. I know there will be some of our former colleagues in Westminster who were with us on that night out who will think that, by leaving Westminster, Steve and I took the easy way out. It was a difficult period for the Labour Party, they will say, and people needed to stick around and work together to sort it out. If I'm honest, I can see why they would say that and I don't blame them for it. It's a valid point of view. In response, I would argue that the reason Labour had got itself into such a mess in the first place was precisely because it was too Westminster-centric. It desperately needed new thinking and new ways of doing politics. In time, I hope people will feel that what Steve and I have created on the outside has delivered that and will help keep Labour relevant in a very different century. In the short term, though, that night left us in no doubt that we had made a few enemies and were swimming in shark-infested waters. We were more than ready to leave Westminster behind and head North.

6

Out of the Bubble

On the 4th of May 2017, I was elected as the first ever Mayor of the Liverpool City Region. It was a brand-new position that had been created as part of a major devolution deal agreed between the government and leaders across our region. The deal meant that the Combined Authority and the new Metro Mayor at the head of it would have many more powers over areas like transport, housing, economic development and skills. It was an exciting opportunity and one that chimed with my growing feelings about the way power is concentrated in this country and how this needs to change. For far too long, decisions about regions like ours had been taken by people hundreds of miles away in London who didn't understand or care about the people where I lived. We were seven years into the austerity programme at this stage and hundreds of millions had been cut from our region's councils. We had been starved of investment and, while I was under no illusions that the money was about to come rolling in, I felt the devolution deal and a new mayoral position would give us more clout and more opportunity to make the most of the resources we did have.

But I had problems closer to home than Westminster. It was actually my predecessor as Liverpool Walton MP, Peter Kilfoyle, who had urged me to seek the mayoral nomination when I was still in Parliament. He was no fan of the then city of Liverpool Mayor, Joe Anderson, who had put himself forward for the regional mayor nomination. I decided to go for it and, as well as Joe, I was up against Luciana Berger, who was the MP for Liverpool Wavertree at the time.

The selection process for the Labour candidacy wasn't straightforward. Funding the campaign was a huge issue and I relied heavily on numerous volunteers. Many of them staffed a phone-bank to contact as many of the electorate as possible during the contest. I spoke to hundreds either face-to-face or over the phone to explain my vision for this new position. Some people thought I shouldn't have run as they believed Joe Anderson should be coronated into this new role as he had been the Mayor of Liverpool. However, I always believed that the position required someone who would represent all of the six districts equally. I certainly didn't start as the favourite but grew into the contest. At the end of the day, it would be for Labour members to decide. I was certain that I had a vision that would be attractive to members across the whole of the city region geography, unlike either of my rivals.

There were hustings events where there were hostile questions and all sorts of shenanigans, with claims that both of the other candidates were leading in the race, although all of our polling consistently had me ahead.

By the time of the announcement of who had won the selection, I thought I had a really good chance of victory. We weren't certain that we had accumulated enough votes to win on the first round, as that required more than 50 per cent for an outright victory. We calculated that I would disproportionately benefit from any redistributed votes if Luciana finished third, which indeed she did. In the end I was well out in front in round one and, when Luciana's votes were redistributed, I received a clear margin of victory.

Being selected as the Labour candidate was such a buzz. My whole family and many of my friends had supported me throughout the lengthy process, delivering literature and staffing phones. After my acceptance speech and a round of media interviews, we all met up in Liverpool city centre for a meal and a couple of drinks to celebrate.

The election process was slightly more straightforward. This time, I had the majority of the Labour family working towards a victory. At the election on the 4th of May 2017 I received 60 per cent of the vote, with the second-placed candidate on 20 per cent. With campaigning now over, my mind turned to the job of delivering for the 1.6 million people in our area.

On my first day as the Metro Mayor, I walked into our office building on the Liverpool waterfront and there were literally no Combined Authority staff – it was just me and a laptop. They didn't even have a desk for me to sit at. From the very start, I felt up against it.

There was a lot of tension with Joe Anderson. He told us that, despite being the Mayor of Liverpool, the largest authority in our region, he would no longer attend meetings of the council leaders from the Liverpool City Region. There was a big row early on about meetings with officials and who should or shouldn't be at them. Staff who were on secondment from Liverpool Council to help at the Combined Authority were suddenly withdrawn and called back to the council, with Joe claiming that they were needed there.

This stuff was appearing on the front page of the local newspaper and it was highly damaging as nobody at this point understood what this new body was all about. To add to my problems, the man who was the interim head of paid service (or chief executive) at the Combined Authority, Ged Fitzgerald, was arrested just weeks into my term. His arrest was part of a Lancashire Police investigation relating to his former employment, as a result of which he is set to stand trial. So, all of a sudden he was out of the picture and the place was rudderless.

It was an extremely chaotic situation that I had walked into. I knew I had to dig in and stay strong. I was in this for the long haul but those first few weeks and months were incredibly tough and I relied on Andy a lot through calls and advice. On my first day, I phoned him and said: 'It's like the bloody *Mary Celeste* in here.' There was literally no one to meet me.

He, by contrast, had walked into a well-established Combined Authority in Greater Manchester with lots of staff waiting for him and ready to start work to deliver his manifesto.

It was definitely a lonely time. Nobody had ever done this job before. There was no handbook for how you could get going and life was being made incredibly hard for me by others. I had to try and put a team together in about ten days and get some of those most basic things in place that just weren't there.

I'm quite a stoic person and will keep going when things get tough. I believed that eventually things would start to fall into place. When I got some people into the office, we were able to build up the processes and the safeguards that I needed. We knew we would have to spend a good deal of time developing the wider strategies that the government would need to see in the longer term if we were to convince them that we were serious about our ambitions.

That was the only way we could get the funding to make a difference. But then there was another headache. The challenge of doing all of this, while also setting up an office from scratch, would mean that the public were not going to see tons of tangible achievements appear immediately. And yet, they had just voted for this new position and were expecting results. So my team and I needed to look for some quick wins too. Dealing with all of this was a challenge that required all of my political skills. It was hard but we pulled it off. And, after the first few months, I had actually started to see my position differently. While the first few weeks were awful, they did give me an opportunity to start with a blank canvas. I could create what I wanted my office to be and put into it who I wanted. Before long, it all came together under my own vision.

When I walked into the Greater Manchester Combined Authority building on the morning of Monday, 8 May 2017, it couldn't have felt more different to the days when I walked into Whitehall departments as secretary of state. Down there, you got the feeling that most of the place was either indifferent or working against you. Walking into a reception full of around two hundred people on Oxford Street in the city centre was the exact opposite. I immediately got the sense that the whole place was with me. Of course, there would have been people in that reception who voted for other candidates at the election four days before. But what united everyone was a burning desire to see our place, Greater Manchester, move forward. I quickly understood that an approach to politics based on the unifying force of place, rather than the divisive force of party, is a much more powerful starting point.

Standing alongside me in the packed reception on that Monday morning was Baroness Beverley Hughes, the new Deputy Mayor I had just appointed. You might recall Bev being mentioned in an earlier chapter as a member of David Blunkett's Northern enclave. I had got to know her at that time and was a great admirer of her style. Like Tessa, she could be both sympathetic and steely at the same time and that is a great combination in politics. Bev was the first person I thought of when it came to gripping the challenge I knew I would inherit: changing the problematic culture of Greater Manchester Police. She would go on to stay with me for the next six years and I will always be grateful for her support and the vital role she played in making a success of devolution in Greater Manchester.

As Steve says, I was taking charge of a Combined Authority which was well established. While Steve had no desk to work from, Bev and I had a full team ready to support us. But there were challenges ahead of us all. The staff of the GMCA had been used to working with council leaders, some of whom were very set in their ways. Already, some of the ten leaders were muttering about my 'Westminster ways'. When I stood for the nomination, I said I thought the task of establishing this role was a Cabinet-level job which required Cabinet-level experience, much to the annoyance of many in local government. Seven years in, I stand by it. My challenge was to put the role of Mayor of Greater Manchester on a par with the established role of Mayor of London. That was going to require a lot of political experience if I was to do it while not going too much against the local grain. I would have to change my style and the local system would be required to change too. It wasn't going to be easy.

One issue that I didn't think was being handled particularly well was homelessness. The rise in the number of people sleeping rough was a huge issue in the mayoral campaign and I had already said reducing it would be my top personal priority. I pledged to donate 15 per cent of my salary every month to the cause and have done so ever since. Before arriving in the reception of the GMCA, I had already done an early morning walkabout of Manchester city centre. Greater Manchester was having to adjust quickly to the reality of having a mayor and some already didn't like me sticking my nose in things they saw as their responsibility. They pointed out that I didn't have any formal homelessness powers. From the start, I was clear that I couldn't let that restrict my approach to the job. If the public of Greater Manchester were concerned about something, I would have to find ways of convening a response to it, whether I had the right powers and budget or not.

Don't get me wrong: I was huge admirer of what had been achieved in Greater Manchester over the years. It was way ahead of other city regions at that stage in terms of its devolution arrangements and economic development. At the same time, there was room for improvement. The emphasis on economic regeneration had created a sense that social issues like homelessness were being neglected. There was also a feeling that there was too much focus on the city centre and not enough on the outer boroughs. When the devolution deal was done with George Osborne, he had insisted on introducing a mayor. In return, the ten leaders had insisted on being given the right to re-regulate the city region's buses. That was the basis on which they shook hands. When the mayor they didn't want finally arrived, it was always going to be a period of painful adjustment for many. To be fair, though, one of Greater Manchester's strengths has always been its ability to manage its disagreements internally. That has held good during my time as mayor. At some of our more difficult meetings, the then leader of Manchester city council, Sir Richard

Leese, would sometimes remind the room that, as far as he and the other leaders were concerned, my only role in life was to re-regulate the buses and they didn't want to hear from me on anything else. It always gave everyone a good laugh and helped to take any tension out of the air.

Steve and I were in very different positions but we were both having to take on some of the ingrained culture that existed in each region. Another thing we had to change was the culture of separateness between the two big city regions. My Liverpool background was not the ideal CV for the Mayor of Greater Manchester, as Gary Neville and Terry Christian pointed out when I decided to stand. There were political risks for me of working with Liverpool, but I couldn't let that stop me. We needed to be more of a 'North West Powerhouse', as Steve liked to put it. So, we started to do more joint appearances, with one photo in particular being derided as a promo for a new gritty Northern detective series from ITV. While a few took the mickey, what we found is that most people in both of our city regions liked the idea of the two places working more closely together. More broadly, I had picked up on some unhappiness from other Northern areas about the attention Manchester was getting, particularly since Osborne had made his big Northern Powerhouse speech in the city in 2014. There was a risk of Manchester becoming seen as the London of the North. So, as well as presenting a united North West front, Steve and I proposed the idea of an annual Convention of the North. As we approach the fifth Convention in Leeds in 2024, it has certainly succeeded in bringing the North of England closer together and increased the power of its political voice.

To succeed in our mission of building something outside of Westminster, I knew Steve would need to change the political culture in Liverpool and that I needed to help him with that. It would be no easy feat. He probably won't like me putting it this way but I think, going into his new job, he knew Liverpool needed to be a bit more like Manchester. More pragmatic and straight-dealing; less political and able to work with the government where possible. Despite our reservations about Whitehall, we had to work with them to get the funding our regions deserved – and for too long Liverpool's approach had been to shout at them from the sidelines.

I don't think the job Steve has done in changing the political weather on Merseyside should be in any way underestimated. What he has achieved is massive. He is the first person to challenge what in the past has been a problematic political culture in the city. He has helped steer Liverpool City Council through its recent difficulties and has built a Combined Authority which is now taken seriously in Whitehall. He probably wouldn't accept a knighthood. But he deserves one.

When I sat down in the office on that first day, with absolutely no one around me, the only thing I could find to read was a report from the charity Crisis about homelessness. It was presenting this idea called Housing First. Originally developed in 1992 in New York by Dr Sam Tsemberis, Housing First uses a different approach to tackling homelessness from those traditionally used by governments and local authorities. The idea is to provide a home as a starting point rather than an end goal and to then build targeted, wrap-around support tailored to that person to help them keep that home and rebuild their lives.

Straight away this felt like something we could do differently with the new powers we had. There was an opportunity to be part of a government-funded pilot project, so having met with Crisis and other organisations working in the field to learn more about the idea, I wrote to the government to put ourselves forward. Of course, I instantly came up against some of the same obstacles. I spent an inordinate amount of time convincing our local authorities that this was the right thing to do. They were resistant to change. But I'm glad we persisted because we have had some incredible results with Housing First. We are now supporting more than 200 people through the scheme with nearly 90 per cent of those people sustaining their tenancy. People are now coming to us to learn about what we have been doing with Housing First, which shows the impact it has had.

But again, it shows what I was up against in those early days. Unabated resistance. As Andy says, I have tried to change the political culture that has existed in Liverpool for a long time. You don't have to like the government of the day, but you do have to try to work with them to get the best results for your people. I believe Housing First is a good example of that. We've shown the government that this works and why they should keep funding it. Previously Liverpool's approach was combative. I was determined to work more pragmatically – even with a Tory government. Some people will never get that and see me as a collaborator with the Conservatives. That can be the nature of our politics in Merseyside. But Andy's right: I was looking at the progress in Greater Manchester and thinking we needed to learn lessons from their success and do things differently for the good of our region.

Steve and I received absolutely no help whatsoever from our own party in the early days of our time as Mayors. Bear in mind that these were completely new positions with new powers. We were trying to unlock the potential of these great Northern regions, build a new type of politics and reconnect people in our part of the world with our party. Huge and laudable ambitions, you might think, but seemingly not ones shared by the Labour Party. They weren't interested. While the Tories barely missed an opportunity to praise Andy Street, the Conservative Mayor of the West Midlands, we felt cut adrift and, looking back, perhaps that was no bad thing. We were free to build an approach in our own way and one we knew would be right for our areas. Devolution doesn't work if you are perceived to be a puppet on a string dancing to the party's tune or taking orders from Labour officials in London. In the early days, we had each other for support and that was it.

One other person who really supported us both in those early days was Michael Bloomberg, the former Mayor of New York. He had offered to assist us in our new roles through his philanthropic organisation. He was a big believer in the power of cities and in localism and took a real interest in what we were trying to do. He invited us both out to join a leadership course at his offices in New York. I'm not a good flyer, and usually try to avoid going anywhere by aeroplane, but I couldn't say no to this invitation, especially as it wouldn't cost the public purse a single penny and there was the potential to attract inward investors to our regions.

The event was a real eye-opener. Over in the United States, the idea of being a mayor has a certain cachet. It has gravitas. I'm not sure this was the case in the UK at the time, certainly not with our new positions because people didn't really understand them yet. I think most people at that stage thought of ribbon-cutting and opening fetes when they heard the term mayor, imagining more of a ceremonial mayor. We knew we had a real job of work to do in selling these positions and the devolved powers that came with them to the public. Over in America, however, mayors had real profile and presence and we were keen to learn from them.

The time we spent in New York in the summer of 2017 with Michael Bloomberg and his team was incredible. We had left a high-powered club in Westminster and, after a period of isolation, it felt like we – and the city regions we represented – were being invited into a new, less elitist and more expansive one. They fed us a philosophy that was a little alien to the British political mind: the power of cities as the twenty-first century force. If the nineteenth century was the century of empire, and the twentieth was the century of the nation state, the new thinking was that the twenty-first would be led by a network of cities around the world.

Bloomberg made a speech at the event which helped us position our embryonic English devolution project in a much wider global movement. Cities would lead the building of the economies of the future and needed to be empowered to do it. It was music to our ears at the perfect time. We were only a few weeks out of the antiquated, top-down world of Westminster and, all of a sudden, a new world of bottom-up possibilities was opening up. Our own country and party had not paid enough attention to the potential of our cities so we were very taken by the fact that this international support network was interested in us and what we were trying to do. In Britain, the narrative was often that cities, and particularly inner cities, were part of the problem. In America, cities were the functional powers in a dysfunctional land and we wanted some of that. Michael has remained a friend and supporter of us both ever since.

Steve went down a storm in New York. I had observed his arrival in Parliament and you could just tell from the start that he wasn't going to fit in with the club down there. I know he always felt that was the case because of his background and his accent. Yet here he was bossing it with Michael Bloomberg and all these big-shot mayors in the States. It makes you wonder how many people from working-class backgrounds have been elected to the UK Parliament through the decades but have never been enabled to fulfil their potential because of the innate hierarchy of the place. There was a particularly memorable moment when we were at a rooftop reception in the middle of Manhattan. I had popped to the loo and was walking back around the corner of this incredible New York penthouse to find a scally from Kirkby in a close encounter with Dr Henry Kissinger, the former US Secretary of State. It turned out, to my great relief, that he had cut his finger and Steve was administering first aid, not a 'Kirkby kiss'. In the list of things you don't expect to see in life, that would come pretty close to the top. It was a surreal moment in a life-changing trip that would mean a lot to us both.

The priority in those first few years in the job was to try to take the meagre pots of money we would get from the government and prioritise them in the areas we felt they could do the most good for our city regions. I had a big focus on homelessness and on helping long-term unemployed people back into work – which is good for people and for the economy. But it was hard. People saw a shiny new job and heard about these newly devolved powers, and they wanted to see instant results. The nature of the situation meant we didn't have big things we could announce early on because we weren't ready for that yet. The one thing I do know from my days in the construction industry is that, if you don't have solid foundations, things can fall apart very quickly. A lack of political collaboration and agreed strategic investment had prevented progress in our area over an extended period. Merseyside should have had a tram network decades before but, while the money was there, the plans fell through on more than one occasion because those foundations just weren't in place. Partnerships frayed and investment was lost. So I knew how important it was to put those things in place first.

One of my big objectives was to strengthen and diversify the local economy. Much of Merseyside's and particularly Liverpool's renaissance has been built on a hugely successful tourism and visitor economy. But, as we saw when Covid struck, this is a fragile base to rely on and we needed to move into different areas like science, technology and advanced manufacturing. This is something I have tried to spearhead with the powers at my disposal.

Obviously, a big part of the job as a Metro Mayor is to work with the government of the day. Unfortunately, thus far, this has always been a Conservative government and there are some people in my region who believe any work with the Tories should be resisted at all costs, despite the fact that every Labour council in the country has to do this. I will always criticise and call out the many things I believe successive Tory governments have done wrong. But the simple fact is, if you don't work pragmatically with government, you will not get the funding you need to make your region a better place. You have to meet the Tories where they are and make it clear why investment in areas like the Liverpool City Region is good for the UK economy as a whole. You just have to be realistic about these things.

One of the significant problems caused by the constant

discord within the Conservative Party has been the revolving door of ministerial appointments. This game of musical chairs creates issues within and outside the Westminster bubble. Every time the long knives are drawn by one Prime Minister or another, it results in organisations like Combined Authorities (and a myriad of others) having to start from square one in explaining their objectives to the incoming ministers. It's like a game of snakes and ladders, with too many snakes and not enough ladders! It is not only in Westminster that I have witnessed this constant change. The devolution agreement we currently have means that my Cabinet is made up of the leaders of our councils. The lack of diversity across the board in local government has meant it largely being constituted by white middle-aged men. Further, in the seven years I have been Mayor, there have been more than twenty people, at one stage or another, leading the six local authorities. Some have been positive, productive figures with whom it has been a pleasure to work. Others have proved obstructive, often seeking to block – without justification – policies on which I had secured an overwhelming direct mandate from the public.

Our region had relied on grants for a long time, often from the EU. But, with that coming to an end and a government that wasn't exactly throwing cash at us, I knew we had to encourage more investment. We've tried to take the pots of funding we have been given and use them to maximise the possibility of getting other investors to buy into our region. Without fully funded devolution, this is the best way to grow the economy and provide the resources for all the things we want to do with these new powers.

Exactly two weeks after I took office as Mayor of Greater Manchester, a terrorist detonated a bomb that killed twenty-two innocent people – including many children and young people – at the Manchester Arena following a concert by Ariana Grande.

What would turn out to be one the darkest days of my life began in very ordinary circumstances. That evening, I had played five-a-side football in Culcheth with my brothers, John Hunt, his brother Andy and all of our kids, before calling on my dad with a bottle of wine for his birthday, which is May 22nd. I headed home to nearby Golborne and was sitting watching *Newsnight* in my full football kit when my phone rang. It was Steve calling and I thought I would just leave it and catch up with him in the morning. A minute later, he rang again and I left it. When he called for the third time, I picked up knowing something was wrong.

'Andy, Andy, my girls are at the Manchester Arena. What is going on?'

I had never heard Steve's voice like that. He was screaming into the phone. This would have been about 10.40 p.m. and, at that point, I didn't know anything was wrong beyond a few noises on social media.

However, as I was on the phone to Steve, I could hear that another call was waiting and looked at my screen to see the words 'Chief Constable calling'. I told Steve I needed to drop off and would call him back. When I answered the call, I was informed of the devastating news that a bomb had been detonated at the arena. In an instant, I felt that same feeling that I had in 1989 when I looked at the scoreboard at Villa Park: sick to the very pit of my stomach. I recall asking whether the bomber was alone or if there was any intelligence that there were others in the arena. It was impossible not to think of the Paris attacks of 2015 which included the attack at the Bataclan. Ian Hopkins, the then Chief, said they didn't know. But the number of casualties from the bomb was high. He would call me back as and when he knew more.

I spent all that night and into the early hours of the morning receiving fragments of information and trying to piece them all together. There were rumours of further attacks in the city centre and in Oldham but, thankfully, they proved to be false. But it all added to the feeling of high anxiety. At about 4.30 a.m., I got myself together and drove into Manchester city centre to the office of the GMCA that I had entered for the first time just a fortnight earlier. I will never forget my surprise at seeing so many people already there around 5.30 a.m. It said something powerful to me about the people and place.

I had spoken in the early hours with Sir Richard Leese and we had agreed to do a joint public statement around 7 a.m. looking into Albert Square from the steps of Manchester Town Hall. As we walked over from my building on Oxford Street, the empty city felt subdued and jittery. I met Richard inside the cloisters on the ground floor and we went out through the old double doors and down the steps to face what seemed like the whole world's media. I began: 'After the darkest of nights, Greater Manchester is waking up to the most difficult of dawns.'

I was very conscious that, for some people, they would only just be waking up and hearing the news for the first time. Police raids were taking place at multiple locations across the city. Many would be terrified. I had to find the right words. Even though many were still not aware of my new role, I knew they soon would be. It would fall to me to lead the city region through this moment of enormous challenge. The weight of that responsibility lay heavily on my shoulders. As I spoke on the steps, I tried as best as I could to begin to reassure people, pointing to the stories already circulating of what taxi drivers and the city's hotels had done to help people fleeing the scene in distress. I said that was the real spirit of Greater Manchester and it would carry us through this time. Manchester would not be divided.

Something of what I said clearly resonated as I began to get messages thanking me for going out there straight away and giving the city region something to unite around. Even though my role was new, this was an immediate example of why it was necessary and important. In moments like this, you have to speak to the soul of the place you are in and that's what I tried to do. My main memory of the rest of that morning is seeing the growing calls on social media for a vigil in the city that evening and discussing it with Sir Richard and Greater Manchester Police. In one way, it felt risky to bring everyone into the city. Richard was clear that we should. Manchester had got straight on with things in 1996 after the IRA bomb and we would do the same here. We couldn't let the place be overtaken by fear as that would be to let the terrorists win. Richard said no politician should speak at that event and suggested that we should ask the poet Tony Walsh to deliver his stirring ode to Manchester, 'This Is the Place'. That call would prove to be utterly inspired.

As the afternoon wore on, my old world of Westminster started to intrude on our best-laid plans. Remember: 23 May was two weeks from polling day in the 2017 general election. We had approaches from all the main parties who wanted senior figures to speak at the vigil. We said no, but Jeremy Corbyn's office were particularly pushy and he ended up doing a photocall with some firefighters against our wishes. It all felt a bit unseemly considering what had happened. It was the first time that the superficial ways of my old world jarred badly with me in my new one.

From early evening, thousands were gathering for the vigil in Albert Square in the bright early summer sunshine. As Tony Walsh walked to the podium to read out his poem, I was standing right behind him. Talk about rising to the occasion. I watched his shoulders physically lift as he gave a nervous and grieving Manchester the perfect tonic. Tony truly and beautifully spoke to the soul of the city that evening. He reminded it of its strength, its solidarity and its swagger and I could see faces visibly change in the crowd. Heads lifted; voices raised; moods shifted. It is a word that can be overused, and misused, but, in a very real sense, that power of that vigil was awesome to behold. We had enabled people to reclaim their city and, from then on, their incredible response carried us through.

The title of this book is *Head North* and implicit in it is the invitation for people to come here and see how things are done. To take their heads out of Westminster and think about what our country would feel like if it was run with Northern values at its heart. Truly, I could not be more proud of how Greater Manchester reacted in the days and weeks after the Arena bombing. How people looked out for each other. How much they donated to support the families and those affected. How they got themselves tattooed with the symbol of the worker bee. How they simply refused to be divided. I remember that evening in Albert Square meeting many people who had come over from Liverpool. That moved me, profoundly. It reminded me of the way people in Manchester had shown solidarity with Liverpool after Hillsborough. The North has always had an ability to come together during its darkest moments and I hope that will never change.

The days that followed the vigil were hard. I barely went home or slept. We had no idea what would happen from one hour to the next. People wanted to be in the city. They were scared, angry but also determined to deal terrorism a show of togetherness that would guarantee its ultimate defeat. In those days, I knew I was in the right place. I had made the right choice. I would have hated to have had to react to that attack from Parliament and then return to the nonsense of the general election campaign. It was an intense time. I spent mine visiting the A&Es that had treated people, attending multi-faith events at Manchester Cathedral and trying to bring different groups together. I was definitely learning on the job and relying on my instincts for a lot of it.

One moment within that week will forever stay with me. I had come back to my office for a breather and found a white box on my desk. Inside was a beautifully iced cake with a picture of Manchester's worker bee on top. The inscription said: 'Stay strong our kid.' Instantly, tears started to roll down my cheeks. It had been sent from a local bakery and it just meant the absolute world to me. I was the new Mayor, born in Liverpool, and had wondered if people in Manchester would accept me speaking for them and representing them at a time like this. Was I speaking for the soul of this place? Do the people here accept me doing it? I had been flying blind, and was full of self-doubt, so that wonderful gesture meant so much. After having felt lost for years in Westminster, I was in the right job and in the right place.

As shadow home secretary in 2015, it had fallen to me to respond from the despatch box in the House of Commons to

Theresa May's statement on the terrorist attacks in Paris, where 130 people were killed. I had asked her at the time whether British cities outside of London were prepared for something similar. I was pretty sure the answer was no. It is why, on my first morning as Mayor, I had asked the then Chief Constable of GMP the same question. I was given assurances about the training exercises that had been done in recent years but, when you look at the failures of emergency services on that night, we now know the answer. Among a wide range of mistakes, the official Manchester Arena Inquiry found that the police failed to declare a major incident for a long time after the bomb was detonated and that firefighters didn't arrive on site for hours.

I immediately asked Sir Bob Kerslake to do a review of the response. I knew we couldn't wait the years it would take for the full public inquiry to complete its work. The Kerslake Report, when it was published a year or so later, enabled us to lift the lid on a fire service that needed major changes. But, in time, it would also reveal a serious problem with the internal culture of GMP. The account they initially gave to the voluntary Kerslake Review would be revealed as inaccurate by the on-oath Manchester Arena Inquiry.

I don't like drawing too many parallels between what happened at the Manchester Arena and Hillsborough. They are very different events. And yet, there are some undeniable similarities, including failures in the emergency response and in being honest about it afterwards.

We will talk later in this book about how we believe we need to rebalance this country in favour of ordinary people and away from a powerful establishment. One important way of doing this will be through a new Hillsborough Law to help prevent future injustices where there is state involvement. Steve and I launched a major campaign for this essential change – Hillsborough Law Now – and will never rest until it is achieved.

There are two key planks to the new law. One is a duty of candour on police and all public servants during all forms of official inquiry. Or, to put it another way, to tell the truth at the first time of asking. It's not a lot to ask. The other is an entitlement for bereaved families to parity of legal funding with public bodies. Only these reforms will prevent public bodies from creating false narratives in the aftermath of tragedies and seeking to shift blame off themselves and onto the victims. They would rebalance the scales of justice in favour of ordinary people. As with our political system, social class and connections count for a lot in our legal and judicial system. Those with power can easily manipulate the system in their favour and against those who don't have it. The rewiring of Britain must include the rewiring of the legal system if we are to create a society that in any way resembles a level playing field.

It was only later in 2017 that I was able to return my focus to my two personal priorities for my first term as Mayor. As we approached the winter, I hadn't yet been able to put in place a comprehensive plan to reduce rough sleeping. It was still far too high. As a start, I agreed with the ten councils that we would offer a place indoors to everyone on every night that the temperature was below freezing. This was better than the national requirement of doing so only when there have been three consecutive nights of sub-zero temperatures. When we reviewed how the plan had worked in the spring of 2018, the consensus was it hadn't. If people are in accommodation one night and then out the next, they can never settle and escape the revolving door of homelessness. Then, in the middle of the meeting, came one of those comments that I wait for as a politician – one that cuts right through the confusion and gives you a new insight. Reverend Ian Rutherford, a senior methodist minister in the city who had thrown himself into our homelessness mission, said the only time our accommodation plan had worked was during February's 'Beast from the East'. This was because people had been able to stay in the same bed for fourteen nights and the teams were able to settle people, get to know them and start to help them turn things around. It was in that moment that our 'A Bed Every Night' scheme was born. From then on, we would endeavour to provide a place for everyone every night. And not just any bed: the same bed. It is now a permanent scheme looking after over 500 people every night and gets us as close as I can to delivering on the promise of ending rough sleeping. I can't stop people going onto the streets. But I can now give everyone an offer of help and we are the only city region in the UK able to do that.

My second passion in my first term was to establish a free bus pass for sixteen to eighteen-year-olds. This was a policy I had wanted Labour to introduce when we were in government. The Education Maintenance Allowance was a great thing but, like any means-tested benefit, created resentment among those who were just over the line. I always felt a simple, universal scheme would be better. Raising the aspirations of our young people is a personal mission for me. I never forget my time working unpaid on the *Middleton Guardian* and how hard that was. Giving people the ability to travel without worrying about the cost at that stage in their life is a crucial enabler of social mobility. The creation of Our Pass, as our youth Combined Authority named the free pass, is still one of the things I am most proud of in this job.

Unlike Steve, who basically had to build from scratch, for me it was about setting a more people-focused direction. Inevitably, that brought tensions with it. Only one of the ten council leaders had backed me for the Labour nomination for the job – the then leader of Wigan, Lord Peter Smith. Manchester's leader Sir Richard Leese had told *Manchester Evening News* that he would be giving Ivan Lewis his first preference and Tony Lloyd his second. He didn't go so far as to add that I would be getting his third. But the good thing about the Greater Manchester culture is the ability to prevent disagreements becoming permanent rifts. It was in that spirit that I invited Richard to become deputy Mayor of Greater Manchester and I like to think that we became a pretty formidable team, particularly during the pandemic. We are very different politicians – I am more instinctive, Richard more analytical – but that is probably what made us an effective partnership. Richard will think through issues carefully and give a pretty blunt critique. His early warning 'not to bring any Westminster ways' felt a bit harsh at the time. But, in retrospect, it was fair criticism and I needed to hear it. This job would only work if I approached it in a completely different way to my old one and his advice has actually stood me in pretty good stead.

The biggest difficulty of my first term was getting to grips with the problems at GMP. Following the Kerslake Report, other issues had come to the fore such as the botched implementation of a new computer system and a damning HMIC report towards the end of 2020. I had come into the role knowing that GMP was not where it needed to be. It had a defensive culture and a huge number of ongoing internal disputes. The HMIC report gave me the evidence I needed to ask the then Chief Constable to step down. Not easy but the right decision. Three years later, the turn-around in GMP under Chief Constable Stephen Watson is complete: the latest HMIC inspection found them to be the UK's fastest-improving police force.

One big eye-opener of my first term was the new perspective it gave me on how national government treats local government. It is quite shocking. Councils are the last line of defence for communities around the country and yet are treated as last in the queue when it comes to a funding priority. Having cut billions from their budgets, the same government then criticises those who dare to fill in the black hole by raising council tax. It makes them bid and beg for fragments of what they used to have through various pots and it seeks all the political credit when the list of winners and losers is announced. The worst one of all is when they take a 'tough on benefits' approach to please certain newspapers but the effect of policies like freezing housing benefit simply places more unfunded pressure on councils because of the increasing number of homeless families they will have to support.

I think everyone who works in central government should be required to spend some time working in local government. That would help them see for themselves how they come over to those at a local level. Who knows, it might give us a more self-aware Whitehall and stop it treating councils with contempt.

7

Hunger Games: Live from District 12

In many ways, the story of what happened during the Covid-19 pandemic could be seen as a condensed version of all the themes of this book. It brutally exposed a number of things: England's deep social inequalities; where power truly resides; how it is used and abused; and how Britain's London-centric system of government thinks it can treat the North. At any one time, my assessment is that only around fifty people in the heart of Whitehall are running this country. In normal times, this is dysfunctional. In a pandemic, it is dangerous.

Myself and the other Mayors made many pleas for closer involvement in decision-making. In particular, we asked for a seat at the COBRA table. This was done in a spirit of national unity and of working together in a crisis. In the end, Sadiq Khan and Steve attended one each. I was never invited at all – which you might think odd given that I was the only living ex-health secretary who had experienced a pandemic. As a result, I often had to resort to the media to get Greater Manchester's perspective across. If you are not prepared to listen to the voice of the big regions of England, how as a government are you going to ensure balanced decision-making in an emergency for all parts of the country? The simple answer is you are not and that is what this chapter will reveal in disturbing detail.

In January 2020, the government decided (without consultation) to quarantine people who had returned to the UK from Wuhan in China at Arrowe Park hospital in Birkenhead. This act was one of many that catapulted our area to the centre of the Covid story. The first moment when I remember it dawning on me how serious this thing called Coronavirus was, was when I was due to go and watch Liverpool take on Atlético Madrid in a Champions League match on 11 March 2020. This turned out to be one of the last major sporting events to take place in this country before the first national lockdown. The situation with Covid-19 was worsening in Europe and in Spain games were already being played behind closed doors. In a bizarre and dangerous turn of events, 3,000 fans who were unable to watch their team play at home, because of restrictions in their own country, were able to travel across Europe and into Liverpool for this match.

The decision to allow that game to go ahead – and the Cheltenham Festival to continue for days after – would later be heavily criticised as potential factors in transmission growth and Covid deaths during that first surge in the UK. A joint report from the House of Commons Health and Science Committees, which analysed the government's failures in those early days of the pandemic response, suggested there were up to an additional thirty-seven deaths at local hospitals after the Anfield match and forty-one stemming from the Cheltenham Festival. They branded the decision not to lock the country down earlier as 'one of the most important public health failures' that the country had ever seen.

Around the time of the match, things were very confusing. The game was going ahead so we mistakenly believed that, as the government had given its approval, it must have been fine to attend. Obviously, I was more worried. It was the first time I had taken hand sanitiser with me anywhere and the taxi driver told me I was being a bit 'overly cautious' as I sanitised my hands on the way to the ground. When I got to Anfield, I tried to keep my distance from other people. But you can imagine how difficult that was. I was starting to become very anxious...

I first got a sense of the seriousness of Covid in January 2020 when I was asked to attend a meeting of our Chinese community who were concerned about relatives in Wuhan, Manchester's twin city in China. This is where the virus had originated and people here were trying to source and transport medical supplies for family and friends. At a meeting at the famous Yang Sing restaurant on Princess Street, I remember being surprised by the level of panic in people's voices and desperation in their eyes. As things got more serious here, I started to develop a sense that the government was not following what I understood to be the national pandemic plan. As health secretary, I had dealt with the much milder swine flu pandemic of 2009. While Covid was different, the principles underpinning the response should have been the same. One of my last acts as health secretary was to commission a review of the government's handling of swine flu. It was published in 2011 and, while broadly commending our response, the Hine review concluded it was too centralised and recommended a more devolved approach for any future pandemic. This would turn out to be the total opposite of what the government did in 2020.

One thing people tend to forget is that, while the Tories had been in power for ten years at this point, the Johnson administration was in effect a brand new government. The general election had only been a matter of weeks before in late-2019. The more moderate ministerial class of the Cameron and Osborne era, and you could also say more competent, had been purged from the Conservative Party. All new governments have a tendency to centralise control in the early days, as New Labour did in 1997. But the government of early 2020 had other, more worrying qualities, including a new breed of small-state, right-wing politicians who had taken the helm. Even at that time, I wondered whether they were ideologically suited to deal with what a pandemic would involve, as well as having the right level of experience.

As things were getting more serious, and people were getting more anxious for information, I remember how, one weekend in February 2020, an article appeared from a health minister. Vital public advice in a health emergency – behind a paywall in a favoured newspaper. It would be a sign of things to come. This was my cue to become more involved in the public debate about Covid – something that would not stop for the next eighteen months.

In the spirit of trying to be helpful, I took to Twitter to write a long thread about swine flu in 2009 and the mistakes I had made with public communications, recognising that it's not an easy task in a pandemic. I recalled how I had alarmed people early on by giving the worst-case scenario for deaths. People react differently to things said by politicians and I suggested that there should be a daily briefing led by the chief medical officer and other experts. I think they were listening to a degree, as the daily Covid briefings started soon after. But they decided that politicians would front them all, which I think was a mistake. We needed unadulterated and clear public health advice, not political posturing.

As we went into March, I remember one weekend getting a long email from Tom Tasker, a senior and trusted GP in Greater Manchester. He was becoming more and more alarmed by what he was seeing in his surgery and hearing from other colleagues. People needed a stay-at-home message – now. I checked this with other colleagues in Greater Manchester and it seemed to be the consensus. On the morning of Monday, 23 March, I was booked to appear on *Good Morning Britain*. I had been waiting in my garden for a good half an hour while Piers Morgan berated Matt Hancock over the confusing nature of the government's messaging. When I finally got on air, I said that I believed the government needed to move now to a new stay-at-home phase of the pandemic. I remember thinking how ridiculous it was that my experts in Greater Manchester could advise me clearly but that the might of the UK government couldn't do the same for ministers. After all, the case rate was much higher in London at the time. As we now know, they were providing that advice but a chaotic operation in Number 10 was incapable of receiving it. After a day of confusion, Boris Johnson would eventually appear on our TV screens that evening telling us all to stay at home.

People's reactions to the crisis differed wildly in those moments. Despite my requests for us to work from home, the Combined Authority told me this wasn't possible. I was left feeling a little frustrated: something needed to happen. And then, two weeks

later, Boris Johnson came on our television screens telling us all to work from home. The next day our entire organisation was doing just that. Things moved and changed rapidly.

One of the major issues that immediately confronted us in that first lockdown was the safety of workplaces that stayed open. While many people could work from home, there were many others who couldn't and were forced to keep going out to work. This obviously included emergency workers but also those in factories and warehouses. This was a big issue for us in Merseyside. We were getting emails from workers who weren't being given personal protective equipment (PPE) or even basic sanitising stations. You have to remember that we were not fully aware of Covid's airborne transmission at that stage. Everyone was being told to wash hands and yet the people being forced to go out to work during a lockdown weren't even given hand sanitiser.

We had a massive outbreak of Covid at a factory in the Knowsley area and we had images that showed there was very little compliance with any of the guidance. Andy had a similar issue with a major clothing retailer at their warehouse in Greater Manchester. It was a nightmare.

It was all new to us as Metro Mayors. Andy and I were keeping in touch with each other as these situations developed and we worked together on responses. Andy is a former health secretary so he was a really good sounding board. But we had never experienced anything like this. We had only been in office for three years and this enormous crisis just landed on us. It was extremely tough. Our determination was to do the right thing by our people. We put place before politics and pulled out all the stops for our areas, although it never felt like this was reciprocated at a national government level. At times, along with other colleagues, Andy and I were the voice of the North.

In this book, we talk a lot about the divides that exist in this country. They were never more starkly on show than when the pandemic set in. All of a sudden, Britain was split into its two different worlds. There was one world in which people on furlough or working from home were sitting in their gardens, doing quizzes on Zoom and sipping cocktails. There was then the other where people were out at work as normal. Except they were more busy than normal as they had more parcels to dispatch to the people sitting in their gardens.

In April, Steve and I started to get inundated with anxious emails from people who were worried about the safety of their working conditions in factories and warehouses. Some were terrified they were going to get seriously ill or die. We looked into the law that the government had put in place for workplaces and it said that employers should observe two-metre social distancing 'where possible'. In other words, it was useless. When we raised these issues with the government, we got a 'well-someone-has-to-get-our-Amazon-parcels-out' type of response. The Health and Safety Executive was conspicuous by its absence. I set up a dedicated email address for people worried that their workplace was unsafe and it quickly became inundated with thousands of messages from all over the country.

Around the same time, Unison North West sent me a report that would bring out another issue which would become huge. A survey of their members working in social care found 80 per cent feared they wouldn't able to self-isolate if asked because it would mean they would have no money. They were on zero-hours contracts and had no access to sick pay. In a pandemic, this was not just dangerous for them but also for the people in their care. While care was the sharp end of the problem, we knew millions of other British workers were employed in exactly the same way – more in the North than elsewhere – and that would present real challenges in controlling the virus in some of our least affluent communities where poor, over-crowded housing would make matters even worse. In that moment, chickens came home to roost. Britain's insistence on a decades-long drive towards a deregulated low-wage economy had left us dangerously exposed. The way Britain's two worlds quickly emerged, and the shocking lack of support for those at greatest risk, tells you a lot about the broken state of this country.

Covid highlighted the many disparities that exist in this country. We had very high rates of the virus in the Liverpool City Region. We could see things were a lot worse in areas of deprivation, high-density housing and where people had long-term health issues.

Employment and the types of jobs people had also presented huge issues. Our region is very reliant on public-facing roles in service industries, such as hospitality, care and the NHS. These were jobs where, however hard you tried, you couldn't really distance yourself from other people. We could see from our own data that these were areas where the virus was spreading rapidly. We were constantly raising this as an issue, that these people needed help, proper sick pay and support. It was very difficult to get that across to anyone in government. Once again, they were taking a 'Westminster-knows-best' view of our local needs.

As I said earlier, the recommendation after swine flu was for the next pandemic to be handled in a less centralised, more localised way. As 2020 wore on, one decision after another confirmed that the government was sticking with a traditional, top-down approach. My fears that they were diverging from the pandemic plan were gradually confirmed. The first big error was standing down local testing teams. I was stunned when my officers relayed to me the instruction they had received in early March. We were best placed to know how testing services should be organised but it was to be done via a national, outsourced operation. Sometime in April, we were informed that our first testing station would be stood up at Manchester Airport. That would not have been our choice of location.

This was followed by another first order failure on data. When the Coronavirus Act was passed at the start of the pandemic, Covid-19 was added to the list of notifiable diseases. This meant, by law, directors of public health would have to be given names and addresses of people in their area who tested positive. This is critical if local spread is to be contained. Unbelievably, by the mid-summer of 2020, we were still fighting to be given access to it. Local testing and tracing had been stood down and, instead, billions spent on an outsourced, centralised test and trace operation. Incredibly, they said the data belonged to them and they wouldn't share it with local councils. We had to show the government their own law to get that changed.

The third huge mistake was to adopt a centralised approach to contact tracing. By definition, this should have been a local responsibility. Greater Manchester repeatedly made this plea to civil servants and ministers. But to no avail. The government was determined to stand up an outsourced operation based on call centres. Our approach would have involved teams on the ground knocking on doors; theirs involved telephone calls from an unknown number. It's not hard to see which one would have been more successful.

After that, we spent weeks trying to retrofit the national system to work better for us. We had a stubbornly high case rate and tried to negotiate a protocol whereby the names of people who had tested positive but could not be contacted by the call centre would be passed to our local teams after forty-eight hours, involving volunteers from our fire service. How else were we going to be able to get a grip on our high case rate? Again, you would think that should have been a straightforward ask. But no. It took until the autumn to get a scheme of sorts going and, in truth, by then it was too little too late.

In summary, NHS Test and Trace did little to stop the spread of the virus. It was a scandalous waste of public money and should always be paraded as the classic example of how Britain's addiction to expensive, outsourced services does not serve us well. Whitehall would rather throw billions at tick-box operations run by private entities than trust local government to do the job, saving many millions in the process. We can live in hope that a big lesson was learned; that there is now a realisation in Whitehall that locally controlled and locally delivered services are more effective. But I'm not sure anything has changed. After the pandemic, local councils continue to be cut to the bone. The root cause of Britain's botched pandemic response was overly centralised, London-centric decision-making. Mayors and local leaders were completely excluded. News of major decisions would reach us on the grapevine with minimal supporting information on implementation.

In late May, I was in my kitchen getting ready to join a Teams meeting of the GM Covid Emergency Committee. My director of communications rang me unexpectedly: 'We're hearing that they are going to change the message from "stay at home" to "stay alert" as early as today.'

Not for the first time, I was stunned by what I was being told.

'They can't do that. Our case rate in Greater Manchester is still too high. Can we seek a meeting to ask them to delay?'

'They've already sent us the new logos to use on our messaging. The decision is made.'

The timing of the lifting of the first national lockdown would set the course of what was to follow in Greater Manchester in the rest of 2020. Covid had originally taken hold in London and then spread up the country through the Midlands to the North. Consequently, there was a lag of two to three weeks on the case rate. By the later part of May, cases in London and the South East were settling down and so our London-centric decision-makers were ready to change course. We would have told them it was too early for us. But they didn't bother to ask.

We were trying to understand what was unfolding at the time as best we could and get the best advice possible. We never pretended to be experts but we got to understand things like the R rate, which was the rate by which the virus was spreading, and this is what we were warning them about. It was often above one in the North West.

I really struggled with Boris Johnson during our exchanges during the pandemic. I never felt confident that he had read his briefing notes or was on top of the detail and the situation. Whenever we spoke on the phone or over Zoom, it all felt very false. He would always be over-friendly and I could just smell the bullshit. He overdid it. I think he wanted to be seen as a sort of wartime leader and was telling us that we were all in this fight together. But we knew that wasn't the case.

By the summer of 2020, we were trying to walk a tightrope between calling out the government when they didn't treat us fairly but also still trying to pull together as part of the spirit of national unity. It got harder and harder to do as more and more bad decisions were made. We had already proved them wrong about the sharing of data but things went significantly downhill at the end of July 2020.

One afternoon, I got an unexpected call from Matt Hancock. He told me that the government was very worried about the high case rate in Greater Manchester and would need to bring in local restrictions on household mixing the next day. He asked me whether we would issue a supportive statement for that approach. I said that we were similarly concerned that cases were too high, but this was very short notice, and I would have to consult the ten local leaders and come back to him. I hastily convened a meeting and, while many concerns were expressed about the need for good information to explain the change, we didn't see we had much choice. I conveyed this back to the health secretary and, within an hour or so, he did a quick TV clip to say that, from midnight, people in Greater Manchester wouldn't be able to visit each other's homes. What we didn't know is that the government would not have the supporting detail we had been led to expect. So, from 9 p.m. onwards, all hell broke loose. My social media was inundated with people who worked in other people's homes – such as painters, decorators and childminders – asking whether they would be able to go to work in the morning. We searched and searched on the Number 10 website for the detailed regulations we had been promised and found nothing until some patchy FAQ material arrived in the early hours of Friday. It was a taste of what was to come in the autumn.

There was never any clarity in the official messaging and things got trickier as different tiers and rules were created for different areas. We wanted to know what was being planned for our regions so that we could tailor our guidance specifically.

People won't be surprised to read that in Merseyside there is a fairly heavy distrust of Conservatives. We knew that we would have to get the communications right and make sure it didn't all come directly from the likes of Boris Johnson or Matt Hancock in order to make sure people paid proper attention. But they never gave us time to do that. They just dumped these massive, life-altering announcements on us without the crucial supporting information and left us to try and deal with the chaos it created.

There were some points where you just had to ignore them and make your own calls. We had an issue with the tolls that are charged for motorists driving through the Mersey Tunnels between Liverpool and the Wirral. During the lockdown, it became very quickly apparent that the only people making these journeys were emergency and frontline workers and it did not feel right that they were being charged to travel to do their important work.

I had a tortuous conversation one day with a minister in the Department for Transport. I said we were planning to scrap the tunnel tolls and was told it was a bad idea. I would set a difficult precedent. A veiled threat was being made about how the government might treat us going forward if we went against their guidance on this. The clear implication was that we might find ourselves in a difficult position when funding announcements were being made. That was the government's style all over. I scrapped the tolls during the first lockdown anyway, because it was the right thing to do. It was a high stakes decision and one I felt we had to take, regardless of what the ministers were saying or threatening.

We are people who care deeply about our regions and there was huge, life-and-death stuff happening. We started to push back more and more against the government in terms of how they were doing things. These problems intensified as we got into the summer and the prospect of different tiers of restrictions for different areas emerged. It became clear that they were just making it up as they went along. They were punch-drunk, staggering from one crisis to another like an injured fighter without any sense of planning or strategy. I think that period in the middle of 2020 sums up the chaos of the Johnson administration. It is being very clearly revealed to everyone by the Covid-19 Inquiry, to which Andy and I have given evidence, that the government was a dangerous shambles.

When we got into September, we were picking up reports that the Eat Out to Help Out scheme, initiated by then Chancellor Rishi Sunak, was driving increases in cases. There was a particularly sharp rise in Bolton. Almost overnight, the government went from encouraging people to go out for cut-price meals to closing all hospitality businesses in Bolton. There was zero financial support for those affected. David Greenhalgh, the then Conservative leader of Bolton, and I formed a cross-party alliance to speak out about how unfair this was. But nothing came back from the government. In the minds of those in Number 10, Bolton could simply be shut down and wasn't important enough to require any further attention from them.

As we approached October, the storm clouds were gathering. Word started to reach us that the government would be moving from a confusing patchwork of ad hoc local restrictions to a structured tier system. The M9 group of mayors were invited to a meeting about it with Matt Hancock and Nadine Dorries. One after another, we made the case that, if they were going to bring in tougher restrictions, they would need to provide financial help to people and businesses affected. I was particularly exercised on this point with the Bolton experience still fresh in my mind. Would there be any help? we asked. Nadine said nothing had been agreed. Sensing our rising alarm, Matt said he would raise it with the Treasury.

The bombshell landed on 7 October 2020 – my twentieth wedding anniversary. Marie-France and I had been out in the Atlas Bar near to Deansgate station and were on the train back to Newton-le-Willows when the next day's front pages started to appear on social media. Marie-France nudged me and showed me a picture of *The Times* headline: 'Pubs to close across the North'.

Once again, a decision with major implications was briefed to the media with no supporting details nor confirmation of any support. We were now getting angrier about how we were being treated. As luck would have it, I was due on *Question Time* the following day and I didn't hold back. Steve and I followed it up with a Saturday lunchtime Zoom press briefing where we laid down a clear ultimatum: we would not accept restrictions without a fair package of support. The temperature was rising and we were on a collision course with the government.

The Chancellor's response was to offer a complicated furlough scheme for the people whose workplaces would be closed – in effect, 67 per cent of their wages. We pointed out that those working in pubs, restaurants, betting shops and bingo halls were on the lowest wages. A two-thirds furlough wouldn't be enough. And how would it be fair when others were sitting in their gardens on an 80 per cent furlough? Just as ministers felt they could treat Bolton differently, they assumed they could do the same with people who served them their drinks and who they barely ever looked in the eye.

Greater Manchester was in a different position from the Liverpool City Region. By this point, we had been in local restrictions for two months. They hadn't worked and people were hurting. We were in no mood to be pushed around. We were sceptical about whether Tier 3 would work and, in a meeting with senior officials, under forensic questioning from Sir Richard Leese, Jonathan Van-Tam, the deputy Chief Medical Officer, appeared to confirm it wouldn't. A few days later, a follow-up Zoom meeting was arranged and, this time, the entire Greater Manchester delegation was placed on mute so we couldn't interrupt Number 10 when they were wrong.

We were resolute in our objection to any form of restrictions without proper support for people. It was a principled stance for equal treatment of all of our citizens. Number 10 briefed local media about local hospitals running out of critical care beds. These were old-school scare tactics and we saw them for what they were. Instead of wearing us down, they hardened our resolve. That process of negotiation over Tier 3 gave us a direct window into a chaotic Number 10. We didn't like what we saw. After having to front up for their poor decisions all year, we weren't having it any more. We were ready for a fight.

During the autumn of 2020, the Liverpool City Region was in a different position from Greater Manchester. We had not been in restrictions for months like them but, belatedly, our case rate was exploding to astronomical levels. It was inevitable that we would need to bring in restrictions or our local NHS would become overwhelmed. The information I was getting was that, if we carried on as we were for another two weeks, there would be no capacity left in our hospitals. It didn't take a rocket scientist to work out what the consequences of that outcome would be.

While I knew that was where we were heading, when *The Times* front page leaked news of a new Tier 3, and listed the Liverpool City Region as one of the areas that would be placed in it, I was determined that the very least we would get was a decent settlement to help us through the crisis.

Andy and I were constantly working together on this, even though we were in different circumstances in terms of the virus. We were in regular contact and it felt like we were fighting this pandemic together and all that came with it. This became more important when we got into negotiations about what support would arrive with these new rules and we realised that the government was trying to divide us and play us off against each other. It's amazing to think they were deploying these kinds of tactics during a pandemic. It was foolish of them to believe they could get between Andy and me.

We were able to negotiate a £45 million package as we accepted the inevitable Tier 3 restrictions, which was a decent settlement and meant we could support businesses that would be hit hardest. But the madness of how they worked out the actual rules caused us more problems. We were informed by Number 10 that there was a prescriptive set of restrictions for areas designated to be in the highest tier. In discussions with local leaders, we were all concerned by some of the places that would be forced to close. But we were told it wasn't an 'à la carte menu' to choose from. The additional restrictions were the additional restrictions. Full stop. However, when other areas followed us into Tier 3, different conditions applied. For example, the Tier 3 restrictions for our region included closing all gyms while bingo halls could stay open. When Lancashire next door to us went into Tier 3, they could keep gyms open but they had to close all their bingo halls. No explanation was given for this. It made absolutely no sense and just caused more confusion and resentment. Some people began questioning our motives and targeted criticism towards us and away from the government. This made some of the local leaders very jittery at times.

It became an incredibly difficult period for me because people were starting to compare my approach with Andy's, as he began to push back in Greater Manchester against the government's proposals. As I've mentioned, we were in a totally different situation with an out-of-control case rate. I just wanted to get a decent deal as we went into the restrictions. Which we knew, in reality, we needed. Greater Manchester had lower infection levels and was a region that was weary from months of restrictions, so Andy was in a different battle. But people drew comparisons anyway. It was the lowest point of my career. People were attacking me for supposedly 'rolling over' and 'selling out' the people of my region. Twitter was an absolute maelstrom of abuse. It felt very unfair because I was just doing my best for our area. It made me feel extremely low. I wasn't sleeping and felt genuinely unwell. My family were worried about me. There was hardly any respite from the constant demands.

Boris Johnson hadn't helped my cause by publicly praising me at the despatch box in Parliament and in his Downing Street press conference – not an endorsement you would ever want in Liverpool. But of course, this was all a tactic to try to divide

Andy and me. By praising me, Boris was trying to isolate Andy, pile pressure on him and make him cave. Unfortunately, lots of people couldn't see through that. How anybody could have believed that I would work against the interests of my own people is perplexing, but when you factor in that the person I would have needed to collude with was Boris Johnson, it became farcical.

I've never had any time for Johnson. Back in 2019, I attended the Convention of the North in Rotherham where the then Prime Minister delivered a keynote speech. After he appeared on stage, he asked to meet with the Metro Mayors: I was ushered into a room to wait for the Prime Minister's entrance with Andy, Dan Jarvis and Ben Houchen, the Mayor of Tees Valley. He came bounding in full of beans and shook Ben's hand, who he knew very well and who he later elevated to the House of Lords in his resignation honours list. He then enthusiastically shook hands with Andy and Dan and exchanged pleasantries. He then approached me and held out his hand.

'I'm sorry, Prime Minister,' I said. 'I respect the position you hold, but I can't in all conscience shake the hand of someone responsible for the hurt caused to the people in my city with the *Spectator* article on Hillsborough.'

He went puce and, with a hand still outstretched, turned to others in the room. He looked shocked and confused. He mumbled something inaudible and then asked an open question with his back towards me. It was an awkward moment. But I couldn't have lived with myself if I hadn't again challenged his unforgivable behaviour. It wasn't the first time we had crossed swords on the issue.

Back in 2004, Johnson edited and published an article in the *Spectator* which inexplicably linked the death of Ken Bigley, an engineer from Liverpool who was publicly beheaded by Iraqi militants, with Hillsborough. He criticised what he saw as our over-sentimentality in response to this abomination because there were plans to hold a two-minute silence in Liverpool as a mark of respect to Ken and his family. The piece went on to

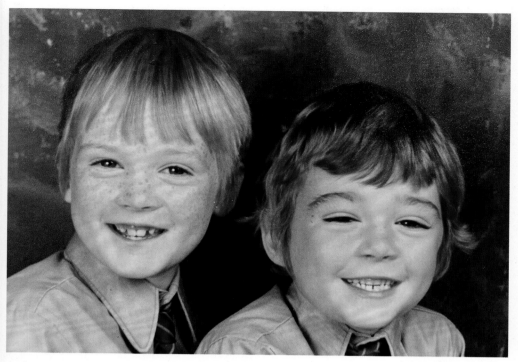

ABOVE: Nick and I, St Lewis's RC Primary, Silver Jubilee Year, 1977. (Andy)

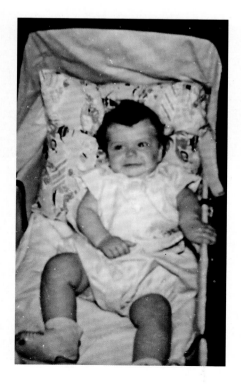

LEFT: The fifth born child of eight, 1961. (Steve)

LEFT: With John, annual family photo at Goodison Park, summer of 1984, wearing 'that' yellow jumper which so offended Nick Hornby. (Andy)

RIGHT: Everton away-days with Nick, London, late 1990s. (Andy)

LEFT: Marie-France finally banishing my imposter syndrome, Fitzwilliam College Ball, 1990. (Andy)

LEFT: Me and fellow Mod, Phil Jones, at Eric's Club, Liverpool, 1978. (Steve)

ABOVE: Bricklaying in the Falkland Islands, 1983. (Steve)

RIGHT: A rare footy shirt photo, 1984. (Steve)

LEFT: Another day that changed everything, Anfield, April 2009. (Andy)

ABOVE: Speaking in the House of Commons, a proud moment 2010. (Steve)

LEFT: A proud day as the new Lord Mayor and Lady Mayoress of Liverpool, 2008. (Steve)

RIGHT: With the other Margaret, who in my opinion would have made a much better Prime Minister, September 2013. (Andy)

ABOVE: Another campaign, but this time for me, 2021. (Steve)

RIGHT: From hero to friend, at Sir Kenny Dalglish's Lifetime Achievement award at the BBC Sports Personality of the Year, December 2023. (Steve)

LEFT: Attending the Bloomberg 'Program for New Mayors' in New York, 2017. (Steve)

ABOVE: Live from District 12: fighting the Capitol over Tier 3, October 2020. (Andy)

LEFT: Delivered to my office, 25 May 2017. Meant the world. Always struggle to talk about it without tearing up. (Andy)

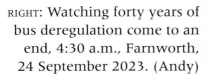

RIGHT: Watching forty years of bus deregulation come to an end, 4:30 a.m., Farnworth, 24 September 2023. (Andy)

RIGHT: Presenting "Rotheram and Burnham" – a new gritty Northern detective series from ITV, 2016. (Andy)

LEFT: Thou shall not pass, charity match at Anfield, May 2021. (Steve)

LEFT: Header North: scoring into the Kop. (Andy)

RIGHT: Arriving with Annie, Rosie, Marie-France and Jimmy for the 2021 Mayoral election count. (Andy)

LEFT: Mayoral election night and family nerves, May 2021. (Steve)

RIGHT: With the Modfather himself, Paul Weller, November 2021. (Steve)

LEFT: Take Over The World: two paperboys from the North West watching The Courteeners, September 2021. (Andy)

repeat untruths of the past and blame the Hillsborough disaster on drunken Liverpool fans in the same manner that Thatcher's press secretary, Sir Bernard Ingham, had done. Furthermore, it accused Liverpool of 'wallowing in victim status' which caused an outcry locally and resulted in the then Tory leader Michael Howard dispatching a recalcitrant Johnson to the city to apologise personally.

I'd only been on the council a couple of years and was sent to intercept him to ensure he understood the anger and resentment of local people and the Liverpool Labour group regarding his unfounded words. *Channel 4 News* were also trying to get an interview with him but, typically, he was being evasive. So we headed around the likely spots where he might turn up. We were at the old Granada studios on the Albert Dock, and had almost given up, when we spotted a small cavalcade heading our way. It was unmistakably him.

As his car pulled up, I quickly stepped forward to confront him. I knew at best I would have a minute or so to put forward my case. He got out of the car and offered his hand. But I refused and instead berated him, explaining he must have known his remarks would cause offence. I said that he clearly didn't understand the tragic story of Hillsborough nor our collective shock at the brutal murder of Mr Bigley. His response stunned me. I had never encountered someone who spoke about themselves in the third person. He asked whether I thought that Michael Howard had ordered Boris to Liverpool to apologise. A little bit taken aback, I said yes. I did believe that was the case. Johnson looked straight through me and flounced into the studio leaving me a little stunned at the encounter.

All those years later, to have people spreading lies on social media, claiming I would enter into a Faustian pact with someone like Boris Johnson, caused me great anguish. The trolls were having a field day. But, when credible threats appeared against my personal safety, I contacted the Chief Constable of Merseyside Police, Andy Cooke, who had been made aware of the situation. He posted a twenty-four-hour police presence outside my house. Despite the murder of my former Parliamentary colleague Jo Cox, there still appeared to be some people on social media who believed it to be fair game to stir up hatred. Some see it as their right to threaten the safety of politicians simply because they are in the public eye. Just a year later, the veteran Conservative MP David Amess would also be tragically murdered in his constituency.

There was an important moment around that time which shows the importance of my friendship with Andy and our unity. We were due to do a joint live interview on *Channel 4 News*. The government was still trying to divide us and cause tensions between the different regions. Some people who should have known better were sucked in by it all. My head was so fuzzy, everything felt like a blur as we went live on the show. I stumbled through the first question, barely able to get the words out. Then they went to Andy. He said:

'The Prime Minister is trying to divide me and Steve. Nothing will ever divide me and Steve.'

It was a big moment for me because it started to dampen down some of the vitriol I had been getting. It didn't stop the abuse but it softened. It showed people that Andy and I were united, despite what the government was trying to do, and that they shouldn't be kidded by Tory tactics. After the interview, my wife Sandra and my kids phoned Andy to thank him for what he had said. They could see how down I had been and they knew that it meant a lot to me. It showed how important our friendship was and that remains the case today.

The government's attempt to divide and rule Liverpool and Manchester revealed more about them than it did about us. They think that everyone can be played off against each other; that everyone and everything can be bought; and that, in the end, people will shaft each other. They don't have the same values as we have here where friendships and bonds mean more than political wins. Where we come from, you are loyal to your mates and I don't think a lot of people in Westminster understand that. The nature of the place, and the bubble that surrounds it, makes it hard for people to form proper, meaningful friendships. Everything is so transactional. People always seem to have one eye on their next move, their next opportunity.

By mid-October, we were having a lot of behind-the-scenes meetings with ministers and officials. We were steadfast that, if Greater Manchester was to go into the highest tier of restrictions, people affected should get the same 80 per cent furlough as the rest of the country. Because they were only pushing the North into Tier 3, they thought they could palm us off with less. But we wouldn't back down. Why should people here be valued less than elsewhere in the UK?

After a crunch meeting with the government produced no progress, we decided to make our position clear via a press conference outside Manchester Central Library in St Peter's Square. I was joined in a socially distanced line under a gloomy sky by Sir Richard, Bev Hughes and Sean Fielding, the then leader of Oldham. 'New Order are getting on a bit,' said one Twitter post.

It was a surreal moment. The city was virtually silent, but we were there to make a noise. I said I wasn't happy with what the government was offering and I wouldn't sell the city short. The government was asking us to gamble with our residents' jobs, homes and businesses on a strategy that may well not work. That last comment was based on the admission from the deputy Chief Medical Officer who had admitted it was not certain that Tier 3 would be effective. When I finally appeared at the Covid public inquiry in late 2023, I discovered it was worse than that: ministers had been explicitly advised that it wouldn't work and yet they still pushed us into it without sufficient support. I will never forgive them for that.

The press event was only intended to ensure that our side of the argument was better understood. As I returned home on the train, I was surprised to see Gary Lineker tweeting about it. More and more people were beginning to tune in to this unfolding story. At that stage, I genuinely hoped that the high public profile of the issue would be enough to make the government see sense and treat us fairly. I felt sure it would be resolved in phone calls over the weekend.

Despite some helpful conversations with Eddie Lister, the Prime Minister's right-hand man, we couldn't get anywhere. He informed me on the Sunday morning that the Treasury weren't backing down so maybe it was time for Greater Manchester to do that instead. I told him politely that we wouldn't. At the same time, we had opened lines of communication with the Labour front bench asking for their backing. I said we were going toe to toe with the government on an issue of principle where I thought public support would be with us. I needed my party to back me and quickly. I felt pretty aggrieved when nothing came back.

By the Monday, I felt isolated and anxious about the week that lay ahead. At teatime, a media report appeared saying that Greater Manchester had until the close of play tomorrow to agree to the government's proposals or Tier 3 would be imposed. It was accompanied by some scurrilous briefing about the lack of hospital beds as they tried to pile on the pressure. The next morning, D-Day had arrived and I headed into the Manchester office. Before long, word came through that Number 10 were on the line asking to put me through to the Prime Minister. Shortly after, Boris came on the phone: 'Andy, you are just going to have to accept this. We've put a generous offer on the table.'

'We don't see it that way,' I said. 'People won't have enough to live on. We will accept the restrictions but we are asking for more help before we do.'

'Well other areas have accepted it and we don't see why you are different.'

'I'll tell you why we're different. We've been under restrictions for months with no funding and people are struggling.'

'What restrictions do you mean?'

'The ones your government put us under in July.'

'Well, I don't know about that but I'm asking you to speak to your leaders, tell them about our final offer and call me back when you've spoken to them.'

When I put the phone down, I turned to Kevin Lee, my political director, and we both looked at each other in disbelief. The Prime Minister clearly hadn't bothered to inform himself about the full situation in Greater Manchester before making the call. We had accepted the July restrictions in a spirit of cooperation but there was zero appreciation of that. And, unbeknownst to me, rather than seeking a genuine resolution, Boris and his team were more interested in winning the game of poker by any means necessary. His comment about speaking to the leaders was not an innocent one. While we had been on the phone, it was clear that Number 10 advisers were going behind my back and trying to get some of our council leaders to peel away. To my relief, when I asked them to stand firm with me, they all did. It meant a lot. I felt emboldened to go back to Downing Street: 'Can I speak to the Prime Minister, please?'

He didn't come back on the phone as promised. Instead, Robert Jenrick came on the line and, in a very high-handed way, told me they would be imposing Tier 3 in two days. When I asked him to confirm that this would also come with the government's final financial offer of £60 million, he replied: 'There are no guarantees about that.'

It was a profoundly depressing conversation. This is how the UK government operated during a once-in-a-generation health crisis. Not like a responsible administration but like a Westminster mafia. We knew that they would already be briefing the press against us so we convened another media briefing outside the Bridgewater Hall. As we walked over, taxi drivers sounded their horns and waved to show support. But, rather than feeling buoyed up by this, I actually felt quite down.

When I began to speak to the media, it was more in sorrow than in anger. I explained that we had stood up for people because we knew many people in Greater Manchester were struggling. People whose workplaces would soon be closing should be entitled to the same furlough as others and we had no regrets about taking a stand for them.

During the question and answer session that followed, Kevin did something quite unusual. In a gap between questions, he walked up to show me a text message he had just received. He thought I needed to see it in case someone from the media got wind of it. It was from Manchester Central MP Lucy Powell who was texting from a meeting in Westminster called by Matt Hancock. This is what the text said: 'On call with Hancock: comes into effect 1 min past midnight on Friday; it's going to be £22m only; they are going to try and pick off individual councils.'

When I processed what it said, my mood changed in an instant. All year, I had tried my best to work with this chaotic bunch. Now, because we had stood up for low-paid people, they were going to administer a public punishment beating. This was the same government that less than twelve months before had been elected on promises to level up the North. My pent-up frustrations came pouring out. How could they grind people down and treat this city in this way? A few passers-by had stopped to listen, shouted the odd word of encouragement and then applauded when I'd finished.

I trudged back to the office and asked Kevin to give me a lift home. I was drained after days of tension. As the tiredness kicked in on the journey down the M62, the feeling of despondency came back and was even more overwhelming this time. I never like letting people down and I felt like I had. I arrived home, turned my phone off and took our dog, Axel, for a walk with Marie-France. When we got back, we put a film on. I had a school-night beer to try to switch off. A couple of hours later, as we were getting ready to call it a day, Marie-France said: 'This'll make you laugh. Pictures of Kevin are all over social media.'

To our surprise, the image of Kevin showing me his phone, and my dejected reaction, had become something of an internet meme. Most of them were positive and I took heart from the fact that people seemed to understand what I was trying to do. It seems I was not the only one who had been getting increasingly frustrated with the behaviour of the government. What happened next encapsulates everything this book is about.

Days after Greater Manchester's Tier 3 showdown, London was placed into Tier 2. These were the same restrictions that we had been under for months with no offer of support; the same restrictions of which the Prime Minister was seemingly unaware. However, for the Capital, he was immediately able to put a financial package on the table. I didn't need to point out the double standards. Millions did it for me. It wasn't much longer after that the whole country went into a national lockdown. We now know that this is precisely what the experts had been advising the government to do for weeks and weeks. They had concocted the Tier system as a last gamble to try to avoid it. They had tried to force the North into an arrangement which they knew was unlikely to work, and was certain to cause damage to people's lives and businesses, on the off chance that it might. Why? Because they could. But, when it was clear that London would have to enter the Tiers, the Treasury opened the purse-strings immediately. I don't think any other episode in our political history has more starkly exposed the dark truth about life in Britain: we may live in the same country, but some people and some places are most definitely more equal than others.

On the Saturday morning after Tier 3 had been imposed, I was down to address a Conference in London by Zoom. It was a strange time. The different parts of the country felt very separated. I genuinely didn't know how people in the conference room down there would have viewed our Tier 3 showdown. I had been quite down for a few days after it but, by then, was starting to come round. To break the ice, I decided to start my speech with a little joke: 'Good morning to everyone in the Capitol. I am coming to you live from District 12, also known as Greater Manchester.' My clumsy reference to *The Hunger Games* seemed to provoke a bit of nervous laughter in the room. Perhaps Boris's divide and rule tactics were having more impact than I realised.

It was just so brazen. During our own negotiations, I had been invited onto a COBRA meeting and the first ministers of the devolved nations were on the call too. When it came to my turn to speak, I said maintaining furlough at 80 per cent was a red line for us. You cannot reduce the amount of furlough you pay to people in a particular part of the country – how would that

be fair? I asked them what they would be doing if what was happening in the North was happening in London. Why should people be treated any differently to elsewhere?

Nicola Sturgeon and Mark Drakeford backed me and said exactly the same thing. But Boris Johnson just came back and said no. He asked Rishi Sunak, who was then the Chancellor, to address my point. He said it may well have been a red line for us but the government would not be moving. As Andy says, everything magically changed when London went into the new tier system. To see that difference in their approach after their hardline stance with us, tells you all you need to know about the disparities in this country. It was staggering really.

When the tide went out in March 2020, we all saw modern Britain more clearly than we had ever seen it before. Things not visible to the naked eye in more normal times were suddenly on full show: the brutal divides; the parallel lives; the broken British state. The question is this: having now seen it, what do we do about it?

We started this book by recounting our experience as young men as tragedy unfolded around us. For us, it was a life-changing experience and revealed things about this country which have haunted us ever since. But we appreciate that Hillsborough did not have the same impact on everyone. However, we have ended the first half of this book with an account of a collective, national experience which has revealed exactly the same flaws as we went through in 1989. The difference is, this time, they were revealed in real time to the whole of the UK population. We all had a ringside seat as an unaccountable state tried to divide and rule and foist decisions taken by a small cabal on millions. We saw private vested interests being prioritised over the public interest. We got proof, if it were needed, that Whitehall does not regard all people and places as equals. If Britain is to be in any way ready for the next pandemic, we need to start planning now for the fundamental rewiring of the British state – and building a broad movement of people determined to bring it about.

2

Our Vision

8
Why We Need to Change Things

If anything brought us both into a life of politics, it was the desire to see our part of the world and its people receive equal treatment with the rest of the UK. If we have learnt anything from our journeys so far, it is this: our goal is not achievable as long as our current political system remains in place. To be honest, though, it's not just the North West which is being held back from achieving its potential. The same applies to every other part of the UK outside London and the South East. For proof of that, look no further than the wide disparity in the standard of transport infrastructure.

So why is Britain one of the most unequal countries in the world?

In this second half of the book, we will attempt to provide a clear answer to this question in the hope that, by sharing a diagnosis of what is wrong, we can start to shape a cross-party and cross-geography consensus on the need to rewire Britain. Our starting point is to share with you the stark realisation we reached after years of trying to advance the cause of the North within the Whitehall world: this is not just a deeply unequal country; this is a deliberately unequal country.

The North–South divide is no historical accident. It is in fact the product of long-term national policy. It is only when there is clarity about this stark truth that everything else starts to fall into place. Look closely at the British Parliament today. You can still clearly see the influence of the feudal society from which it evolved. Wealthy families granted large land interests in centuries past are still making your laws in the unelected House of Lords. There are more people in the Lords who went to Eton than there are peers who were born in the Liverpool City Region or

Greater Manchester. Meanwhile, over in the House of Commons, there are clear echoes of the ancient 'rotten boroughs' in a first-past-the-post system which gives some people and some places more influence than others.

So, if our national Parliament has never represented all of Britain's regions and nations equally, is there any real surprise that there is such disparity in living standards across our land? Obviously not. But the make-up of Parliament alone doesn't describe why things are as they are in an unequal Britain today. There is a deeper question of where power truly lies and how it is used or misused. Our experience of the Parliamentary whip system is that it has the effect of transferring power out of this flawed Parliament and into a small number of hands – largely unelected – in the heart of the Whitehall machine.

At any given time, a majority of MPs in the Commons will be required via the whips' offices to back the official line, which often tends to be the long-held positions of various Whitehall departments. It is almost as if those who built Britain's system of national governance over the centuries took great care at every step of the journey to give away as little power as possible to the people and their representatives.

When we were first elected as MPs, and entered Parliament, we were labouring under the misapprehension that we would have real power to change some of the things we came to see as wrong when we were growing up. It was not long before we realised that was a mirage. Unlike the US, where elected representatives are allowed an independence of thought, the UK's whip system turns representatives of the people into human rubber stamps – or, in a phrase MPs use knowingly about themselves, 'lobby fodder'. The MP's main role in life is to nod through the decisions of the fifty or so people who really run the country; most of whom, you won't be surprised to learn, are unelected and hold London-centric views. This latter adjective also accurately describes the permanent policies people in these powerful positions seek to protect and promote. It suits them to hoard resources and power in the place where they live rather than allow any upstart rival power bases to spring up elsewhere in the UK and weaken their position.

For decades, the Treasury's Green Book has set out the rules against which potential investments must be tested. In short, it gives a higher score to projects which will produce the most returns for UK plc in the shortest possible time. In other words, it is a formula to give most to the already-affluent parts of the UK – mainly to be found in London and the South East – and least to areas that are struggling. This policy hasn't just helped create the North–South divide; it is a mechanism by which it is continually widened.

To summarise: Britain is wired for regional inequality – and its impotent Parliament has so far proved itself incapable of changing that. By keeping MPs trapped in party-based tramlines, the whip system has so far successfully prevented a cross-party rebellion of the English regions in support of a fairer national investment strategy. Beyond regional disparities, there are other ways in which this over-concentration of political power in one postcode is not conducive to the public good. It is a system in which already-powerful interests find it far too easy to get their way. Corporate lobbyists have few people to persuade to land the contracts they want. Manipulative media outlets only have to hold a few powerful people to ransom to make the nation dance to their divisive tunes. And, through the decades, when disaster has struck, the institutions of government have only had a few phone calls to make to get the cover-up underway.

What else explains how an entire English city could cry injustice for twenty years, with complete justification, only to be completely ignored? For Liverpool in the 80s, read Derry in the 70s and Aberfan in the 60s. Think Grenfell, contaminated blood, Primodos, Windrush, and the nuclear test veterans. Watch the recent ITV drama Mr Bates vs The Post Office. The tactics deployed against the sub-postmasters and postmistresses were also used against all of the victims of the scandals mentioned above. It is a pattern that keeps on repeating down the decades and a playbook as old as time: a powerful centre plays divide and rule, creates false narratives to turn public opinion against powerless people and places and then casts them into the wilderness. It is the unelected British state at its very worst. How can it do it? Because of the near-unlimited power of people at its centre.

If Peter Hain hadn't made that mistake with his election expenses, it is almost certain that neither the second Hillsborough inquest nor the Infected Blood Inquiry would have happened. That justice for thousands of innocent people hinged on a random turn of events Whitehall couldn't control, rather than the democratic process, is a truly mind-blowing thought.

The main check on the near-unbridled power of Whitehall is the Cabinet minister. Junior ministers are easily ignored or worked around. If a powerful Cabinet minister is determined to change his or her department's official position, they can do it. We know things only changed for us on Hillsborough because one of us was a Cabinet minister and was able to persuade the Prime Minister of the day to open things up. Similarly, we appreciate that, in the 2010 to 2015 Parliament, the fight for the truth was only kept alive because Theresa May clearly saw the moral imperative of making sure the Hillsborough families were given it. We will always be grateful to her for that. It is what happened after Theresa May left the Home Office, which we witnessed first-hand, which gives you a shocking glimpse into how brutal this system is in the pursuit of its own interests.

We will always maintain that the full and final truth about Hillsborough will not be known until the same is established in respect of events five years earlier during the Miners' Strike at the Orgreave Coking Plant. Bear in mind that both events took place five years apart and involved the same police force, South Yorkshire Police (SYP). Even though there has not yet been an independent inquiry into Orgreave, it is a fact that the SYP deployed precisely the same underhand tactics against the miners who had attended the mass picket as it would later do to much more devastating effect against the Liverpool supporters. On the first day of their trial in 1985, the case against the miners was thrown out by the court because of mass manufactured police statements. It was all part of a crude attempt to portray the miners as the villains – and turn public opinion against them and their strike – even though many were victims of indiscriminate police violence on the day.

We believe that, before she left the Home Office, Theresa May was persuaded of the critical connection between Hillsborough and Orgreave. By mid-2016, there was a growing expectation in Westminster that, following the conclusion of the Hillsborough inquest, an inquiry into Orgreave would be announced. Then came one of those unexpected Westminster moments that the Whitehall machine pounces on to use for its own ends. The surprise departure of David Cameron after the EU *referendum led to Theresa May's sudden entry into 10 Downing Street. Her promise on the steps to correct 'burning injustices' shows where her mind was at. However, within weeks, her successor in the Home Office, Amber Rudd, would make an abrupt statement to Parliament ruling out an Orgreave Inquiry, to the shock of those present, on the basis that 'no one died'.*

As we suspected at the time, this was not the real reason. In her 2020 book, Diary of an MP's Wife, *Sasha Swire recalls Amber Rudd confiding in her that she was planning to rule out an Orgreave Inquiry because it would 'slur the memory of Thatcher and the party won't like it'. We can imagine the scene inside the Home Office shortly after Theresa May's departure and the huddle of civil servants around her newly arrived successor.*

'Are you sure you want to proceed with this inquiry, Home Secretary, given that it may well be a little uncomfortable for your colleagues?'

And so, forty years on, the facts of one of the most significant events to have happened here in the twentieth century are still being denied to millions of people across the North of England by a handful of people in Whitehall, acting out of entirely unscrupulous and self-serving reasons. Of course, if people were to know what truly happened, it might build public support for radical change in the way the country is run. That is precisely why it suits the system to continue to keep a lid on it all. They can do this because they have the power. But they shouldn't have that power. They shouldn't be able to deny people in the North the ability to know our own story. It is only by seeing clearly how we were governed and policed in the twentieth century that the next generation of Northerners will be able to change things in the twenty-first.

Every step of our journey – from Hillsborough to Tier 3 – we have had to fight back against a Whitehall machine which thinks it can treat our people as second-class citizens. That won't change until power is transferred back to a reformed Parliament and then passed out into every part of these islands. In the next chapters, we will set out our plan for the complete rewiring of Britain. In our view, nothing else will allow the North to fulfil its potential and the English regions to enjoy a level of equality with the rest of the UK.

9

A Written Constitution and a Basic Law

Part 1 of this book exposes the serious shortcomings in the way Britain is run, charting the paths Steve and I have taken and the barriers we have come up against. We left Westminster to start the process of trying to change it from the outside. We didn't know whether we would stand any chance of success but, seven years on, we feel we have made a decent start. To some extent, we have managed to rebalance the political debate. At least the voice of the North is being heard more loudly now than it was before. That said, we have to accept that what we are doing will not, on its own, be enough to secure equal treatment for the North and its people. If you need proof of this, look no further than the government's decision to impose Tier 3 or, more recently, its decision to scrap HS2 without any consultation with Northern leaders while holed up in a hotel in Manchester for the party conference.

Part 2 of *Head North* is all about a bigger vision of what the North could be in the rest of this century and the wider changes needed to the governance of Britain to get us there. Alongside that, it is our hope that it will help mobilise a stronger movement across all regions in support of the call for change. If we are to achieve that, we need a simpler description of the problem we need to fix. So let me try.

Imagine a rambling stately home. It has a rickety old electricity system which means that the power is only on in some rooms. In the main living room, and those adjoining it, the lights work well. Let's call that part of the house Greater London. Upstairs, directly above the living room, is the main bedroom. There, the lights flicker but they do work. Let's call that room Scotland. Down the end of the landing, there are two smaller bedrooms where the lights work but are much dimmer. I think you know where this going – they are Wales and Northern Ireland. A few other rooms have a bit of murky light – these are England's big city regions – but the rest of the rooms are dark.

I like to think my stately home is a pretty good analogy for creaky old Britain and its antiquated political system. It is a place where power does not circulate evenly. If we want the lights to come on in all the rooms – so that everyone in the house has the same living standards – we won't be able to achieve that by patching up the old electricity system. We will need to carry out a top-to-bottom rewiring of the house.

This is a book about power and how unevenly it is distributed across Britain. If people and places don't have access to sufficient power, it is very hard for them to improve their living standards. In Westminster, there is a received wisdom held by people on all sides that changes to the way Britain is run are not a priority for the voters. Hence they are always put off. But it is time for this flawed thinking to be challenged. The things voters do cite as priorities – better homes, better transport, better jobs – won't be available to everyone unless places across the UK have the power to deliver them. Therefore, constitutional changes are first order issues.

If we want a country where all people and places have the same living standards, we need nothing less than a complete rewiring of Britain. Of course, a major part of that is a radical reform of Parliament itself. It is an astonishing state of affairs that, in 2024, our national Parliament does not provide equal representation for all the regions and nations of the UK. Beyond that, significant power has to be taken out of Westminster and devolved to all parts of the UK. Finally, this transfer of power needs to go right down to the individual level, with people given new rights to the essentials of life.

We will set out a ten-point plan for a rewired, revitalised Britain. We hope it is a plan that can unite people from all places and all parties. We will come to the details in later chapters. But we start with the recognition that none of it will work unless we agree a new set of principles and rules for the running of the British state and the rights of its citizens; or, in other words, unless we build the new Britain on the strong foundation of a written constitution.

Like anything in life, if you have strong rules, you have a chance of a level playing field. If you don't, it is a recipe for the powerful to dominate. This simple truth explains why practically every other country in the world – over 190 of them – have a written constitution. Many have been developed after internal conflict and contain commitments to balance the rights of their different peoples and regions. Britain sits alongside Saudi Arabia, Israel, Canada and New Zealand in being one of the five countries that doesn't have a constitution. Why is this? I believe it is because Britain, unlike other countries, has never had a moment of modern nation-building. Our system of governance has slowly evolved from the feudal state, the remnants of which are still clearly visible in Parliament today. Power has only been wrested out of the hands of the powerful when they've had no choice.

Our failure fully to set out the rules for how the country should be run is one of the principal reasons why Britain is one of the most unequal major countries in the world. Our unwritten and murky constitutional arrangements have had the effect of hoarding power in a small number of hands – in Whitehall and Westminster and, by extension, in the powerful networks of institutions and vested interests that surround them. Because there are no written rules, everything is done through negotiation. But they are never equal negotiations. What chance does a local council have negotiating with the might of the Whitehall machine? The separate roles and responsibilities of local government and national government should be recognised and respected, but our failure to do this means the latter constantly rides roughshod over the former. Conversely, because power is concentrated in SW1A 0AA without clear rules for its use, it is all too easy for private vested interests to hack the system and exploit grey areas for their own benefit. There is a reason why Britain is the outsourcing capital of the world and local government is on its knees. NHS Test and Trace anyone?

Under the current system, ministers are able to do different deals with different regions based on the different relationships they might have. They are free to play one area off against another. Forget the merits of your case or the level of your needs. If you can get in with the relevant minister, you could soon be quids in. Because this is how money is given out by Westminster, it very much keeps power in the hands of those fifty or so people who run our country. Regional and local leaders are constantly required to bid for funding and go on bended knee to the Palace of Westminster. Everyone is kept in their place. And let's be clear: we are not just talking about the North of England here. People in Cornwall, East Anglia and the Midlands are treated just the same as us and are just as frustrated by the lack of fairness.

Beyond the imperfect Barnett Formula, there is no wider formula for the fair distribution of funding around the country. There is, however, the Green Book which, as I explained earlier, is a covert formula for keeping the funding flowing into the wealthier parts of Britain. Beyond the baseline funding given to the main public services, places have to beg and plead for individual deals and pots of money. The government holds all the cards. If we had a more balanced approach, where councils and mayors were dealt some cards too, we would have a much more functional, mature country where no one has to carry round a begging bowl and the age-old divide-and-rule tactics would be no more.

So, where in the world do we look for inspiration for a country like this?

The irony of ironies is that it is to one which Britain had a big hand in shaping in the post-war period. After the Second World War, the Allies drew up boundaries for the new German states in a bid to prevent a future concentration of political power in Berlin. In the constitution, those states – or *Länder* – were given a high degree of autonomy. Following this, in the second half of the twentieth century, Germany began to prosper in an impressive and equitable manner. When the Berlin Wall fell in 1989, it had to set about the enormous task of maintaining this social progress, while reunifying and levelling up East Germany with West Germany. To ensure a perception of fairness, and build a sense of unity between the two halves which had spent fifty years apart, Germany decided to add a Basic Law – or *Grundgesetz* – to its written constitution. The Basic Law stipulates that there must be 'equivalent living standards' between all of the German *Länder*. To achieve this, the wealthier states are required to pay into a central system which ensures that funds are redistributed around the country to achieve the law's central requirement. When you visit Germany, you can see and feel the success of this policy. In all German towns and cities, there is high quality public transport, public realm and infrastructure not seen in England outside London and the South East.

So, Britain has played a big part in creating one of the most levelled-up countries in the world. It's just a shame that it's not our own. Modern Germany stands as a model of nation-building. Britain's ancient, ad hoc arrangements, by contrast, have taken us to a very divided, unequal place.

If you want to release the latent potential of areas around a country, then you need to move towards a more federal structure. This is the obvious lesson from Germany where many areas across the country are flourishing, not just the capital. In England, London and the South East are on fire economically with the rest of us desperately trying to catch up. We are finding this very difficult because all the levers and resources we need to make progress remain in the capital. John Burn-Murdoch and Professor Sir Michael Marmott have produced data that explains the health inequalities that arise from the economic imbalance in our country. If you take the best performing areas out of each of the leading economies around the globe and then distribute the remaining wealth, the rest of the economy is maintained due to equal levels of investment in other areas within that country. However, the data clearly identifies just how concentrated wealth within this country is. Removing London from the UK positions the rest of the country's average wealth below that of Mississippi, which is America's poorest State.

We understand that changes aren't going to happen overnight, but even some movement towards a Basic Law that funds the different regions of this country fairly and equally based on need would make a huge difference – and it would do so quickly. A Basic Law for the English regions could release all sorts of potential that would benefit the whole nation. This isn't just about the money itself; it is about how that money is spent and on what. Currently, as the Mayor of the Liverpool City Region, I have to bid for different pots of money that can only be spent on certain things – the funds are ring-fenced. The money always comes with strict rules for how it can be used. Those rules are decided by the government. Under a Basic Law, combined authorities like ours would have much more autonomy for making the spending decisions that we know will most benefit the people of our regions – and we would have the fair funding settlement we need to do it.

Can you imagine how Britain would look and feel today if, after the war, we had created English regions with more autonomy, a written constitution and a Basic Law? We would be living in a very different – and I would say better – country from the one we live in now. There would be much less poverty and inequality. Manchester would probably have an underground system and Liverpool would certainly have a tram system.

In early January 2023, I invited Carsten Schneider, Minister in the German government for East Germany and Equivalent Living Standards, to address delegates at the Convention of the North in Manchester. It was a very deliberate move to lift the debate about 'levelling up' and start a conversation about the serious rewiring needed to make it happen. If Britain has created a framework for a levelled up country before, why can't we do it again?

Steve and I proposed the creation of the Convention shortly after being elected in 2017 to build a sense of greater unity across the North. But it was also a very deliberate attempt to start flexing the North's political muscle. If the North is speaking with one voice to Whitehall, it's a brave minister or a senior civil servant who comes to the Convention and tries to tell us what we can and can't have. In 2019, Boris Johnson came onto the stage at the second Convention of the North in Rotherham to zero applause. When he cracked his customary jokes, there was a stony silence. When he made some of his wilder claims and promises, a few grumbles could be heard. I was sitting in the audience thinking: 'Great, this Convention is really starting to work.'

By inviting Herr Schneider to address our Manchester gathering, we wanted to show the government what real 'levelling up' looks like. It was the late, great Lord Bob Kerslake who compared the gap between the North and London and the South East as being akin to East and West Germany after reunification. Well, unlike Boris in Rotherham, here was a minister from a country that has actually done the heavy lifting of levelling up. Carsten Schneider told us:

> 'The goal of creating equal living conditions everywhere in Germany can even be found in our constitution. There are good reasons for it. If regions are drifting apart, it is bad for everyone. If a variety of regions flourish, the whole country will prosper.'

His words resonated around the cavernous space of the former railway station where the Convention took place and with the people gathered there from every corner of the North of England. From the 80s onwards, we have all lived through the drifting apart of the UK's regions and nations and experienced how bad it has proved for everyone, with two divisive referendums in 2014 and 2016. Unlike in Germany, where traditional industry was given transitional funding to modernise, the North's big industries were allowed to fall into steep decline and the areas in which they were based went the same way with them. The Thatcher government developed an economic model for Britain based around the success of the City of London. A supercharged financial sector would bring in enough for UK plc to pay for everywhere else. In 1997, New Labour had a chance to reset things and rewire the country. There were good intentions at the start. Deputy Prime Minister John Prescott put forward a vision for a new regional policy across England and more devolved arrangements. Observing things from the inside, I could tell that the New Labour machine allowed John space to put these ideas forward. But it was always sceptical about them. They never really got behind him. At no time was this more evident than when the North East went forward with the first referendum on regional devolution in 2003. At the time, I was part of a steering group called Yes For The North West alongside the legendary Anthony H. Wilson. The idea was that, when the North East endorsed devolution, we would be the next to go. But John was on his own. When he looked over his shoulder, the big beasts of New Labour were nowhere to be seen. Perhaps a referendum like this could never have been won. I don't know. But the Labour Party should have given John's Northern Way project much more backing than it did. Beyond some high-profile North West successes, like the 2002 Commonwealth Games in Manchester, Liverpool 08 and the relocation of the BBC to Salford, the New Labour years did not bring a determined drive to rebalance the country and reignite the regions. Instead, focus was soon switched back to the capital and all available public investment for infrastructure was swallowed up by London 2012.

By the time the Coalition government arrived, resentment was building in the regions. Poorer communities were dealing with some of the impact of the expansion of the EU but not getting the help nor the investment that they needed. There seemed to be no vision for them beyond a low-skill, low-wage, call-centre economy. When people in the more neglected parts of Britain got the chance to tell the powers that be that Westminster and Brussels combined wasn't working for them, they took it.

When it comes to funding, the idea of a British Basic Law is a simple one. It means a requirement in a new UK constitution of equivalent living standards across the regions and nations. If you look at Andy and me, we currently raise money in our city regions through what is called our mayoral precept. When we do that, we put all the money raised into a pot and we look at how we can distribute it fairly to communities, projects and areas that we feel need it most. That small amount raised provides capacity for us to secure significant additional funding streams without which the opportunity to bid would be lost.

The government obviously raises money through tax on a much grander scale. A lot of revenue is raised from London and the South East, because it is an economic powerhouse. A lot of it goes back into those areas rather than being properly redistributed around the country to the areas that need it most, thereby improving their economies to increase the revenues back to the Treasury. This is why £19 billion has been spent on the new Elizabeth Line, further enhancing London's already impressive public transport network. Yet people still can't reliably travel between Liverpool and Manchester by train. It is why HS2 was ceremoniously dumped between Birmingham and Manchester but will still connect Old Oak Common to Euston station at huge cost.

If you don't fairly spread the funding around the country as the Germans do, then the areas that are already behind will continue to fall further behind. This is the opposite of levelling up. In the current structure, you just keep people and communities where they are and you don't give them the chance to flourish.

If you look at what happened during the Covid-19 pandemic, it provides a vivid case study of why a German-style Basic Law is needed in this country. Bolton saw its hospitality closed with no financial help and no comeback. By contrast, when London went into Tier 2 in late October, the cheque book was immediately opened. We had this perverse situation where the government was trying to undermine me, while praising Steve, so that they could win over public opinion in favour of a less-than-fair funding settlement for people in Greater Manchester who had lived under restrictions for much of 2020. It was Westminster divide and rule at its very worst – made possible by the lack of basic rules in the way public administration should work. The pandemic revealed in real time that there is no equal treatment and no commitment to equal living standards.

A written constitution for the UK – with a German-style Basic Law at its heart – would make the handling of the next pandemic much different from the last. It would create a framework for English devolution so that, in time, all parts of the country can work towards equivalent devolved powers. A small group of people making major decisions for millions was never going to work. A more devolved response to the pandemic would have been a safer response.

A constitution could also protect local government from abusive and bullying behaviour by Whitehall. One of the things that has shocked me most since leaving Westminster, looking at things through the other end of the telescope, is just how badly Whitehall treats town halls. Local government fulfils a range of essential functions in every community. Indeed, I would describe councils as their last line of defence. And yet, they are seen in Whitehall as an easy and unimportant target. The hollowing out of councils, which has taken place since 2010, has drastically reduced their power and influence to the point where, one after another, they are now issuing Section 114 notices because they are on the brink of bankruptcy.

There is no doubt in my mind that the funding decisions that are made in this country are political. The most obvious place to look for evidence of this is local government and how cuts to councils' funding have been meted out. In 2019, the Centre for Cities think tank found that cities and urban areas across the North had been the hardest hit by local government cuts since the Coalition government began the austerity programme in 2010. The top three local authorities in terms of cuts to council spending were Barnsley, Liverpool and Doncaster. All Northern, all Labour.

The perverse nature of these highly political decisions means that areas with the highest levels of deprivation, where more resources are needed to help people, have actually been hit the hardest in terms of the removal of central government funding. How could that decision be made on anything other than a party political basis?

Take my home city of Liverpool, for instance. An enormous £500 million of cuts have been handed out since 2010 to a city that has some of the highest levels of deprivation and need in the country. What conclusion could you possibly draw from these decisions other than this is a Labour city where the Conservatives are unlikely to pick up many votes? Now, under this government's so-called 'levelling up' agenda, these same councils that have been unfairly battered by cuts for fourteen years are being asked to put further resources into bidding for small pots of funding for specific projects. The levelling up fund is another programme that has been totally skewed by politics. It has rewarded Rishi Sunak's wealthy Richmond constituency with £20 million, given £14 million for Sajid Javid's Bromsgrove, and yet could not provide any funding for Huyton in Merseyside – an area classed by the fund as a high priority. How can that possibly be described as 'levelling up'?

The methodology behind these funding decisions is a total mystery. None of us knows how it is worked out and I think there is probably a reason for that. Things moved from blurry and opaque to downright Kafkaesque when we found out that some of these cash-strapped councils were paying out money to put bids together for funding that they were never going to be allocated, because the government had changed the rules around who could receive cash awards. It is just a ludicrous way to govern a country.

A Basic Law would not allow this to happen in this way and would ensure that places that needed money the most would get it through a fair and transparent process. It would mean that funding for particular areas would be considered a right and not a gift for the government to give to whoever it favours. It would banish the murky practices used at present to decide these things. A Basic Law would also make it easier for regions and local leaders to challenge these decisions, to question the methodology and potentially get decisions overturned. There would be a reference point in law that could be used to show that the proper processes have not been followed. At the moment, there is very little that you can do to challenge any of these decisions.

The current arrangement gives central government so much power and local government so little. We firmly believe things need to be weighted back towards the local and regional level. If developed correctly, a UK constitution would achieve this rebalancing. It would protect the important role of local government in the running of the country and codify Whitehall's responsibility to ensure that all councils have sufficient funding to carry out their statutory functions. It could also prevent what unfolded in Manchester in October 2023.

A decade before, in 2014, the then Chancellor of the Exchequer came to Manchester and promised us a 'Northern Powerhouse'. He said he would bring the great cities of our region together by building new world-class infrastructure: modern railway lines linking up the North from west to east and a high-speed line to Birmingham and London. People were sceptical at the time as to whether it would ever happen. But, of course, Greater Manchester had to go with it because of the huge opportunity it represented. There were people in our city region who, in good faith, devoted their careers to developing the plans for HS2 at Manchester Airport and Manchester Piccadilly. They were constantly given reassurance from the top that it would all happen. Indeed, exactly five years after George Osborne's speech, Boris Johnson came to Manchester in 2019, stood in front of Stephenson's Rocket and promised the same and more.

Fast forward to the autumn of 2023 and rumours started to circulate of the government's intention to scrap HS2 to Manchester. The Prime Minister would be due in Manchester in the first week of October and, together with Bev Craig, the leader of Manchester City Council, I wrote to him asking for an opportunity to discuss a decision which would have momentous implications for Manchester before it was made. For four surreal days, the Prime Minister and his team were camped out in the Midland Hotel, just yards from our offices, but refused to give us even the courtesy of a phone call. On the Wednesday of that week, he stood up in our city and tore up in our faces the promises the Conservative Party had made in Manchester a decade before.

There is a serious question which flows from this: should it even be allowed to happen? Should the government be able to cancel a huge project, upon which local stakeholders have incurred massive expense, without even talking to them? Given that major national infrastructure goes beyond the life of any Prime Minister and government, and by definition has a huge impact on local communities, should they be able to work in this unilateral way? I honestly don't think they should.

For me, the HS2 decision was a rerun of the Tier 3 stand-off but with much more serious implications for the running of the country. In what other country in the world would the massed ranks of the governing party be gathered in a city and refuse to speak to its local leaders before taking a decision which would have huge implications for it? Beyond the obvious dictatorships, I would say barely any. And make no mistake: the rest of the world have noticed Britain's mishandling of HS2 – and repeated failure to deliver infrastructure – and it's nothing short of embarrassing.

In earlier chapters of *Head North,* we have spoken about the Green Book, which is a methodology used by the UK government to appraise spending and evaluate funding decisions. The Green Book has been around since at least the 60s and applies to all policies and projects that the government might consider funding. It is part of the Treasury orthodoxy that every funding decision is assessed using a benefit–cost ratio (BCR) to decide if it is worth the Exchequer spending money on it.

As part of our vision for reform, we believe that the Green Book should be torn up and that decisions should be made on a different basis – based around the social case for funding areas that need it the most. The Green Book methodology will always favour London and the South East over the North when it comes to funding decisions. This is because the BCR can more easily be met in London, where that investment will obviously see a quick and guaranteed return in an economy that is already thriving. Making the case for investment is therefore a lot easier in London than in areas like ours because we would struggle to make the same case for those same immediate returns to UK plc. It is harder to prove a business case for a project that could take a long time to revitalise an area left behind for decades. There is no social deprivation weighting folded into the decision-making. If that were to happen, then overnight those factors could transform decisions and areas like ours.

You don't just have to listen to us on this. In 2020, the Treasury's own review of the Green Book found that it failed to support the idea of 'levelling up' the regions. It concluded that this was because the process 'relied too heavily on cost–benefit analysis'. It said the BCR placed too much weight on benefits that could 'easily be assigned monetary value, with insufficient weight given to whether the proposed project addressed strategic policy priorities.' Even they knew it needed to change but, subsequently, nothing has happened.

A good example regarding the limitations of the Green Book in our region is our plan for a project called Mersey Tidal on the River Mersey. The Liverpool City Region has one of the UK's largest tidal ranges and we believe we have a unique opportunity to harness the power of the Mersey to generate a plentiful and reliable supply of clean, green and predictable energy for generations to come. This project could create enough renewable energy to power up to one million homes and thousands of green jobs. We are yet to convince the Treasury to fund it because the Green Book test makes it too difficult. I have no doubt that if this project was in London, the government would have approved and funded it. When they needed a Thames barrier, they just went ahead and did it.

Another example is Liverpool Central rail station, which lies on our regional Merseyrail network. This is the most frequented underground station in terms of footfall outside of London, serving 40,000 people every day. The station is now at the point of its lifespan where we are starting to worry about safety. We are already beginning to regulate the numbers coming through one of the city's most important transport hubs. If this situation was replicated in London, the station would automatically qualify for government investment. The Green Book's BCR test would be more easily met. Because Liverpool's economy is worth less than London's, we are finding it very difficult to make that economic case stack up. In reality, redeveloping that station would cost a fraction of the price of what was spent on any of the stations on the Elizabeth Line.

It is much harder for us to make the purely economic argument for investment. We believe that any funding decisions should also be based on a social case. The Treasury should be asking different questions: what would this decision mean for people in the North?; how would it help the city and region to grow?; what are the consequences of not doing this? If these questions were considered alongside the pure economic criteria, we might actually start to see some real levelling up.

There is a great irony here. It was the European Union which funded infrastructure on a social basis. By leaving, the neglected communities who voted for Brexit felt they were going to get more infrastructure investment from our withdrawal. The reality is that it is more difficult now. It is entirely within the government's gift to create a formula for infrastructure funding that is based on social need. They have failed to do this. Promises of 'levelling up' have come to nought and the Green Book's economic test remains firmly in place.

There are few cities in the country that have felt the loss of EU funding more than Liverpool. Waves of EU money were invested into the city after the dark and difficult days of the 80s. Among other things, this led to the creation of the city's waterfront arena and the cruise liner terminal. To be clear, this funding would not have been given if we were reliant on the Green Book test of the Treasury. The investments had to be made with a long-term ambition to build Liverpool into something better. EU funding acted as the catalyst for other private investments such as the Liverpool One shopping district. Once other developers saw things starting to change in Liverpool, they wanted to get involved as well. Many areas like ours didn't vote for Brexit but we have been left to suffer the consequences.

If we want something built up North, we are expected to go to the pound shop, while London continually gets to shop at Waitrose. This was reflected in the government's decision to downgrade plans for Northern Powerhouse Rail (NPR) – a vision for a high-speed rail link connecting the cities of the North of England from west to east. Instead of agreeing to build the full network from Liverpool to Leeds via Manchester and then Bradford to Hull, the government announced a cut-price proposal in 2021. They opted for upgrades to existing lines while also shamefully throwing out the eastern leg of HS2. This Westminster short-sightedness became full-blown myopia in 2023 when Rishi Sunak cancelled the Birmingham to Manchester leg of HS2, meaning no part of this enormous infrastructure project will now reach the North.

Grant Shapps was the transport secretary at the time of that 2021 NPR announcement (as part of the Integrated Rail Plan). We had been in discussions with him and his team about the plans for the Liverpool to Manchester leg. There were five different options originally on the table. For all the reasons highlighted in this book, we didn't go into those talks with grand expectations of getting everything we wanted. There was a 'Rolls-Royce' option: a high-speed line between Liverpool and Manchester, with an underground station at Warrington. In all honesty, after years of broken promises and unfair treatment, we never expected to walk away with that.

We were more realistic. With five options on the table, we felt if we conceded on the gold-plated one, then options two or three might be in play. Shapps had said he wanted to have open and honest discussions with us. We made it clear that the fifth option, the cheapest option, was a red line. We wouldn't accept it. Well, I'm sure you can guess what happened next. The remaining options were whittled away with the government claiming each one in turn was unaffordable. We were left with the two least attractive options. Despite our protestations that the cheapest option was unacceptable to us, because it would shut Lime Street station for two years, they just went ahead and announced it as the one that would be moving forward.

I was absolutely furious. We knew we weren't ever going to get the 'Rolls-Royce' option, but we certainly weren't going to accept a three-wheeled Reliant Robin in its place. I went in to speak to my chief executive and said I was going to have to respond strongly because we had been screwed over again. It was telling that he was worried that my reaction might affect us in terms of future government decisions for funding allocations. He recommended caution but I was having none of it. I think that exchange tells you a lot about the power dynamics at play. We had been badly let down by the government in a decision that could hold our region back for years and yet officials were worried about me reacting publicly because then we might lose out on future schemes and funding. It was like being told not to upset your mum or dad as they might withhold your pocket money. That's why fair funding should be a right and not left to the whim of a transient minister or politically controlled civil servant. The power imbalance is deeply dangerous for our democracy. They hold all the cards and they know it. It's a way of keeping people and places down and making them dance to the government's tune – this is what we want to change.

I'm pleased to tell you that I ignored my chief executive's concerns. I released a statement in which I legitimately criticised the decision. I said that this was a once-in-a-generation chance to transform rail in the North but that they had chosen a 'cheap and nasty' option instead. Shapps snapped. He didn't like that at all. He hated it actually. I have found him to be pretty thin-skinned. He was so affronted by my criticisms of their plan that he bizarrely launched a scathing attack on me in the pages of the *Yorkshire Post*, labelling me 'irrational'. It turned into a massive falling out. He claimed that I had called the whole project spend for the entirety of the link from Liverpool to Hull 'cheap and nasty' when he knew full well that I had specifically called into question the downgraded leg between Liverpool and Manchester. The whole episode just summed up how unhealthy the relationship currently is between the government and regional leaders. If we think of it in terms of popular daytime TV programmes, we had been promised *Grand Designs* and were then expected to welcome a *60 Minute Makeover*. A written constitution would protect the right of an elected mayor to call out a demonstrably unfair decision by a Cabinet minister, without fear of petty reprisals.

A written constitution would also protect Whitehall from itself. The culture of the ministerial merry-go-round, with regular reshuffles, creates the conditions for the constant chopping and changing of national policies and projects. This is what imports delay and complexity and ultimately leads to spiralling costs. Whitehall is simply not set up to deliver major infrastructure. By contrast, England's regional combined authorities take a long-term, place-based approach and, in my view, if given more responsibility to deliver major projects, would do a better job. To do this, the constitution would need to contain a commitment to equal and fair funding for all places consistent with the Basic Law. The time has come to tear up the Green Book and the Barnett Formula and replace them with a modern funding formula which works for the English regions and the home nations. This is critical if we are to lay the foundations to make Britain a more successful nation in the twenty-first century.

The Barnett Formula was first used in 1978 and is named after its founder Joel Barnett, a former Labour chief secretary to the Treasury. It is still used by the UK government to allocate funding to calculate the yearly change in the block grant given to the devolved administrations of Scotland, Wales and Northern Ireland. The idea is that, for devolved services, the formula calculates the same pounds-per-person change in funding as the UK government is spending in England. Crucially, the devolved administrations can choose how they spend that money.

However, the formula is far from perfect and for a long time there have been calls for reform. In 2014, the Institute of Fiscal Studies found that the formula was protecting Scotland and Northern Ireland from hundreds of millions of pounds of cuts that were being wrought on England and Wales. Indeed, the English regions have been more exposed than anywhere in the UK to the austerity of the last fourteen years because of the combined effect of the Barnett Formula and the Green Book.

As we've explained, the Green Book drags funding towards London and the South East. This is then badged as 'English' funding. The Barnett Formula then adds on consequential funding to the home nations as a result of this. While it aims to protect the devolved nations in terms of funding, there is no corresponding funding protection for the English regions. This is why the English regions continually miss out. We are all affected by a pincer movement between the Green Book and the Barnett Formula.

Joel Barnett made an appointment to come and see me when I was chief secretary to the Treasury. He made a passionate case to me to get rid of the Barnett Formula. As you know, politicians usually ask for their name to be added to things, not taken away. So I was more than a little surprised by his request. Joel said he couldn't defend it because of the way it unfairly skewed money across the UK and didn't want to be associated with it any more. It was only ever meant to be a short-term fix to deal with political problems in the 70s and, he told me, was now highly unfair to the North of England.

What we are looking for is an equity formula. When I first came into the job of Liverpool City Region Mayor, the entirety of our first three-year transport settlement from the government was £172 million. This was meant to cover every transport scheme across the whole area. Now that might sound like a lot of money. But it starts to look less impressive when you understand that the government spent more than £800 million on just one station on the Elizabeth Line.

Despite the lack of government ambition for our area, we became the first authority in the country to purchase our own trains. We invested £500 million in the UK's most sophisticated rolling stock fleet for Merseyrail. They were designed in partnership with local rail passengers to be fully accessible, so there is no step and no 'mind the gap' to contend with. It was an 'invest to save' initiative and is the very essence of devolution in action. Just imagine what we could achieve with equitable funding in the North, where we are currently allocated just a fraction of the transport investment that London receives.

When the Prime Minister announced the scrapping of the HS2 leg to Manchester, he said that the savings from the project would be allocated to transport initiatives across the North and the Midlands. This redistributed money had the potential to fund schemes and to improve local infrastructure. We were quite hopeful about receiving this money during early conversations with the transport secretary. However, instead, some of the savings from HS2 have been allocated to projects far from the North and the Midlands, including a bizarre Department for

Transport announcement that it would fund the repair of pot holes in the capital. It appears that, along with many other failings, geography isn't one of Rishi Sunak's strengths.

What we need is a new formula covering the whole of the UK and including the English regions as separate entities. If London were to get investment, there would be consequential investment for everywhere else. Greater Manchester and the West Midlands are soon to move to an arrangement with Whitehall which is more like the single block grant given to Scotland and Wales. In time, this should be available to combined authorities across all of England. Under the new formula, funding would be allocated to the regions and nations based on social factors and levels of need. This is how the EU used to allocate infrastructure investment to Britain's more deprived areas and there is a cruel irony that Brexit threatens to make them even worse off without the influence of Brussels.

Of course, it is now entirely in Britain's gift to create its own funding formula to deliver a British Basic Law. If we don't do something like this, and we leave existing processes in place, the North–South divide will only widen in the decades to ahead. If we do, the dream of a Britain with equal living standards becomes a distinct possibility.

10

Rewiring Westminster

If the UK government is operating permanent policies like the Green Book, which are inherently biased against the North of England, it follows that both it and the other English regions will need to rely on the backstop of a strong Parliament to correct the unfairness. Sadly, in its current form, the elected house does not have the required power to stand up to the executive. Even worse, the unelected house does not represent all people and places equally. So, there is no path to a more equal Britain which does not take in a major reform of the UK Parliament. Steve and I went there hoping it would be where we could achieve our goal of doing some things to advance the cause of the North. It took me sixteen years, and Steve seven, to realise that, far from being the means to our solution, it was part of our problem.

Despite my frustrations with it, I have a lot of good memories of my time in Parliament and affection for the place. The vast majority of the people who work there – both MPs and staff on the Parliamentary estate – are thoroughly decent and in it for the right reasons. I can honestly say that I gave my all to those sixteen years and, while of course I made mistakes, I am proud of what I achieved. Westminster was mainly a friendly place to work, although always dysfunctional. The mood darkened in the period after the EU referendum and the pandemic seemed to drain the life out of it. When I go back there now, I struggle to recognise the place I entered in 2001.

I have given a lot of thought as to why I progressively fell out of love with Westminster. My main reflection looking back is that the job is not what you think it is when you go in and, for that reason, you become increasingly frustrated the longer you spend there. Put simply, you don't have the power people think you have. There is a big difference between the privilege of being able to write strong letters on House of Commons paper and having actual leverage to make change happen. MPs have no executive decision-making powers and nobody, not even your local council, is under any obligation to listen to you. It comes as something of a shock to the system when you realise this shortly after the privilege of sitting on the green benches for the first time.

The House of Commons should be the place where the big decisions are taken about every aspect life in Britain. In reality, because of the way the Parliamentary whip system works, it spends the majority of its time rubber-stamping decisions taken elsewhere. For that reason, the whip system is a big part of the problem. Every general election, 650 people are elected with the votes of millions and big ideas about the things they want to change. Then, the minute they walk through the door to take their seats, the power given to them by the public is removed and effectively handed to a small number of their elected colleagues and many more unelected advisers who set the party lines and positions for which they are required to vote. As a result, the whip system disempowers MPs, diminishes their status and, over time, disconnects them from their constituents. It makes you say things you're not sure about and vote for things you don't believe in. At its worst, the whip system unfairly makes good people seem like frauds.

We believe that a major reform of the whip system – or even its total removal – will empower Members of Parliament. The change to this way of organising Parliament would mean individual MPs would no longer be considered simply as voting fodder by their political parties and leaders. That's how it currently works. You get told: this is what we're going to do and you need to vote with us; this is a three-line whip and you have to vote with your colleagues.

As a backbench MP, I felt powerless. Labour was in opposition for all of my time in the Commons, so that made it even harder to feel like you were able to change things or make a difference. It is only when you step away from Westminster that you realise how dysfunctional it really is and how many people have become institutionalised down there. As an MP, you might be made aware of something that is an injustice that needs to be put right. Maybe you will put down an early day motion, which calls for a debate on the matter. Then the debate happens, a few people turn up for it and nothing changes. You have done your bit in terms of the levers of our constitutional democracy, but you haven't really changed anything. This is what we mean about the limitations of the role of an MP.

Many of the debates seem pointless because everyone knows which way they are going to vote before they even start: they have been told how to vote. Don't get me wrong, I've sat through some absolutely fantastic speeches in that chamber. But they often don't make a blind bit of difference as everyone just votes on party lines.

You would hope that in a healthy democracy, you could go into debates on serious and moral issues with an open mind: a mind that could be changed or affected by the arguments put forward by your colleagues. In reality, on most occasions, the decisions have already been made for you.

Of all the places on earth, the green benches of the House of Commons should be a place where people really engage in debate and discussion. But the system is such that they don't. They know how they will vote and so they spend most of their time in that chamber shouting, trying to put people off or not even listening. I know I did. It just doesn't work. The whips know the exact number of people in their party who will be voting a certain way before the debate has even started because they have called around everyone to establish their position and warn those who might possibly rebel.

For me, this didn't have a huge impact. I've explained earlier how I made it clear from the moment I set foot in Westminster that I had no ambitions to progress through the Labour Party structures. This made me less vulnerable to the warnings from the whips. But I saw the impact that behaviour had on many others.

Despite my lack of desire to progress, I am first and foremost a Labour loyalist. Regardless of the ups and downs, I love my party and did not want to be seen as constantly critical. At the same time, I always felt very uncomfortable being told how I should vote on issues before I had listened to a single word of a debate.

If you ask anyone in Westminster whether we need to improve trust in politics, most would almost certainly agree. If you then ask how we do that, very few would call for reform of the whip system. That's because it is so hard-wired into the mentality of the place and the running of the system down there. The received wisdom is that removing the whip system would cause chaos and the country would be ungovernable without it. My view is the complete opposite. It would result in the immediate empowerment of MPs and the House of Commons and bring better decisions that would benefit us all. Nineteen times out of twenty, or even ninety-nine out of a hundred, most MPs would probably vote in the way their party asked. But it is on those isolated occasions, when the government has gone too far, that the public needs more independent MPs to be the ultimate guardians of the national interest.

When life changed overnight in March 2020, so many things about Britain were revealed more clearly than ever before – and one was the frightening way we run things. As the Covid Inquiry is confirming, Parliament was effectively bypassed during the pandemic. That small group of fifty or so people at the heart of the Whitehall machine foisted ill-thought-through decisions on millions. This is not a safe way to run a country.

If someone has managed to be elected to a national Parliament, you would like to think they have the judgement and skills to analyse subjects and form sound opinions. In my experience, the vast majority of MPs from all sides are exactly those kinds of people. Popular opinion holds that 90 per cent of MPs are scoundrels and 10 per cent are decent. In my experience, it's the other way round. Yes, there are certainly plenty of villains in the place. But don't fall for the claim that they all are. Instead, they are good people working in an antiquated system which does not give them the authority they deserve and, at times, unfairly undermines their integrity.

I think back to my time as an MP and some of the big votes which threw the Parliamentary Labour Party into complete turmoil, such as those on Iraq, student fees, foundation hospitals and the Welfare Reform Bill. On these occasions, and many others, the government I served in would have helped itself if it had trusted the majority feeling in the PLP rather than continue to force on it the preferred position of a small number of people at the heart of government. Is it in any way healthy that decisions of major consequence are made with the threat of being ostracised or a black mark placed against your name?

My worst experience in Parliament was undoubtedly the vote in 2003 on Iraq. It was traumatising on every level. I voted for the action; that is a matter of public record. What people might not understand is just how trapped we felt as MPs in making a simplistic, binary choice about something as huge as taking military action in another country. There was no ability to insert any conditionality on the military action nor vote about the exit strategy or plans for the future of the country in the aftermath. The rushed nature of the process only added to our anxiety because it was clear we were dancing to a different timetable set on the other side of the Atlantic.

I struggled with my decision. What eventually swung it for me was when the Labour MP Ann Clwyd, who had done a lot of work in support of the Kurds in Iraq, invited in the Kurdish leader Barham Salih to speak to MPs. He pleaded with us to vote to remove Saddam. I asked him whether he thought there were weapons of mass destruction in Iraq. His answer had an impact on me. He said he genuinely didn't know but it was that uncertainty which Saddam exploited to keep his grip on power. Because people thought he might have them, they were too frightened to rise up against him. That was why he would never let the weapons inspectors complete their work. When I look back, that was the only meeting which gave me any clarity about what we were being asked to decide. I can still justify now the decision to remove Saddam. What I can't justify was the complete absence of a credible plan to secure the country in the aftermath. Had I known that then, I would have voted against military action. But, of course, I wasn't being asked about this, only whether we should take action or not. I learnt a painful lesson from this experience and, in the years following, tended to vote against taking military action whenever those decisions came before the House.

What I know for sure is that the whip system is entirely inappropriate when considering questions of this magnitude. Whips will pile pressure on people who are already struggling to hold it together and raise a range of other considerations to make people comply. There is something very unseemly about that. If Labour MPs had been given a free vote on Iraq, it would have shown to the outside world that the decision was being taken on its merits and nothing else. That matters on an issue like this. I also think there is a good chance that there would have been a majority against military action, given how borderline people like me were.

Put simply, the whip system transfers power from the elected to the unelected. As I have said before, no more than fifty people are running the country at any given time and less than half of those people are elected. The rest are advisers and senior civil servants. The whip system has the effect of giving great power to people who are not sufficiently accountable to the public. MPs spend much of their time nodding through things which these people decide and which are not always popular with their constituents. It also creates fake debates in what is supposed to be the cockpit of the nation. When an important issue is being discussed in the Commons, and people all over the country are tuning in to hear it, it is often the case that they simply cannot understand how the vote comes in as it does. This is because the debate will often reflect the passion of MPs who turn up to speak. However, what people will not realise is that there are many more who are not listening to a word of the debate and will emerge from their office or the Strangers' Bar when the division bell sounds to vote as they are told. This does more damage to trust in politics and Parliament than people in there realise.

The whip system also promotes a party-first rather than place-first approach. At some point, all MPs will face the dilemma of being asked to endorse a policy decision that is detrimental to the area they represent. But the whip system doesn't make allowances for that. If MPs had more independence and were able to organise in the interests of place rather than party, I think Parliament would have done a better job than it has of standing up for the North. Instead, it has watched impotently as the North–South divide has widened over the decades.

Hillsborough is a stand-out example of this problem. When I gave my speech to the Commons after the second inquest, I'll admit to doing so with a feeling of barely contained rage towards the 'mother of Parliaments'. I had left Liverpool with Steve early that morning, after spending the day before with the families, with a growing feeling of anger at the way these dignified people had been treated by their own country. By the time I stood up at the despatch box, I was ready to unburden myself of all the frustrations that had built up over the years with a political system that often doesn't serve the public interest. How could an entire English city have been left in the wilderness for twenty years crying injustice and no one in its national Parliament was listening? When I posed this question, I remember scanning round the entire Commons chamber, looking directly into the eyes of as many MPs as I could and wanting them to feel as uncomfortable as possible. It is a question I have asked many times since. I am still waiting for anyone to offer an answer.

If MPs could operate differently, the Hillsborough cover-up would not have lasted as long as it did. In 1998, the Stuart-Smith inquiry could have been exposed for the stitch-up it was. Instead, MPs were expected to get in line and accept it. And the worrying thing is Hillsborough is no exception. There is a shamefully long list of other injustices, and accompanying Whitehall cover-ups, that a supine Westminster culture has left in place for decades.

Possibly the worst example is the contaminated blood scandal. The public inquiry which reports soon will finally bring an end to a cover-up that has lasted the best part of half a century. When I gave evidence to it in 2022, I described how, as secretary of state for health, I was given the line by civil servants that no one was knowingly given unsafe blood products. Whitehall had been dug in behind that claim for decades, leaving the thousands infected in the wilderness. In 2009, when I included this line in an official letter to a campaigner, I was unaware that it was a lie.

It was only after the Hillsborough second inquest had concluded that I turned my attention to contaminated blood. My great friend Paul Goggins, who we sadly lost in 2014, had repeatedly told me it was at least as great an injustice as Hillsborough and that I should look into it in the same way. I had promised him I would but had taken time to get round to it. By the middle of 2016, the blood campaigners were feeling dejected after their hopes of a breakthrough were dashed by David Cameron's sudden departure from government. To be fair to David, he did follow through on his promise of more financial support for victims in his final days as Prime Minister. But it was not the comprehensive package people thought they were getting. It was at that point that I was approached by Diana Johnson MP, whose campaigning on this issue has been truly outstanding, to speak to her All-Party Group on whether there were any parallels between Hillsborough and contaminated blood that could give their campaign new life.

This was the prompt I needed to fulfil my promise to Paul. When I began to think deeply about what I would say to the group, I had a penny-drop moment. The big parallel between the two disasters was the evidence of a criminal cover-up. In the same way that my knowledge of amended police statements was the key to the Hillsborough lock, I suggested to MPs on the group that our collective knowledge of deleted, missing or amended medical records should be our starting point in unravelling the injustice. By this point in my Parliamentary career, I wasn't listening much to the whips. I was preparing to leave for Manchester and, for my valedictory speech, asked the then Speaker John Bercow if I could have an adjournment debate on contaminated blood.

When the day came, I didn't hold back. It had taken me a while to get the measure of the House of Commons. By the end, I like to think I had got it. That day, I felt none of the imposter syndrome that had hung over me as a new MP sixteen years earlier. I told the Commons that contaminated blood was a criminal cover-up on an industrial scale and that I would go to the police with the evidence I had of that if the government did not order an inquiry by the summer recess. I had learnt by this stage that MPs have to establish leverage in creative ways. It is revealing that cracks only began to appear in the blood cover-up when I threatened to go outside of Parliament to get to a truth that it had ignored. Right back to the 70s, thousands of MPs had written countless letters to ministers in the Department of Health in support of constituents who were victims. Debates were held year after year. But they achieved nothing other than a few scraps of financial support thrown off the table. This goes to the heart of the question of where power lies. Is it with MPs? Clearly not. If it was, a wrong like this would never have stood for five decades.

As with many of the proposals we make in this book, Andy and I are not saying that reforming the whip culture in Parliament would be a panacea for our politics; that on its own it would provide us with a fit and functioning democracy. There is no perfect solution. But, it would be a positive step forward. What we are highlighting are the gaping flaws in the current system.

We are trying to show how whipping MPs disincentivises and disempowers them. We want our politicians to be able to stand up for the people that they represent and speak and vote accordingly. This change we are discussing is about empowering Members of Parliament within our nation's democracy.

In my younger days, the whip system certainly had its desired impact on me. When you go into any workplace, you want to fit in and get on. By instinct, I am a team player and certainly not one of life's natural mavericks. I didn't come into it to become an outsider, always criticising the system. Instead, I wanted to show that I could be a proper Parliamentarian. That meant going with the grain of the place and accepting its strange ways.

However, as my time in Parliament progressed, I did start to think: what am I actually doing here? Am I being true to myself? That is the effect of being told how to vote week after week, year after year. As I went up and down the West Coast Main Line every week, I was witnessing the North–South divide getting wider and I didn't feel I was achieving what I came into politics to do. This probably explains why, when the role of culture secretary came along in Liverpool's Capital of Culture year, I threw myself into it and used it to reconnect with home. When Steve invited me to the twentieth anniversary, it prompted a personal crisis. Was I in Parliament to make a difference on things I cared about or not? My personal and professional lives were in a head-on collision. I could no longer find a way to accommodate them both as they were. Of course, I could have done the Westminster thing of going and making a platitudinous speech without any commitments. But that was a non-starter for me. The choice I had was to continue to be a Westminster insider or true to my roots. It is revealing that you can't be both of those things.

I took my first steps out of Westminster on that day and was never the same MP after it. I had understood what had to be done to make an actual difference and how to use power differently and effectively. I couldn't fit back in with the existing structures after that and I know without a doubt in my mind that I became a much better MP for it. I started to rattle the cage a lot more and open up issues which Whitehall wanted to leave alone. But this is my point: the whip system is intended to stop MPs doing that, to keep them in their place, and that is not healthy in a democracy.

In general, I think the standing of politicians in the eyes of the public would rise if they were able to speak more independently and vote more freely. It would raise the status of MPs and make them more authentic. I know there will be some people in Westminster who will think Steve and I have lost the plot. Whenever you raise this idea of removing the whip system, they like to dismiss it out of hand as political naivety. What I would say back to them is this: political naivety is seeing the dangerous decline of trust in politicians and doing nothing to change the system which has brought that about.

As well as looking at the whip system, we do need to talk about electoral reform. There are many ways in which this can be achieved. Personally, I am keen on the systems that are more proportional and yet retain a constituency link. This is something Andy and I differ on slightly (that does happen from time to time). Scotland is a good example of this. In the Scottish Parliament elections, every voter can cast two votes, one for their constituency and one for their region. So, they are choosing an individual to represent them and also a party or independent candidate at a regional level. The winning individual has the highest number of constituency votes, but the regional members of the Scottish Parliament are elected using a formula. It means every vote counts and the number of seats a party gets across a region is proportional to the percentage of votes cast.

I have stood for election to Parliament four times on the first-past-the-post system and twice on a preferential vote system at the 2017 and 2021 Mayoral elections, although the government has wrongly forced us to use first-past-the-post for 2024. The proportional system strikes me as far superior. It guarantees that over half of the public have given you their blessing and that is important for political legitimacy. In elections to the House of Commons, it is entirely possible for over half of those voting in a particular constituency to be opposed to a certain candidate and yet that person can still be elected on a minority of votes. It is also the case that over half of the voting public can be opposed to the idea of a particular party forming a government but, under first-past-the-post, they can still do it any way. Analysis from the Electoral Reform Society calculated that, at the 2019 general election, 22.6 million votes did not in any way count towards the result. In other words, nearly three-quarters of the votes cast simply did not matter.

If we are going to rewire Britain, and make power flow properly right through the land, we surely have to move to a situation where every vote counts towards the make-up of the Parliament and the colour of the government reflects what a majority of country wants. If we can give a clear message to the public that every single vote matters, surely that is the best way of reversing the long-term decline in turn-out at elections?

First-past-the-post has been in place in the UK since 1884 and the third Reform Act. It became the system we recognise today in 1950 when the Representation of the People Act ensured that every Member of Parliament would represent a roughly equal area in terms of population.

In my view, 140 years of the first-past-the-post system cannot be said to have done anything to reduce regional inequalities. When it came in, the North of England had strong regional powerbases in its industrial Victorian cities. That was the last time we saw large-scale infrastructure being built in the form of new railways and waterways alongside grand civic buildings. We are still heavily reliant on that infrastructure now. Over the twentieth century, the power drained out of the North and Parliament did nothing to prevent it. If anything, first-past-the-post has only strengthened the grip of the London-based establishment on the running of the country. London-centric policies proposed by successive governments have not been effectively challenged by Parliament and regional inequalities have seriously widened right under its nose.

We need to correct this. Alongside the removal of the whip system, we should move to a system of proportional representation for the election of the Commons. The combination of the two would result in an entirely new way of doing politics and one which I think would better protect the interests of the English regions and resonate more strongly with the public. Every person and every place will only be equal when every vote is equal. Under the present system, some people and places are more equal than others. First-past-the-post creates weathervane constituencies which in turn leads to a hierarchy of places. As we have seen in the Johnson, Truss and Sunak era, more than ever before, public funds have been blatantly funnelled into places which are prioritised for political reasons.

There are a number of PR systems that could be introduced but one option could combine a regional list system for the election of MPs and a constituency link. A system of this kind is used in the Scottish Parliament. I know Steve favours retention of the constituency link, as do many others, so this could be an acceptable compromise. However, I do think it is important to introduce the regional dimension. Together with the removal of the whip system, it would encourage MPs to work on a more place-based, cross-party basis. Sometimes, MPs can be too parochial and effectively operate like super-councillors dealing only with very local issues. If a number of MPs were elected from a regional list, it would encourage Parliament to have a more strategic focus and that can only be a good thing. If MPs across the entire North organised more effectively together, they could, for instance, vote to disapply the Green Book so the region can begin to get the infrastructure it needs.

PR would also give us better government. I used to be of the view that the strong majority governments created by first-past-the-post were better for the country. What I have observed through my life, however, is the tendency for one incoming government to scrap things established by the one before it simply because it was brought in by the other side. I certainly felt a huge frustration when good things brought in by the Labour government, such as the Education Maintenance Allowance and School Sports Partnerships, were immediately scrapped by the Coalition without any real objective analysis of the difference they were making. This habit of governments scrapping things means public services are constantly being chopped and changed. I know that is hugely frustrating for those who work in them. PR would encourage more cross-party agreement about things which in turn would bring a more stable, grown-up approach to the policy direction of the country. That can only be a good thing.

The third area of change that Westminster needs, alongside the Whip and the voting system, is House of Lords reform. In this book we are calling for the removal of the House of Lords in its current form. We would like to see it replaced by an elected Senate of the Nations and Regions of the UK, as recommended by Gordon Brown. It should remain as a revising chamber, scrutinising the work of the House of Commons, but it should be elected and representative of the whole country.

It is important to say that not everything about the House of Lords is negative. Many government Bills are improved in the Lords through detailed scrutiny. Incisive speeches are made by peers with extensive life experience. However, there are very serious issues with how people are appointed which reveal a major democratic deficit. Look no further than both Boris Johnson's and Liz Truss's resignation honours lists. They put the tin hat on it for many people. The former appointed a thirty-one-year-old former assistant, while the latter appointed both a Tory donor and an architect of the Brexit campaign who was alleged to have broken electoral law. In this period of Conservative government, similar to appointments to the Supreme Court in the US, government appointments to the Lords have become highly politicised.

Overall, when it comes to making Parliament more proportional and representative, I think the neatest solution is the one proposed by Billy Bragg known as the 'secondary mandate'. This uses all votes cast under first-past-the-post for the House of Commons to elect a proportional second chamber on a regional list basis. This system retains the constituency link in the Commons, with a local MP elected, but it also means that, even in the safest seats in the country, every vote counts towards something.

As the MP for Liverpool Walton, I did feel very tied to my constituency. I was from the area and lived there. I wasn't the MP for just any place; it was the place that meant a lot to me. I cared about the area and fought for it. However, I understood constituents who asked what was the point of voting given it was such a safe Labour seat. Under this proposed system, I could have said to them that, even if your vote was unlikely to alter the result in terms of electing an MP, it would make a difference to the composition of the second chamber. I think that would mean something to people. For me, there are few more powerful symbols of the need for House of Lords reform than the sight of David Cameron waltzing up Downing Street in November 2023, ready to take up the position of foreign secretary, knowing he doesn't have to face scrutiny in either the Commons nor at the ballot box. It's unbelievable really.

This was Sunak identifying that there was no one in his band of MPs with the ability to take up one of the main offices of state better than a failed and discredited former Prime Minister; the man whose weakness led the country out of the greatest trading bloc of which we have ever been part. What does that say about the paucity of talent on the Conservative benches and how the political elite rewards failure? If you are talking about the dysfunctional and anti-democratic nature of British politics as it currently stands, well you have it there in a nutshell.

There are different ideas and different approaches to reforming the House of Lords but we believe the mood in the country is increasingly in favour of a total overhaul of the antiquated system we currently have when it comes to our second chamber.

It is quite frankly scandalous that, in 2023, our national Parliament does not equally and fairly represent all parts of the UK. The Electoral Reform Society found that, in 2022, 55 per cent of those in the Lords who were willing to state where they reside said they lived in London, the South East and the East of England. In other words, many parts of the country are massively underrepresented in our second chamber. How on earth can we build a sense of national unity and fairness for as long as that remains the case? More importantly, how much longer is the North of England going to put up with this? Not much, I hope.

It wouldn't be so bad if the Lords didn't do anything. But these unelected, unaccountable Lords are making more of your laws than you probably realise. As I said earlier, the Commons tends to rubber-stamp government Bills without changing them because of the strength of the three-line whip that is applied there. In my experience, Bills are much more likely to be changed in the Lords. So this means we have a situation where people who have been put in there as political cronies, or who have a whole heap of outside vested interests, have more ability to influence and change legislation than their elected counterparts down the corridor.

I don't see how anyone could call this a properly functioning democratic system. It's actually a national embarrassment. We have an elected chamber that nods Bills through unchallenged and an unelected chamber heavily drawn from the higher social classes and one part of the country which regularly rewrites legislation. It's wild when you think about it. Parliament has got things the wrong way round and that's why we need reform of both houses.

The other major issue with the current make-up of the House of Lords is how weighted towards London and the South East it is. Because people are not elected to the Lords and therefore not proportionately drawn from all over the country, the institution is dominated by the capital and those living inside the M25. This is yet another example of how regions like ours do not get fair representation or a fair crack of the whip within our biggest democratic institutions.

An elected second chamber of the regions and nations, voted in using a proportional voting system, would provide an accountable, geographically spread second chamber, with voices from all over the UK ensuring the different places get a voice in the upper house.

The House of Lords may have been intended to be a meritocracy, with peers appointed based on their expertise and achievements, but it is a far cry from that these days. Now it is much more about who you know, for whom you worked or to whom you were loyal. How can that be the best basis for appointing people to a chamber that scrutinises the laws of our land? Well it can't be and it isn't.

This is an issue Andy and I have both spoken about with Gordon Brown. Gordon is a powerful advocate of an elected second chamber of nations and regions and, in 2022, he chaired a commission that outlined ambitious proposals for how this major reform could work under a Labour government. At the heart of Gordon's proposal is a second chamber with a regional focus, which, as you can imagine, is music to our ears. His vision is for an elected Senate truly reflecting the different regions and nations of the UK, which would monitor regional inequality and scrutinise all legislation.

Like so much of our national democratic system, the House of Lords is disproportionately weighted towards and influenced by the capital. It takes power away from the rest of the country and the people in those communities. There is clearly a lot more detail to be worked out about exactly how a new Senate of the Nations and Regions would be created. But we feel we are now firmly on the road towards this vital constitutional reform.

We need to replace the Lords with a proportionally elected second chamber based on a list system. Ideally, it would be as simple as asking the public to cast two votes at the General Election. If we wish to move more quickly, we could use the 'Secondary Mandate' idea championed by Billy Bragg, where the Lords is elected proportionally using votes cast under first-past-the-post for the Commons. This could be a good interim step on the reform journey and easily introduced at the likely 2028 or 2029 general election if the political will is there to do it. We should be ashamed of ourselves if we let the unelected Lords continue into the 2030s. There is simply no excuse for it.

This chapter has presented three reforms – removal of the whip system, PR for the House of Commons and a Senate of the Nations and Regions to replace the Lords – that would make the UK Parliament more powerful, more functional and more representative of us all. The public can see how dysfunctional our political system is and there is a growing appetite for a radical rewiring of it. The longer we delay it, the more we risk losing what remains of public trust in politics.

11

A Federal UK through Full Devolution

Step by step, it is possible to see a roadmap taking shape for how Britain could be converted into a more functional, modern democracy where Parliament is more representative, the civil service is more accountable and the public have more power to make national politics work for them. And yet, that can only be seen as half of the job of the complete rewiring that the UK needs. To stretch the analogy of my old stately home, every room will only offer higher living standards when the electricity works properly everywhere. This means laying new cabling to every corner of the house.

On the foundations of a written constitution, a Basic Law and a reformed UK Parliament, we must complete the process of devolving power out of Westminster to all parts of England, Wales, Scotland and Northern Ireland to allow all the nations and regions to do much more for themselves. Only then will we usher in a new era where people and places can be masters of their own destiny, and free to collaborate, without everything having to pass through the distorting lens of Westminster. Encouragingly, this is one area where Britain has already made huge progress.

The year 2024 marks a decade since Greater Manchester signed its ground-breaking devolution deal with the government, establishing the position I now hold. In what has been a fractious and divisive decade, the cause of English devolution has stood out as a rare point of cross-party agreement and positive progress. It is probably fair to say that English devolution is the most notable and important legacy of this period of Conservative-led government.

According to the Institute for Government, 41 per cent of England's population is currently living in an area with mayoral devolution. This equates to 49 per cent of its economic output and 14 per cent of the land area. After the coming mayoral elections in May 2024, this is set to expand significantly with two new Mayors elected and another covering the expanded North East Combined Authority area. It is expected that, in May 2025, Norfolk and Suffolk will follow suit. At that point, 51 per cent of the population will live in an area with devolution, equating to 57 per cent of its economic output and 33 per cent of its geography. It would be fair to say that, by then, English devolution will have been irreversibly established.

But, of course, it's still work in progress. If the process stalls, resentment towards a two-tier arrangement could grow and that could risk undermining public support for a more devolved England. Equally, if there is a continued failure by national government to shore up the financial position of local government, then the foundations upon which combined authorities are built will fracture to the point of putting the whole project in jeopardy. So we are at a critical point in this journey. To maintain momentum, the ambition for English devolution over the coming decade needs to be clearly articulated.

Put simply, and for the reasons I have given above, we need to complete the job by 2034. That means all parts of England having a devolution deal in place, supported by a clear policy framework which allows them to deepen the extent of their devolution deals over time at a pace that is right for them. As we go further on this journey, I appreciate that we will find more areas that are not overly keen on the idea of an elected mayor. True devolution should mean they shouldn't be forced to agree to this to prise powers out of Westminster. We will need to see the development of more flexible arrangements to allow everywhere to be included.

At the coming general election, I believe it will be important to get the main political parties to agree this path for a more devolved nation so that we maintain what is an important consensus in

British politics. If we can arrive at a point in 2034 where all parts of the UK have devolved arrangements, underpinned by a written constitution and a Basic Law requiring Westminster to work towards equivalent living standards in all of those places, then it is possible to see how the course of the rest of the twenty-first century might be a more positive one for the UK than what it will be if we stick with the status quo.

Our passionate belief is that the roadmap set out above is a journey towards a more functional, contented nation. It would allow for more transparency over the allocation of funding between the English regions and home nations. It would allow the Barnett Formula to be replaced with a new arrangement that is demonstrably fair to all. It would also bring a different way of doing politics to all people and places. Steve and I often talk about the great strength of the devolved systems we lead being that they allow for a place-first approach rather than party-first. Place is a unifying force. Whatever people's political allegiances, they will usually share a pride in, and passion for, the place where they live. If we start with that common ground – rather than the divisive, party-first approach of Westminster – experience shows that we will build more public engagement with what we are trying to do.

In this regard, I do think it is important to encourage Scotland, Wales and Northern Ireland to pass down more of the devolved powers they hold to their towns and cities. In Scotland in particular, power has been drawn out of its regions and up into the national level. This can be seen, for instance, in the centralisation of the police and fire services. In the UK context, when all dialogue between Scotland and England is conducted through Holyrood and Westminster, it becomes inevitably tense and political. If we can imagine a world where Greater Manchester and the Liverpool City Region can collaborate with a Greater Glasgow with similar powers, or the new North East Combined Authority doing the same with Edinburgh and Dundee, it would make the UK a more practical, positive place. As Steve and I learnt when we were introduced to the Bloomberg network, the rest of the world sees cities as the drivers of the twenty-first century economy, leading digitalisation and decarbonisation from the bottom up. If a significant number of UK cities are shut out of that network, and left in low power mode, that will only be to their detriment and that of UK plc in the long run.

When we talk about devolution, I think public transport is one of the most important facets of what we are discussing. Public transport is the most visible symbol of whether a society is fair and functioning. We've said this a few times in this book but let's look again at Germany. Public transport is excellent in Germany and that is across the board. Even medium-sized cities have integrated networks of buses, trams and trains that easily move people around. Canada is also a federal structure and has excellent public transport with rapid transit systems and good integrated bus and rail links. I am not arguing that only federalism leads to an integrated transport system, or that non-federal systems aren't capable of excellent local networks. What I do know is that our current provision isn't good enough and that devolution could be used to catalyse improvements to connectivity. These countries' federal structures mean that high quality public transport networks are run at a regional level, meaning the different services are integrated and work in tandem with one another. The price of travel is also far cheaper compared with public transport in our regions.

Here in the North West of England, or any part of the country outside of London, frustrated passengers are paying through the nose for a broken, fragmented and dysfunctional public transport system and they are understandably furious about this. There might be the odd functional part here or there but none of it makes sense as a coherent network.

As Metro Mayors, we have oversight of public transport. But, once again, the way our transport funding is calculated counts against us. London has seen continual investment in its public transport infrastructure and I say good luck to them. But, if the country doesn't soon take real action to close its huge public transport divide, people's patience will run out.

One of the great selling points for devolved systems like Greater Manchester is that we can break down the silos between Whitehall departments, join the dots and make public services work better for people. The best evidence I can provide of that is a study of the first five years of health devolution in Greater Manchester, published in the *Lancet* in 2022, which found that we had improved life expectancy faster than expected and particularly so in some of our most deprived areas.

People sometimes ask me what the difference is between my old job of health secretary and my current one. My answer is that, from the Department of Health, I was effectively looking out of a telescope at what was going on across the country. I could see numbers but not names. As Mayor of Greater Manchester, I ask my teams to do the opposite: to take a names-not-numbers approach. There is honestly a world of difference between those two things.

The good news is that our new Trailblazer devolution deal, signed in March 2023, will allow us to take this approach to the next level. At the next spending review, it will move Greater Manchester and the West Midlands to a 'single-settlement' with Whitehall – in effect, a similar arrangement as Wales and Scotland. At present, the GMCA's £1.5 billion or so budget comes from 150 separate Whitehall funding streams, each with their own bureaucracy and targets. The single-settlement will consolidate that funding into an arrangement that will give us much more flexibility over how the money is spent. We will be able to take the names-not-numbers approach to the next level and that will most probably mean that we will spend public money in a much more person-centred, preventative way, rather than the crisis interventions of traditional Whitehall public service provision. In an era when public spending will most probably remain constrained, combined authorities represent the country's best chance of securing maximum value for public money. If the whole of England could be moved to this single-settlement approach, perhaps by the middle of this century, it would create the conditions for the replacement formula to the Barnett Formula to be fully introduced.

I believe Michael Gove, Greg Clarke and George Osborne deserve credit for developing English devolution to the point where this kind of thinking is possible. Of course, the majority of the promises in what was first called the Northern Powerhouse have not been delivered. But it would be wrong not to recognise the significant step change that has been achieved. Alongside improved results for people, we can also see now that devolution is beginning to achieve what has long been considered the Holy Grail – higher productivity and growth in the regions outside London. One look at the modern Manchester skyline tells you that something is happening in our city. We have been growing faster than the UK economy in recent years and are predicted to do so for the next two years at least. In the last five years, we have been Europe's fastest-growing digital and tech hub. It's all a far cry from the Manchester to which I returned from Cambridge in 1991. To be fair to Whitehall, we are noticing that more and more people are seeing these results and starting to buy into what we are doing. That was certainly our experience of negotiating the Trailblazer deal. It felt like we had more allies in the Whitehall system than ever before and the conduct of the conversations was more constructive than they have been in the past.

But we still need to see further change. There are pockets of resistance that need to be challenged. For instance, the Department for Work and Pensions still seems to be clinging to a top-down, tick-box approach to running the benefits system. We are certain that localising much more of their funding in a names-not-numbers approach will get better results in supporting people into work.

There is also the question of greater fiscal autonomy for the devolved parts of England. In this space, I accept the need to walk before we can run. But we need to start talking about a world where England's big city regions are able to raise more money directly. We all need to improve public transport to increase productivity. If the government refuses to give us the subsidy to do that, which London received for decades, then I don't think it's reasonable for them also to deny us the chance to raise more ourselves. An obvious early candidate would be to allow the big city regions to levy a modest tourist tax. This is common in large parts of Europe and I don't see why it can't be made to work here. Equally, why shouldn't we be able to use a land value capture approach to support the funding of transport infrastructure, where some of the increase in land values resulting from the new infrastructure is clawed back over time? If Steve and I were able to use that approach on the building of the new railway between Liverpool and Manchester, we could deliver the most ambitious version of the scheme – with a new station in Liverpool and an underground at Manchester Piccadilly – rather than the 'cheap and nasty' version on offer from Whitehall.

You can totally understand people's frustrations when a bus no longer travels to their town or village, or only comes once an hour, or the final service ends at 6 p.m. In the deregulated system, the private bus companies prioritise keeping profitable routes. But this is not how a public service should be determined.

In London, buses are regulated and the fares are subsidised. This creates an efficient service that is accountable to local political leaders and is affordable for the public. Outside of the capital, things feel vastly different. The disastrous impact of the deregulation of bus services outside of London in the 80s was summed up well by former United Nations special rapporteur on human rights, Philip Alston. In a 2021, report he said the move had 'provided a masterclass in how not to run an essential public service, leaving residents at the mercy of private actors who have total discretion over how to run a bus route, or whether to run one at all'. He added: 'In case after case, a service that was once dependable, convenient, and widely used has been scaled back dramatically or made unaffordable.'

I couldn't have put it any better myself. For decades, people in communities outside of London have been asked to put up with a second-class service and to pay more for it. This cannot be allowed to continue. Like Andy, we introduced fare caps meaning that any single bus journey in the Liverpool City Region costs no more than £2 and this made a big impact. Once again, though, our ability to keep subsidising costs is constrained by our funding settlements. However, the cost of a service is just one aspect – we need to make sure those services actually work for the half a million people in our region who use the bus every day. This is where franchising comes in.

Bus franchising means taking our bus services back into regional public control. It means giving locally elected leaders control over setting routes and fares and it means operating bus services in the interests of local bus users and not in the interests of the shareholders of private companies.

We are moving forward with this in the Liverpool City Region. Reregulation which will mean that we can start to level up the injustice that regions outside of London have suffered when it comes to our buses. This may seem like a big and radical move, but in reality we are once again just trying to level the playing field.

To do that, we are having to take big financial risks. London has never had to buy back its bus depots but we are having to do that out of our funding. The government forced us to sell them off in the 80s but there is no government subsidy to help us get them back. So it is a risk, but for us it is one well worth taking if we are ever to construct the first-class public transport system our people deserve.

As it develops, English devolution is allowing us to focus on things long neglected by Whitehall. I describe our approach as 'fixing the fundamentals' – repairing the essential services which have been holding back our economy and society. Technical education is one subject very much in that category, as is social housing, and in the following chapters I will describe the new thinking we are beginning to apply to both. But Steve and I have started with the issue which has the most visible impact on everyday quality of life and the economy overall.

When you look at public transport in the North of England compared with London and the South East, I don't think it is hyperbolic to say that it could be two different countries. It is actually quite shocking that Westminster has allowed such a disparity to happen. The issue isn't simply that the city regions outside of London have been denied the powers to improve public transport over many decades. It's worse than that. The powers that they once had to run buses were transferred to the private sector which then proceeded to run a bus network which worked for their commercial interests but shredded the public interest. When Margaret Thatcher deregulated bus services in England outside London in the mid-80s, she promised 'lower fares, new services and more passengers'. In reality, the precise opposite has happened. Across England, fares shot up, services were cut and passenger numbers fell.

In my acceptance speech after the 2021 mayoral election, I asked how it could be fair that a single bus journey in Harpurhey, Manchester (£4.50) could cost three times as much as one in Haringey, London (£1.50). It obviously pricked the conscience of somebody who was watching. When the Conservative Party came to Manchester later that year for their annual conference, I found out that, in advance, an adviser from 10 Downing Street rang Transport for Greater Manchester to query whether the fares I had quoted were true. While grateful for their interest in the then much-neglected issue of bus fares, it is somewhat revealing, and depressing, that people running the country did not at the time have the first clue about the level of bus fares outside of London.

But, to be fair, it did prompt some action. Early in 2022, I said that Greater Manchester would be moving to introduce a £2 cap on bus fares and Steve committed to the same. A few months later, the government was forced to follow suit and it has now become something of a national policy. This is a simple but powerful example of how devolution is changing the policy debate in England. The increase we have seen in passenger journeys since introducing the cap shows it was exactly the right thing to do.

When it comes to public transport and devolution, trains are another essential service that too much of this country has been badly let down by, and for too long. Money has been diverted into the back pockets of rich shareholders leaving the service poorer for it. Let's look at the debacle with TransPennine Express (TPE), one of the North's main rail operators. In 2023, the company was effectively brought under government control as an 'operator of last resort' as their performance had dropped to such an unacceptable standard, despite millions in bonuses paid to the failing operating company. This follows another of the North's main operators, Northern, meeting the same fate in 2020. TPE was chaotic and provided months and months of an appalling service in which trains would be cancelled at the last minute for thousands of passengers. Being late for work or for appointments is a daily reality for people in the North.

The Guardian's North of England editor Helen Pidd described perfectly the daily anguish of rail passengers in our part of the country in an article for the newspaper in May 2023:

> People in London used to think I was making it up when I told them what an ordeal it was planning a journey on TPE. It sounded so absurd. The angst began as soon as you dared to book a ticket, wondering whether the train you had chosen would actually run. The niggling feeling: maybe I should drive.

Pidd went on to describe how there were regularly fifty cancellations each day and sometimes as many as a hundred. She exposed how the operator was actually taking advantage of a legal loophole in order to vastly underreport the number of cancellations it was making in its submission to the Office of Road and Rail.

We believe the problems with TPE caused around a £40 million hit to our economies in the North but I think it goes beyond just an economic impact. You cannot always measure or estimate the effect that a situation like that can have on people. You have to think about the missed hospital appointments, the school plays people couldn't see and the awkward discussions with bosses after someone was made late for work – again. We say it a lot in this book, but the test always has to be: would this have been allowed to go on for months and months in London? The answer is a resounding no and actually that is how it should be. In comparing things to London, it is not about dragging the capital down or holding them back. It is about other places also having similar standards, opportunities and funding.

Andy and I fully believe in a publicly run railway that works for the public and on behalf of the public. Our current network can only be described as a dog's dinner. It is deeply fragmented and allows operators to get away with providing an appalling sub-optimal service while continuing to hike prices.

I like to think that English devolution came of age on Sunday, 24 September 2023. This is when the Bee Network began operations and, after forty years of deregulation, Wigan and Bolton saw the first buses in England to go back under public control. The fact that Greater Manchester was able to reverse a key part of the Thatcher legacy from the 80s is proof of the growing influence of English devolution.

Our vision is to create a London-style tap-in, tap-out system over bus, bike and tram by January 2025 and then bring commuter rail services under the Bee Network banner by the end of the decade. Given that our trams already run on renewable energy, and the pace with which we are now introducing electric buses, we are on course to have the country's first zero carbon public transport system at street level within a decade. In the Northern context, this is revolutionary but, as we keep saying, this book is about rewiring systems to redistribute power back to people and places. Reregulation of buses does exactly that. In the deregulated world, if a bus turns up late, or doesn't turn up at all, there is nothing the public can do about it. There is zero accountability. The bus operators are able to go where they like, charge what they like and keep all the proceeds that come via the farebox. In the Bee Network, they are answerable to the public. If they fail to deliver a good service, they can suffer financial penalties. This is exactly how it should be.

This speaks to a wider point running through this book. Contrary to claims about consumer choice, deregulation and privatisation often serve to strip power from people and communities. We will come back to this theme in Chapter 13. For now, let it suffice to say that there is something truly miserable about communities across England being unable to control something as basic as bus services. Whatever the shape of the next government, they should legislate immediately to allow all parts of England to retake control of bus services – whether they have a devolution deal or not – and allow publicly owned operators to return to England's streets.

I don't think there can be a person in the whole of the North of England who would oppose this model of local public control being applied to our trains too. After all, nothing could be worse than sticking with the status quo. For five years since the May 2018 timetable change, rail services have been chaotic. On a weekly basis, they are ruining lives and damaging businesses. And yet the operators have still walked away with large salaries, profits and dividends for their shareholders. Bringing accountability back to our railways must be a high priority in the next Parliament.

Just when you have grounds to be optimistic about the prospects for English devolution, there is always something to remind you where true power lies, how Whitehall thinks it is entitled to treat the North and how far we still have to go. The scenes that unfolded in Manchester city centre in October 2023 were in many ways worse than the Tier 3 argument of October 2020. With the massed ranks of the Conservative Party gathered in our city for their conference, the Prime Minister stood up inside a former rail station at the Manchester Central convention centre and cancelled the promise of a new railway line for the city that George Osborne had made a decade earlier. I believe the

Tories took a deliberate decision to make that announcement in Manchester. They wanted to show that the Prime Minister could front up tough decisions in challenging environments. I don't think they succeeded. It just made them look disrespectful and rude.

It says a lot about the political culture of the country that those who run it think they can behave like this and get away with it. Once upon a time, they could. But not any more. This has to be the last time we see scenes like these. A written constitution should give regional and local government, as a bare minimum, the right to be consulted when decisions of major, long-term importance are being taken. More than that, we need to move to a world where the fate of a place is not entirely within the hands of Whitehall. We need the fullest possible version of devolution in England so that, if national government decides to withdraw support or funding, regions should have the power of looking at alternative ways of achieving their ambitions.

But as we wait for that time to come, we can take heart from the fact that English devolution has already changed the country for good. People are questioning things and answering back. The voice of the North is louder than it has ever been. We are not going back to the way things were before.

12

Two Equal Paths in Education

Changing the way power works in Britain requires more than the rewiring of the political system, as important as that is. If we are truly to lay the foundations for a more equal Britain, we need to rewire the education system so that it becomes a true engine of social mobility. At the moment, it is wired primarily to support the needs of the university route and can actually be a generator of social division rather than promoting the more equal country we wish to see.

The different paths that Steve and I took in life, even though we were born only three miles apart, are an illustration of Britain's two worlds and its great social divide. In March 2020, it is probably fair to say that the majority of people who were drinking cocktails in their garden were more likely to have gone to university while those still out at work didn't.

My good fortune in my mum and dad being determined to guide me towards university certainly opened up many more opportunities for me than perhaps would have been expected for someone born in 1970 in a modest semi-detached home in a Liverpool suburb. By contrast, Steve was clearly capable of attending a top university, as were my parents, but his life circumstances, the era in which he grew up and an education system which was then, and is still now, very responsive to the influences of class, social connections and money meant it was probably a non-starter. But it says something that, in the 90s, he and Sandra became determined to do the same for their three beautiful kids, Steven, Hayley and Samantha, as my parents did for Nick, John and I.

In England, there has always been a serious snobbery at play when it comes to education. For decades, the university route has been allowed to dominate the whole system. When I managed to scrape into the O Level set at St Aelred's in 1984, I had a sense at the time of how important that was and that's why I knuckled down afterwards. Truthfully, if I hadn't copied my neighbour's work, God knows how my life would have turned out. It certainly wouldn't be anything like the way it has. Back then, the O Level/ CSE divide was the equivalent of the grammar/secondary modern divide of the 50s and 60s. I was in the penultimate year group to take O Levels in 1986. Ken Baker, the then Conservative education secretary, scrapped O Levels in 1988 realising how they were unfairly dividing young people into two paths at fourteen, with the technical one considered distinctly second-class. He has been a long-standing champion for parity between the academic and technical routes and deserves great credit for that.

However, in England, the desire to make kids feel inferior at fourteen never quite goes away. In 2011, when I was shadow education secretary, the government introduced something called the English Baccalaureate or EBacc: a set of core GCSE subjects considered essential to many university degree pathways. In summary, ancient languages are in the approved list; engineering, business studies, art and music are out. Schools are judged by the government on how well students do at the EBacc subjects. I made the criticism at the time that the EBacc was elitist, arbitrary and divisive and I stand by it now. In all my time in Westminster, I truly hated the way people in both main parties, and particularly my own, were sneering about comprehensive education. To my dying day, I will champion it as a positive thing.

I want as many people as possible to go to university. But I don't believe it is inherently better than a technical path. Both academic and technical qualifications are essential for the proper functioning of society. That's why I have always said that the Labour government I was in was wrong to set a 50 per cent

ANDY BURNHAM & STEVE ROTHERAM

target for the university route and even more wrong not to set a clear ambition for the other 50 per cent on the technical path. Similarly, the Coalition government was wrong to ask OFSTED to judge all schools in England on their success at preparing young people for the university route. How can Britain's political class justify skewing the entire education system towards one group of students and not creating one that works for everyone?

In Germany, academic and technical education are regarded as equals. I believe that is the clear principle upon which we need to rebuild the English education system. At fourteen, all young people should have two clear, equal paths laid out ahead of them: one academic towards university, the other technical towards work. Critically, they must not be rigid paths. They should be designed in such a way so as to allow easy switching between the two should students have a change of plan as they move beyond secondary school.

One of these paths is already clearly laid out. The journey through EBacc to A levels, UCAS and then university is well established and understood. The fact that there is no clear alternative path says something about this country and the way it has been run for decades – and it is not positive. It is clear evidence that, for too long, Britain has been run more in the interests of some rather than everyone.

The country's failure to build an education system for everyone has serious economic and social consequences. It creates an obvious risk of skills gaps and high vacancies across the economy and public services. More seriously, if young people can't see a clear path ahead of them at fourteen, they are at risk of taking a direction that could prove harmful for them and everyone. Greater Manchester is the only part of England to my knowledge which carries out an in-depth study of the thoughts and feelings of its teenagers. The ground-breaking Bee Well survey asks our Year 10s, among other things, whether they have hope for the future. The good news is that four out of five say that they do. But it troubles me greatly that, at fourteen, one in five of our teenagers are not able to answer this question positively.

206

This takes us back to the issue of power again. We have somehow ended up with an education system in England which is hugely empowering for some young people but disempowering for many others. I have heard many say that, because they are not an EBacc student, they can feel their school starts to focus less on them. How appalling is that? To me, it is nothing short of a disgrace that we continue to allow so many young people to pick up a sense that they are a second-class citizen in their teenage years. And, let's be clear, we are not talking about small numbers here. After more than a decade of the EBacc, 64 per cent of young people in Greater Manchester are not taking it. Think about that for a minute – we have ended up with a school system in England not designed for two-thirds of the kids in it.

When I think back to my time as shadow education secretary, I regard it as the most frustrating front-bench position I ever held in Westminster. I was regularly stunned by the elitist and snobbish views I heard, even in my own party. Perhaps this is a reflection of the over-representation in the UK Parliament of people who went to private schools. A report called 'Elitist Britain', published in 2019 by the Social Mobility Commission and the Sutton Trust, found that, at the 2017 general election, 29 per cent of the MPs elected went to private school. This is four times higher than the proportion of the general public who did the same. Unsurprisingly, the figure is even higher in the House of Lords where 57 per cent of its members have been educated privately. Given these numbers, is it surprising that, over decades, Westminster has comprehensively failed to build an education system that works for everyone?

I don't think Westminster in its current form will ever build the kind of education system that I want to see in England. So, this is an area where the devolution of power in England needs to come into its own. If I am re-elected as Mayor of Greater Manchester in May 2024, I will make education my driving mission and the goal of creating an education system in our city region which offers a clear path for all young people. There are reasons why England has never fixed the issue of technical education. There is the fact that British Cabinets have pretty much always been dominated by people who went to the top universities. But there is also the issue of the absence of devolved structures and decision-making at the regional level. By definition, for technical education to work, it must be linked to local employers and the needs of the regional economy. Britain's top-down approach to education is one reason why initiative after initiative in the technical space coming out of the Department for Education has failed to land.

Things were better in the post-war period up until the 80s. Back then, across the towns and cities of England, there were large local employers who operated well-understood apprenticeship and training programmes. People like my dad worked during the day and then went to night school in the evening to secure their technical qualifications. When those large industries went into decline, those important ladders for young people went with them. Sadly, successive governments did not do anything meaningful to replace them.

The good news is that England finally has regional structures capable of stepping in and, in Greater Manchester's case, a Trailblazer devolution deal which gives us permission to do so. I have been a critic of Michael Gove's education policies in the past but I do give him credit for negotiating the ability for our city region to shape its post-sixteen technical system. While I have never been a supporter of his EBacc, I accept that it could be more justified if it was balanced by an alternative for the 60 per cent of students nationally who don't take it.

Based on the recognition that the technical path needs to lead directly to local employers, I am proposing the creation of the Greater Manchester Baccalaureate or MBacc. Whereas the EBacc focuses on the preferred GCSEs of the Russell Group universities, the MBacc will give our fourteen-year-olds clear advice about the GCSEs most favoured by local employers. It will guide them to seven gateways at sixteen which represent the strongest sectors of the Greater Manchester economy. Employers will work with our colleges to create T Levels, with accompanying work placements, and other qualifications to lead them towards good jobs in those sectors. By naming those employers, and giving our young people clear visibility of the opportunities they offer, they will bring the prestige to our technical path which the names of the Russell Group give to the university route. So, in summary, alongside the well-worn path of EBacc-A Levels-UCAS-university, we will have a new equivalent path of MBacc-T Levels-Greater Manchester Apprenticeship & Careers Service (GMACS)-apprenticeship.

This change will come at an important time for Greater Manchester. When I graduated from university, I came back to the North West and wanted to stay there. But, by the early 90s, the good jobs had gone. Like so many Northerners of my generation, I realised that to get on in life, I had to go south. From the mid-90s, and many would say specifically following the IRA bomb attack on the city centre, Greater Manchester began to change. Major employers were persuaded to take a presence in the city region, a trend perhaps best symbolised by the move of the BBC to Salford and the creation of Media City. As a result, the number of good graduate jobs in Greater Manchester has dramatically increased. In recent years, the city region has been the fastest-growing digital and tech hub in Europe. But, even with this growth in good jobs from the mid-90s to now, they have largely gone to people who came to the city to study or were relocated by their employers.

The next chapter in Greater Manchester's development will be the most exciting of all. It will be about opening up paths into the new, fast-developing sectors of the city region for all the diverse young talent growing up here. At present, it is hard for a young person in Hulme or Old Trafford to see a path for them into some of the new skyscrapers they can see from their bedroom. But, through the MBacc, we are going to give them one. The ten boroughs of Greater Manchester are teeming with streetwise talent which, in the past, has not been given its chance to shine. But, when this city region of ours is unlocking the potential of all of its people, it will finally be punching its weight in the economy and even above it. Our integrated, employer-driven technical education system, the UK's first, will give global businesses a clear reason to invest in Greater Manchester. This is how we hope the city region's success story will keep on building.

I believe that the MBacc could become a template for the reform of technical education across England. The truth is the content would be largely similar in all places and the same framework could be used everywhere. But obviously the gateways into the local economy will need to be adjusted according to its needs. For instance, in the West Midlands, there would need to be an automotive gateway. In Liverpool, you could see an LBacc with a gateway for shipping, ports and marine. The point is this: by directly connecting education with the place, and giving young people a clear line of sight into its economy, we will make it relevant to them and raise their aspirations.

One last point. When we create our new technical route, there is no reason whatsoever for it still to be regarded as the second-class route. In fact, it could take people to precisely the same destination – a degree or a Level 6 qualification – but via a different path and without incurring all the debt that comes with the traditional university route. I think there are many people in Greater Manchester who will see that as the superior option.

What Andy is doing with the MBacc is exactly the sort of thing that we also want to create in the Liverpool City Region. But, of course, the package of sector specific subjects is likely to be different in our region to fit the specific needs of businesses in our area. For example, we talked earlier about the Mersey Tidal project. It would be great to gear students towards technical subjects that could skill them up for work in the renewable energy sector, where we are expecting to create the jobs of the future.

Digital skills would also be essential in any programme we put together. We are working to make the Liverpool City Region the most digitally connected region in the country and work has now been completed on a 132-mile ultra-fast fibre network. This network stretches across the whole region and is connected to a supercomputer. We have the Hartree supercomputer – one of the most powerful in the country – situated in our region. This joint venture infrastructure investment has resulted in our area having the fastest digital speeds in the country and the capacity for big data analytics, which dovetails nicely with our civic data co-operative. These are the raw ingredients to make our area a national and global innovation hub.

The possibilities in this sector for young people are huge so we need to make sure we can tailor the education options in our schools to make the most of this. Our award-winning online careers portal called Be-More collates the opportunities available. But I want to attract investment in growth sectors and we will need to create the skills pipeline to service that demand. We are also making big strides in health and life sciences, with a new Pandemic Institute complementing the brilliant ongoing work at our universities and hospitals. Our innovation prospectus could deliver billions in economic growth and is only constrained by the lack of ambition at a national level. Once again, it is our people that are losing out.

The point here is that we believe we will be creating those good jobs of the future and we need to make sure we have the skilled workforce to fill them. At the moment, we cannot influence the types of skills our young people are gaining, which is a problem. This is why what Andy is doing in Greater Manchester is so important.

For someone like me who went down the technical education route before stumbling into academia, the MBacc plans are exciting. I think university is absolutely the right option for many young people – but it is absolutely the wrong option for many others. As a country – and certainly as a Labour Party – we have concentrated far too much on the university route and not nearly enough on the other side of things.

It is right to raise the aspirations of young people that a place at university might be a route for them to start a career. But there is currently no parity of esteem between the technical and academic routes into the world of work. In this country right now, I genuinely believe that someone with a high level technical qualification, such as an NVQ level 7, would be looked down on by a prospective employer compared with a graduate with a third-class honours degree from Cambridge. We need to change perceptions.

I think there is a big difference between being qualified and being educated. I was an apprentice and obviously I went to university in later life. I found some of the people I met there were very good at regurgitating facts to pass an exam, but they didn't have other important life skills that you can pick up through the technical route. I've met people who could design rockets to land on Mars but lacked common sense and who couldn't see the obvious. The dynamics of our university-led approach mean that, for a long time now, we have been churning out young people with degrees, often in subjects that have no relevance to the line of work they are heading into and without the skills to fill the jobs that are being created. What we are proposing is to strike a better balance to align supply and demand requirements for our local economies. It is also about raising aspirations so that mums and dads think that a technical route is a good route for their child to take; one that gets them a good job and won't see them accrue £50,000 worth of debt.

As well as improving the system itself, we need to help people to better understand the options available. This is where independent advice and guidance comes in. The coalition government got rid of the Connexions service that provided a lot of important advice to young people about their options for the future. That was a big blow for young people, especially those from working-class backgrounds. It has led to a situation where some schools with falling pupil numbers are now urging kids to stay on at sixth form, even if it is not the right move for them, because it is the right thing for the school financially. That is not a system that is working for young people and that is why we need independent advice and guidance.

Slowly but surely, devolution in England is fixing things that Westminster has long neglected. Its obsession with the university route has failed too many young people and left us with an education system in England which does not work for the majority. It gives some young people confidence, connections and social capital but leaves others with doubts about their self-worth. It creates a world where doors are flung open for some but feel slammed shut for others. Changing this is about changing the way Britain has traditionally worked.

Think instead of the power of having two clear, equal routes open to all kids at fourteen. It is a word used too often these days but I think transformational is justified in this context. Professions which have been dominated by people from a certain social class, and with all the connections that come with that, could finally be opened up. Social capital could at last be more evenly distributed. If all that leads to more young people in places like Greater Manchester growing up with a sense of hope for the future, and a feeling that they are being backed to succeed rather than written off, then the economic and social benefits will truly be huge.

13

A Grenfell Law

It's pretty remarkable and deeply worrying that, in the sixth richest economy in the world, the essentials of life for many people remain painfully out of reach. In reality, despite our wealth, we have one of the greatest levels of social and economic inequality in Europe. As things stand, our political system does not have the capability to address this inequality and this is why we advocate so strongly for further devolution and the tearing up of the old economic order that has led us to this point.

When you look around Britain today, you see the results of failed economic and social policies everywhere. From privatisation to deregulation and austerity, we now live in a country where many people simply do not have access to the basic essentials, the very things that allow you to sustain a life. It shouldn't feel radical to create policies that provide people with access to basic human rights like safe and decent housing, good working conditions and the ability to get health and social care – but, in Britain today, it does.

In this chapter, Andy and I are calling for people to have a fundamental, legal right to the essentials of life, starting with housing, and we will explain how we believe this can be achieved. It requires power being taken away from vested interests and handed instead to local councils, regions and, ultimately, to people.

You will probably have worked out by now that I am not the kind of politician to go out of my way to praise Margaret Thatcher.

I think many of today's problems can be traced back to the 80s and her divisive ideology. It was the time when the mantra that the market is the answer to everything became firmly planted in the mindset of Britain's political class. It has remained there ever since – to our country's cost.

Our inheritance from the Thatcher era is a problematic one: it left the essentials of life – water, energy, transport – in private hands and the British public paying higher prices for them; a race-to-the-bottom labour market with people's job security and protections whittled away; and, most seriously, a deep-rooted housing crisis. As a result, when the pandemic came, we found ourselves dangerously exposed to it and the cost-of-living crisis that followed. When the tide went out in March 2020, we could see the true state of modern Britain and everything underneath it more clearly than ever before.

We were shocked by the sheer number of people whose terms of employment were so insecure that they couldn't stop working, even when ill. We drove past kids crowded around McDonald's because it was the only place they could access wifi to do their homework. And we realised just how many people were living in poorly maintained, overcrowded homes which are damaging to their health and well-being.

A society living with this level of insecurity isn't just bad for those directly affected: it's bad for everyone. If a person is forced to stay at work when ill because they have no access to sick pay, that is harmful for everyone in that workplace and wider community. The pandemic reminded us that we are all connected and that, if some people don't have basic rights and protections, everyone suffers.

As I said earlier, the mission of English devolution in this current phase should be to fix the fundamentals of life that were broken up and sold off in the 80s. We can't achieve the high ambitions we have for our city region without first ensuring that all of our residents have the security of the basics: good homes, good work and good care when they need it.

I grew up in a working-class household in a poor area of Merseyside and we didn't have much. But what we did have was a home. It was a council house and it offered us a level of safety and security that we needed. When Margaret Thatcher came to power with a mission to sell off council housing under her disastrous Right to Buy policy, there were promises that some of the money gathered from tenants purchasing their council-owned homes at discounted rates would be reinvested in replacing the social housing that had been lost. The reality, of course, was very different. The Thatcher government put conditions on the use of the proceeds which meant little was used for that purpose.

As the New Economics Foundation points out, investment in new social housing has been consistently cut since the 80s, with government spending instead directed towards the spiralling housing benefit bill. The foundation argues that Right to Buy disincentivises the creation of new social housing because councils won't want to build homes only to sell them at a discount and lose out on reliable income from future rent payments. While some people were happy to be able to buy their council homes, the policy and the way it was managed fuelled the housing crisis we see today as those who were able to buy their council houses then moved on, selling up to private landlords. Four in ten Right-to-Buy homes are now owned by private landlords, with tenants paying double what they would have done in a council-rented property.

In places like Liverpool, a lot of the houses went to arms-length social housing providers and, while some of them are decent, there are plenty across the country which aren't up to scratch. We read countless stories of tenants living in mouldy, damp conditions while chief executives earn exorbitant salaries. And, of course, many of these homes are still being sold off to private landlords. In 2021/22, 21,600 social homes were either sold or demolished, while just 7,500 were built. The decade between 2012/13 and 2021/22 saw a net loss of 165,000 social homes.

Those statistics were gathered by Housing charity Shelter whose chief executive Polly Neate said:

'The social housing deficit is at the heart of the housing emergency. The fundamental lack of genuinely affordable homes has pushed millions of people into insecure, expensive and often discriminatory private renting. It is why we have over a million households waiting for a decent social home, and thousands of homeless children are growing up in temporary accommodation.'

We have written a lot in this book about how our current political system is damaging for the country and this of course impacts housing as well. If you build houses to a good standard, they will last for generations. If they are council houses, then people will be paying reliable and affordable rents in those properties for potentially decades and will not need the same level of subsidy from housing benefit. So it is a fiscal win as well as a social win.

My mum was paying rent in her council house for forty odd years but the council still owned the house. If you build more council housing, it is not a financial risk; there is a solid and reliable revenue stream that can be reinvested into more housing to address market failure. It's Keynesianism and it works. This is affordable for the country over the long term, but these days governments never plan that far ahead because they are so worried about the next election. We need to stop thinking in electoral cycles and plan for the years and decades to come in a strategic manner. Local councils should be able to plan to meet housing targets and to build and maintain an area's housing stock – but they can no longer do this because they have lost powers and have had their budgets smashed to smithereens.

If we are talking finances – and, let's face it, this is the language the Tories speak – then improving the conditions inside Britain's homes could also be a massive boost for the

National Health Service. Our current situation, where people are being made physically ill by the condition of their homes, is awful for them and adds pressure and cost to our struggling health service. Some collective thinking might just improve the health of the nation and the health of its finances too.

Perhaps the most devastating legacy of the Thatcher era is today's entrenched housing crisis. Since 1980, when Right-to-Buy was introduced, Britain has lost over two million homes from the public sector. Many have ended up in a barely regulated, poorly maintained private-rented sector with high rents fuelling a rising housing benefit bill of around £25 billion. Solving the housing crisis requires adopting a completely different philosophy from the one that has dominated housing policy for decades. Rather than viewing homes as investment opportunities for some, we need to see them as an essential foundation for all. You can't have good health and a good life without the foundation of a good home beneath you.

Millions of our fellow citizens don't have that security and, as such, are deprived of the power to improve their lives. They go to sleep worrying about whether they can pay the rent and wake up worrying about feeding the kids. Released in 2020, the 'People in Housing Need' report from the National Housing Federation found that 3.8 million people were in need of social housing, with some on waiting lists for almost two decades. The lack of availability forces many into the private-rented sector where the standard of landlords and properties is highly variable. Some are decent but many, sadly, are not. The lack of regulation allows the worse to operate without any real accountability. They can hike rents, ignore requests to fix problems and evict people far too easily. In short, it is a system which places all the power in their hands and leaves tenants at their mercy.

Contrary to Margaret Thatcher's claims that deregulated markets empower the consumer, they in fact do the opposite. They create a huge transfer of power to private vested interests. Two basic things sold off in the 80s – Britain's buses and homes

– stand as incontrovertible proof of that. People in private-rented housing are living in the wild west. There is very little in place to regulate either the behaviour of landlords or the condition of their homes. Tenants know that, if they ring the landlord to complain about rent rises or poor maintenance, they can easily be removed under the 'no fault' Section 21 eviction process. Even if it is repealed, as we hope it soon will be, it won't solve everything and private landlords will continue to hold most of the cards.

The problem with poor regulation of housing goes beyond private landlords. In the 80s, 90s and 00s, Right-to-Buy was accompanied by a drive to transfer the management of public housing stock to housing providers and associations outside of the democratic control and oversight of local government. The claim was that councils were unresponsive and inefficient and, by bringing in a more private sector ethos, services to residents would improve. Instead, consistent with the same trend towards arms-length organisations in other sectors, the bit most imported from the private sector was the tendency for senior management teams to overpay themselves.

In November 2022, an inquest verdict found that two-year-old Awaab Ishak was killed by the damp and mould in the poorly maintained one-bedroom flat where he lived with his parents in Rochdale, Greater Manchester. Requests to fix the problem from the family to the landlord, Rochdale Boroughwide Housing (RBH), went unanswered. Indeed, it was a full two years after Awaab died that RBH got round to checking other nearby properties and found that hundreds of other residents were living in the same conditions.

In a similar way to the *Cathy Come Home* drama of the 60s, Awaab's death sent shockwaves through Britain's housing sector. The chief executive of RBH was revealed to be earning a salary of £170,000. Local councillors had been removed from the board because they had criticised plans to demolish hundreds of flats.

The most devastating example of the accountability gap in housing is Grenfell Tower. The fire that killed seventy-two people in their own homes was the direct result of the failed ideology on housing that has dominated this country over the past forty years. Matt Wrack, the general secretary of the Fire Brigades Union, put it well when he said: 'The Grenfell Fire was not inevitable: it was a crime caused by decades of deregulation, privatisation and the prioritisation of profit over safety.'

The absorbing by Britain's political class of the market-driven mantra of the 80s, and their aversion to so-called 'red tape', has had so many devastating consequences. We heard at the inquiry how government ministers were urged to tighten the rules on seven different occasions in the decade before the tragedy but failed to do so. More broadly, the drive to hive out crucial public services has left us with an unaccountable state. There are now a whole range of quasi-public institutions – housing associations, academy schools, foundation trusts – who operate outside of true local democratic control.

If we are going to change the way power works in Britain, we need to start by adding the housing system to the list of things that needs to be rewired given its fundamental impact on people's lives. We need a major transfer of power away from social and private landlords and towards tenants.

In Greater Manchester, we are starting this process by introducing a Greater Manchester Good Landlord Charter based on our successful Good Employment Charter. Alongside it, we are introducing a new ability for tenants to request a property check and strengthening enforcement. This is an area, however, where devolution can take us only so far. At the national level, we need a complete sea change in England's approach to housing policy. We need to follow the lead of Finland and make 'Housing First' our guiding national philosophy. That means we should make a good, secure home a human right in UK law.

It is a damning fact that, in 2021, 3.4 million homes in England failed to meet what is known as the decent homes standard. Allowing that situation to persist stores up so many problems for the NHS. And remember: many of the landlords who own these homes are in receipt of significant funding from the public purse from the benefits system yet fail to reinvest it in the upkeep of their properties. There is a strong case for introducing conditionality into the housing benefits system. If properties are to be rented with the help of the public purse, they must be maintained to the decent homes standard. If landlords refuse, those homes should be compulsorily purchased and returned to local public ownership.

In the end, the only real way to solve the housing crisis is to bring about a huge increase in the number of homes for social rent. It starts with suspending Right-to-Buy to stop making the problem worse. But it must quickly get into the job of building a new generation of homes for social rent across England on the same scale as the post-war period. In Greater Manchester, we are ready to lead the way with our plan for 30,000 net zero homes for social rent. We hope to be backed to build them in the next Parliament by the incoming government and establish a template that could be taken across England. These will be homes that will be cheaper to rent and cheaper to run and will make a massive contribution to the drive to raise living standards and reduce inequality.

People will rightly ask: who will be responsible for delivering this right to a good, secure home and how will it be funded? On the former, we need to make local councils once again the overall guardians of housing in their areas and re-empower them with a comprehensive package of funding and powers to ensure delivery of the new right in their communities. On the funding, well that is not as daunting as people might think.

In a reformed Westminster, I would expect to see more long-term thinking than we currently do based on stronger cross-party consensus. No other policy area is more ripe for this approach than housing. A long-term national policy of expanding the number of homes for social rent will bring long-term savings to the housing benefit bill. But much bigger savings to UK public spending will come from giving all citizens access to a good, safe home that they can afford. By setting people up for success in life, rather than leaving them living constantly on the edge, we will all benefit in so many different ways.

That ideology of deregulation discussed at the Grenfell Inquiry is one that has dogged Britain and put people at risk. We have heard Conservative politicians boasting about a bonfire of red tape, referring to the reduction and removal of regulations. This is about making it easier for developers to build properties and for others to make money from it. Whether we are referring to the deregulation of housing, transport, health and care services or banking, it is all about making money – if it puts people at risk, well to hell with them, basically.

The Shrewsbury Pickets of 1972 fought for improved pay but also for better working conditions as Britain's building sites were littered with deaths and serious injuries on a weekly basis. I saw things in the construction industry which caused me great concern. Health and safety regulations were ignored so that developers could build with less hassle and make more money. Of course, this meant more people at the bottom of this chain, those working on building sites, could face greater risk and could get injured. But profit was always king. Grenfell is a prime example of this culture and this ideological desire to remove regulations that keep people safe. But hey, why worry about things like that if you and your family are very unlikely ever to be directly affected by such decisions? I wonder how many out of the many thousands of Tory MPs in history have seen their children working for a living on a building site? Or how many live in high-rise blocks and believe cladding such buildings with combustible insulation is worth the reduction in material costs? I would hazard a guess at not very many. Maybe this could be a factor in their lack of understanding that health and safety hasn't in fact gone mad. The madness lies in ignoring its importance to people's lives.

As we write, we await the final report into the terrible disaster at Grenfell Tower. When it comes, I hope that it will be a moment of sombre reflection for a country which has ignored the importance of housing for too long and allowed deregulation to go too far. Nobody should ever be at risk in their own home.

Everyone should have a right to a safe and decent home. Our council house in Kirkby was the foundation which helped my brothers, sisters and me to succeed and I want the same for everyone. I can think of no better way of remembering the seventy-two people who perished in the fire than for the country to commit to introducing this right in a new Grenfell Law, guaranteeing that nothing of this kind could ever happen again.

In an earlier chapter, I talked about the work we are doing with Housing First in the Liverpool City Region, an approach that Andy is also delivering in Greater Manchester. Housing First is an innovative way of tackling homelessness that provides people with a secure home as a starting point, and builds wraparound services for those who are struggling with issues such as addiction and poor mental health which may have contributed to their housing problems in the past.

This policy gets to the heart of what we mean in terms of a safe and decent home being the essential foundation from which people can build – or rebuild – their lives. Finland is a tremendous example of the impact Housing First can have. From 2007 onwards, the country used Housing First as its main approach to tackling long-term homelessness. The results are remarkable. The estimated number of long-term homeless people in Finland dropped from 3,500 to 1,000 between 2008 and 2020. It is a policy that works to empower people. Rather than treating homeless people with complex issues like a burden to be passed around, it immediately places them in a position where they can start to rediscover a sense of self. Services and support are then wrapped around that person to ensure they are able to sustain that tenancy.

We have been taking part in a pilot project of Housing First for several years now. It is currently supporting 220 people across the Liverpool City Region. Crucially, more than four in five of those placed in properties through the programme have kept them. Housing First has been successful in Merseyside because it is a totally different way of doing things. We've exhausted all the contrasting ways that local authorities can intervene in homelessness and this has elevated the issue. Our local authorities are of course still doing good work on a daily basis to try to alleviate homelessness and rough sleeping, but in Liverpool, for instance, the bill to tackle this issue has escalated, increasing nearly tenfold in just a few years. The big concern isn't just the visible aspect of having people on the streets, but also all the hidden homelessness with the people in temporary accommodation or sofa surfing. Liverpool city council have struggled with the budgetary pressures caused by the exponential growth in homelessness. Just three years ago, they were spending hundreds of thousands on temporary accommodation. The latest figures show that this year it will have grown to £19m and its trajectory is upwards for future years, which is unsustainable without government intervention.

With Housing First, it's about trying to provide somebody with a sense of permanence, a roof over their head and appropriate support. We believe this will save money for the country in the long run. We've seen how invaluable it is to people who have lost their way. These people haven't had intensive support like this before. They've often been passed around the system, feel totally unloved and lost without a home base from which to try to rebuild their lives. This is a very different approach from that of the present government's sanctions regime. We are giving people more than one chance. At present, if someone who is struggling with mental health misses a benefits appointment, they get sanctioned. This means they struggle to pay their landlord and go into arrears, which often results in them getting kicked out onto the streets. Housing First isn't there to punish people; it is designed to work to help people, even if they slip up. It demonstrably works and the outcomes are amazing. We are now getting people furthest from the job market off benefits and into jobs in some cases. It is an approach that treats people like human beings and helps them to improve their individual circumstances. That should be the hallmark of a decent society: setting people up for success rather than continually paying for the costs of failure.

Given that Britain is likely to face another pandemic in this century, and potentially a much more deadly one, we will betray our children and grandchildren if we allow Britain to go into the next one as exposed as we were to the last.

I will always recall a reality check which stopped me in my tracks in the early stages of 2020. It was that survey of care workers in the North West I referenced earlier which found that 80 per cent were worried that they would be unable to self-isolate if asked to do so because they either wouldn't be paid or would have no access to sick pay. Ten years before this, as health secretary in 2010, I had said that a major overhaul of social care was needed because of its malnourished state and the consequential poor treatment of care staff. But even I found it a shock to see this stark fact in black and white. You would think that giving people who care for others the guaranteed ability to take time off work if they are unwell is basic common sense, wouldn't you? Sadly, basic common sense seems like it got lost somewhere along the way as Britain's obsession with privatisation took hold.

If we are to respond properly to what we saw in the pandemic, and learning through the Covid public inquiry, we need to take dramatic steps to change the governance of Britain and improve the resilience of our people and communities. So, alongside a law requiring good homes for all, we need to raise the everyday living standards of millions in Britain who can't afford the basics. The best way of achieving that is making sure everyone in work has a good, secure job.

In Greater Manchester, we have developed a comprehensive Good Employment Charter. Following the pandemic, we took the decision to link it to public procurement and, in particular, to the process of reregulating the buses which is currently being implemented around our city region. The results have been revealing. Before we introduced this requirement, people probably did not realise that many people working in our deregulated bus system did not have access to sick pay. The effect of the regime we have established is that, going forward, the Greater Manchester public will know that every person driving our buses on the new Bee Network will be supported to go home if they are ill.

But it all begs a bigger question: how have we allowed large parts of the private sector to get away with such low employment standards for so long? If they are creating a situation where the public is put at risk by people in public-facing roles staying in work when they are ill, how on earth does that improve customer service?

I don't think the majority of the British public realises how many retail or other service staff they interact with in the course of any given day are not covered by sick pay. If they did, they would probably be outraged. But they would be even more outraged if they were to realise that politicians' obsession with privatisation has also left some outsourced staff working in our hospitals, as porters or cleaners, in that same precarious position.

For me, one of the biggest take-aways from the Covid pandemic is this: the people who were sitting in their gardens in March 2020 need to start doing much better by those who weren't. An unhealthy culture of excessive pay combined with poverty pay has become the norm. It is time to narrow the gap and make good employment an entitlement for everyone.

We want to do the right things to encourage people into work but we also need to protect them when they are working. This is why another of our calls is for a legal right to secure work with proper protections around things like sick pay. We saw in the pandemic that far too many people did not have the basic employment rights to protect them and this was damaging for everyone. Far too many people faced losing their pay if they stopped going to work and this massively hampered the country's efforts to bear down on the virus. We had this perverse situation where care home workers with potential symptoms of Covid-19 were still having to go into work because they couldn't afford to isolate at home.

Statutory sick pay (SSP) amounts to 21 per cent of the median

weekly earnings of workers in Greater Manchester and 22 per cent in the Liverpool City Region. I don't think most people could survive on that. Then there are those workers who aren't actually entitled to SSP because their incomes are too low; many of them are on zero hours contracts where, if they don't go in to work, they get no money. Imagine not knowing whether you will get any pay from one week to another. Imagine weeks without a single pound to your name. There are around 90,000 people in this position in Greater Manchester and 47,000 in the Liverpool City Region. They all had an impossible choice during the pandemic. Either continue to work and potentially pass on the virus or stay at home with no pay whatsoever. They were forced into this invidious position because the government ignored them, along with three million self-employed and freelance workers who received no support whatsoever.

In the Liverpool City Region, we have set up a Fair Employment Charter that businesses can sign up to. It contains important directives around fair pay, job security and workers' rights. We've got hundreds of companies interested and signed up, which is great as we believe we are setting new standards for the workplace. Perversely, though, it is not the good companies who are signing up who we should be worrying about; it's the ones who don't sign up. These are the ones who were more likely to have coerced workers to continue working in potentially unsafe conditions during the pandemic, often without the appropriate PPE; there is evidence that even those working in our NHS and social care faced similar risks. Our charter is not enforceable in law as things stand. However, if there was a legal right in legislation for things like secure contracts and sick pay, then that is something we could enforce locally – and thereby drive up employment standards.

We cannot talk about the essentials of life without talking about health and social care. At the time of writing, the NHS and social care are at risk of being overwhelmed by a perfect storm of mounting pressures from every conceivable angle.

Fifteen years ago, I warned that, if nothing changed, the social care system in England would eventually collapse and that would have the effect of dragging the NHS down with it. That prospect has come closer over the course of the last decade and is now staring us right in the face. The broken nature of privatised social care in England was exposed by the pandemic. If nothing changes, it could soon get even worse. According to the Health Foundation, an extra 600,000 extra care staff are needed over the next decade to meet the needs of our ageing population. When I look at the famished state of local government finances, I see no prospect that they will be recruited.

Social care is prevention. It is everyday support in people's homes. It helps to stop people ending up in hospital from falls and infections and speeds up the return home for those who do go in. As public investments go, it's one of the best. And yet, despite having been warned for decades about the social care crisis, Britain's dysfunctional political system has failed to address it. The reason? Cowardice on the part of countless politicians.

This modern fear of taking on a difficult argument about tax is now risking public safety. As society's problems have got bigger, our politics has got smaller. In the end, something is going to have to give and my fear is it will be the NHS.

Just as with Hillsborough, social care was another issue which made me a Westminster outsider. When I called for a radical reform as health secretary, I broke the rules of the modern political game. But I have no regrets about it. I will never stop arguing for what I believe to be the only solution: social care provided on NHS terms and funded through taxation. In the twenty-first century, only that can give everyone the peace of mind of good everyday care when they need it.

People always respond to ideas like this by asking where the money will come from. Undoubtedly, taxation would be needed to fund free social care. But there is also an awful lot of money that can be saved through the integration of health and social care systems. We are currently wasting enormous sums of money because people cannot get the step-up or step-down treatment they need. Cutting local authority funding has had a real and predictable consequence for patients waiting to be discharged from hospitals. We are in a situation where people who need acute care cannot get through the front door or are left waiting for days in emergency rooms. Meanwhile, many people who may not have needed acute care in the first place are in that same emergency room because they didn't access preventative care. On any given day, thousands of hospital beds are occupied by older patients who are well enough to leave but can't because there are no social workers, care packages or places at care facilities available. As Andy says, it is a perfect storm and it needs a big solution.

Councils have responsibility for social care in their local areas but, after years of brutal cuts to their budgets, they are finding it increasingly difficult to cover even the most basic, statutory services. Many spend the majority of their entire budgets on care costs. The government's response to this has been to allow local authorities to raise council tax to fund social care. But, as we know, council tax is a regressive form of taxation and fundamentally unfair. Also, areas with higher needs have less capacity to raise money in this way because of the types of housing they have. If you have a propensity for low-band properties in an area, it means there is less money that can be raised from council tax. So, this whole issue needs to be approached differently and paid for properly.

Good homes, good jobs, good care. These are the essentials of life and the foundations on which everything else is built. In the midst of Britain's forty-year market experiment, we lost sight of this basic truth. If we don't recognise that now and change it, the next pandemic could be much, much worse.

14

A Hillsborough Law

We have talked a lot about power in this book: who has it; who doesn't and what it means when that power is taken away from people or abused by the establishment. When the Hillsborough disaster of 1989 left ninety-seven football fans dead, their families were powerless to secure justice for them as different branches of the state closed ranks to cover up exactly what had happened and who was at fault. If this was a military junta, a totalitarian state or a dictatorship abusing power, influence and control against its own citizens, it would gain widespread criticism from democracies like ours. For it to happen and be orchestrated here demonstrates how our country has become corrupted by a tiny minority who will stoop to any level to protect reputations and vested interests. It was only through extraordinary and tireless campaigning that the truth of what happened on that day came to light, when new inquests in 2016 ruled that those Liverpool fans who died were unlawfully killed.

Despite achieving this truth, the Hillsborough families have never received anything close to justice. Only one person has been convicted of anything related to the disaster, with the former Sheffield Wednesday FC secretary Graham Mackrell fined £6,500 for a safety offence. Other than this, nobody has been held accountable for ninety-seven unlawful deaths of British citizens. This is not justice for the ninety-seven innocent football fans. This is not justice for the families of those fans who had to campaign for three decades against an establishment that sought to lie about them at every turn. It is not justice for a city besmirched by a certain section of the media who were in cahoots with the British government.

This lack of accountability related to the Hillsborough disaster clearly demonstrates just how weighted this country's legal system is against ordinary people. It is a crucial example of where power lies in this country. This is why Andy and I continue to call for the creation of a Hillsborough Law which has the clear purpose of preventing other ordinary people going through the same gruelling experiences as the Hillsborough families only to face a complete denial of justice. We will also make reference to another near-fatal football match in Paris that demonstrated how the Hillsborough playbook of shifting blame, denial and obfuscation is still being utilised as a mechanism to deny accountability.

If you want to find a place where social class, connections and accent still matter, just spend a day in a British courtroom. The whole set-up is designed to be a demonstration of where power lies; who has it and who doesn't. When we visited the main trial following the second Hillsborough inquest, Steve and I were surprised to find the defendant sitting in the body of the court rather than in the dock. We asked ourselves whether it would have been an option on offer to a young person standing trial from Toxteth or Moss Side.

You would like to think that, in a country like ours, a courtroom would be a level playing field where everyone is truly equal in front of the law. In reality, it is the exact opposite and more like a casino: the lower your social standing and the less money you have, the more heavily the odds are stacked against you from the moment you walk in.

Shortly after the conclusion of the second Hillsborough inquest, Steve and I invited Margaret Aspinall down to Parliament to speak to MPs and peers about her experience at the hands of the legal and coronial systems. As the packed room listened in silence, she described preparing for the original inquest and having no choice but to cash the cheque she received from the Criminal Injuries Compensation Authority in respect of the death of her son James to fund her contribution to the families' legal costs at the first inquest. Even then, she had to top it up with help from family and friends. If all that wasn't bad enough, she would soon after be catapulted into the cold light of the courtroom, raw with grief, only to find herself with the other families up against the best QCs in the land hired at taxpayers' great expense by police and public bodies. She was left feeling as though it was her son who was on trial, alongside the other Liverpool supporters.

This is by no means an isolated experience. Even today, bereaved families attending inquests where the state is involved can go through something very similar. It is far too easy for false narratives to be set, for victims to be blamed, and for circumstances to be created that families will find retraumatising in the many years in the wilderness ahead of them.

Sometimes people get a little bit confused when they hear about a Hillsborough Law. They seem to think that this is still about trying to get justice for the families of the ninety-seven Liverpool fans who were killed. It's not. Unfortunately, all the legal avenues for those families have now been exhausted. They fought for truth, and they got the truth with the verdicts at those second inquests, but they did not get justice as no one was held to account for how their loved ones died.

The Hillsborough Law is a considered attempt to rebalance the scales of justice by using the experiences of the Hillsborough families to stop others going through the same nightmare; to correct some of the massive flaws in our legal system and offer a fairer process. Myself, Andy and others, including current Members of Parliament, are sponsoring the campaign for this law, but the initiative comes directly from the families. From the manner in which these families were regarded by the legal system, you would have thought that they were the accused in this case. They were the victims of events that took the lives of their loved ones and of catastrophic processes that denied them closure. They were put through harrowing experiences as they tried to get justice. Surely being able to pursue that in respect of a loved one, without barriers being put in your way, is a basic tenet of a democratic society?

We have a system that is so stacked in favour of those with the deepest pockets that the public sector and agencies that have millions of pounds at their disposal were able to drag something on for as long as possible to try to exhaust these grieving, working-class families in an attempt to deny them natural justice. They all believed that the passage of time would count in their favour and, unfortunately, it often does. We have seen that with other injustices where ordinary people are ground down by the process and run out of energy and hope. But they picked on the wrong people when it came to Hillsborough. As the late Bill Kenwright rightly said, they messed with the wrong mothers. Parents and families who were never going to give up. That is why we now have the truth. But not justice.

Nuclear test veterans. Aberfan. Bloody Sunday. Shrewsbury. Contaminated blood. Primodos. Orgreave. Hillsborough. Post Office. Windrush. Grenfell.

Different scandals from different decades but a list that bears witness to three uncomfortable facts: how easy it is for agents of the British state to cover up; how difficult it is for ordinary people to secure justice and how not enough has been done to break this pattern. It's a depressing list and by no means exhaustive. Behind every single one of the justice campaigns that the public know about, there are thousands more relating to individual families or smaller groups who face an even bigger uphill struggle. If I go back to that day in Parliament with Margaret, something happened straight after she had finished speaking which brought that over to me. When I asked if anyone would like to ask a question, immediately a hand shot up belonging to a young woman dressed all in black with an orange flower on her lapel at the back of the packed room in Portcullis House.

'Margaret. What happened to you is happening to us right now.'

That person was Nicole Gbangbola, wife of Kye, and mother of a young boy called Zane who was killed in a flooding incident in Chertsey in early 2014. The same event had put dad Kye in intensive care and left him permanently disabled. Nicole said that, prior to the flood, it was known that the family lived near a hazardous landfill site. Shortly after it, representatives from Porton Down were on site quickly. The presence of hydrogen cyanide in the family home led to other nearby properties being evacuated and wider local health warnings. Even 10 Downing Street was forced to make a comment about the incident following a COBRA meeting. And yet, despite all this, the inquest did not admit crucial evidence and there was a rush to pronounce the cause of death as carbon monoxide poisoning – meaning, effectively, it was the family's fault.

The striking thing about the experience of the Gbangbolas at the hands of the system is how like Hillsborough it is but in a microcosm. All the same ingredients are there. Nicole speaks of being made to feel like the accused. There were unfounded slurs against Kye. And, like the Hillsborough families, there was no legal funding to fight back against all of this.

Why does this pattern continue to repeat itself and why do these injustices often stand for decades before they are over-turned? One answer is the huge power imbalance in the legal system and the David versus Goliath battles between the state and those whose lives have been turned upside down by bereavement. Another goes back to the nature of our political system. Victims of tragedies and scandals will often find to their cost that Parliament doesn't have the power they thought it had. In the aftermath of inquests, when they seek the support of MPs, they will often find that the letters they write in good faith, and the questions raised in the House, will simply bounce off an intransigent executive. This is the practical effect of the whip system which transfers the power of MPs to the unelected state. It leaves victims coming face to face with the 'patronising disposition of unaccountable power' – the description given by Bishop James Jones in his powerful report on the experiences of the Hillsborough families.

We believe this pattern of injustice can only be broken by the passing of a comprehensive Hillsborough Law. We will never level up the scales of justice in favour of ordinary families unless we change the balance of power. There are two core elements to the proposed law: first, a legal duty of candour on police and public servants to tell the truth at the first time of asking; second, parity of legal funding for bereaved families at inquests where the state is involved.

You would think it an uncontroversial requirement on public servants to tell the truth. But experience shows it is needed. Decades after Hillsborough, it is still far too easy for public bodies to create false narratives that impact on ordinary people. I know from my experience that the vast majority of civil and public servants are good people. The problem is often not them but the culture of the institutions in which they work. Many would willingly tell the truth if given the chance but fear of what would happen to their careers prevents them. When an organisation as powerful as a Whitehall department or a police force is dug in behind a lie, it takes a brave person to step forward and challenge it from the inside. The duty of candour would protect them in doing so.

In an earlier chapter, I described how as health secretary, in 2009, I was given a letter to send to a campaigner on contaminated blood which stated: 'there is no evidence that individuals were knowingly infected with contaminated blood and blood products'. I didn't know then, but do now, that there was in fact plenty of evidence inside the Department of Health to the exact contrary. I consider it truly breathtaking that it was put on my desk for me to sign. When there is an official cover-up, what chance do ordinary people have of prising the lid off it if the lies are going all the way up to Cabinet ministers?

The second core component of a Hillsborough Law is the requirement for parity of legal funding for bereaved families. Currently, if bereaved families come up against an attempt to establish a false narrative or blame victims in court, it is very hard for them to fight it if the legal resources at their disposal are a fraction of those available to public bodies. If the requirement to have parity of funding was set down in law, it would create an incentive to put a limit on the amount of legal spending by public bodies which would ensure a much more level playing field.

The legal system dragged out the already unimaginable pain that was suffered by the Hillsborough families for decades. What they needed was someone giving them the genuine reasons why their loved ones died so that they could begin the process of moving on. When you speak to the families, that's what they always wanted. They didn't want to become campaigners. They were forced into that life by the failures of the system. They could not allow the lies and smears to be the end of the story. They could not let it drop and it is to their eternal credit that they never gave up.

I find it difficult to comprehend just how they did that. I was at Hillsborough and I have spent a considerable amount of my life campaigning around it. But I have been able to switch off at times and continue with my own life. Those families have never been able to do that. Their first morning thought will be about the precious person they lost on that day and every occasion when they were vilified or lied about. Their day will start with all that pain being brought straight back to the forefront of their minds.

I think many of the ills of our society were exposed by Hillsborough and that long campaign for the truth. We still see many of them in our society today. Politicians at the highest level who tell lies and believe they are above accountability. The establishment conspiring to cover up injustices like the Post Office scandals. These are endemic issues in modern Britain. We need to fight against them and redress the power imbalance for natural justice to prevail. But maybe it's an issue endemic in other countries too. When French authorities tried to use similar smear tactics against Liverpool fans during the

Champions League final in 2022, it demonstrated that often the first duty of those in power appears to be to save their own skins. Football supporters appear to be an easy target whom to transfer blame.

In 2014, Andy asked me and my mate Billy to join him for a trip to France to watch Everton versus Lille. They were both looking forward to the game but I decided to join them specifically to observe how fans of another football club were treated, as I had only ever been abroad to watch Liverpool. What we witnessed was disgraceful treatment meted out by overzealous police dressed in robocop armour. When we returned to the UK, we wrote to the French authorities but didn't even get the courtesy of a response. This clearly demonstrated the disdain that the French authorities had for English fans. The treatment of Liverpool fans in Paris a few years later could have led to much greater consequences. It was due to the self-stewarding by the supporters themselves, many of whom had witnessed the events of Hillsborough, that prevented a chaotic event turning into a catastrophic one.

Beyond issues raised by Hillsborough and other injustices, there is a strong case for a much more fundamental reform of the courts and the criminal justice system. Steve and I are still reeling from the fact that the main criminal trial after the second Hillsborough inquest did not allow evidence to be admitted from that inquest, which was the longest and most comprehensive such process in British legal history. Surely a provincial crown court should not be able to discount something of that magnitude and seek to start again? Slurs about Liverpool supporters disproved by that inquest were allowed freely to circulate once again around that Preston courtroom. How on earth could that even happen when the supporters had been completely cleared on all counts by the second inquest?

Elsewhere in the system, it is not hard to find evidence of other injustices. Although it is over a decade since they were abolished, it is shocking that there are still over 1,000 people in prison on indeterminate 'imprisonment for public protection' or IPP sentences. They are literally being left to languish in prison with very few protections in law. Likewise, I have huge concerns about the way joint enterprise cases are sometimes handled. In 2017, eleven teenagers from Moss Side were jailed for a total of 168 years for their part in a killing in the same Preston courthouse and by the same judge who oversaw the main trial after the second inquest. While it must never be forgotten that there is a victim's family at the heart of this case, it must also be remembered that there are other families deprived of their sons who dispute that they played any significant role in what happened. On the face of it, it is hard not to conclude that this cumulative sentence is anything other than disproportionate. If you look into how the joint enterprise rules are used, it won't take you long to find widespread concerns about them and how black, working-class young men are particularly affected. It is a common complaint that unfair stereotypes about 'gang culture' abound in the courtroom.

The blunt truth is this: courtrooms are places where some lawyers will exploit issues such as social status, social class (as denoted by accent) and race. The whole atmosphere and environment works against people who are not used to it. The wide discretion afforded to coroners and judges creates circumstances in which natural justice does not always prevail.

We have talked about how our political system strips people of power. So too does the legal system – and, for most people, this is the one with which they are more likely to come into contact at some point in their lives. The two systems are interlinked: people can exploit the power imbalances in one to gain advantage in the other. Both can be easily played by those with power, connections and money. Parliament should be the back-stop against these abuses but, as we have seen with Hillsborough and countless other injustices, a supine Parliament can often take decades to overturn them, if it manages to do so at all. This is not a criticism of MPs but more of the antiquated system in which they are required to work.

At the Labour Party Conference in Liverpool in September 2022, party leader Sir Keir Starmer started his keynote speech by confirming that an incoming Labour government would put a new Hillsborough Law on the statute book in a bid to prevent further injustices where there is state involvement. Speaking at the conference, Keir said: 'We've repeatedly called for the Hillsborough Law and making it a reality would be a priority of my Labour government.' He said he had met with Hillsborough families, adding: 'Their raw pain was matched by their inspirational courage. Nobody should ever have to endure what they've been through.' It was undoubtedly a big moment. Here was the leader of the Labour Party, and the likely next Prime Minister, committing to a Hillsborough Law for which many of us have been campaigning for a long time.

It is vital that we continue to keep up the challenge and ensure that, if Labour do come into power, this remains a priority. We know how much legislation gets pushed through the system when a new party comes to power and the machine can get clogged up. So we will need to be vigilant to ensure that this new proposed law comes into statute as quickly as possible. That's because we know the profound difference this piece of legislation could make to ordinary people who are unfortunate enough to get caught up in a tragedy or a disaster, and who deserve to hear the truth.

In the King's Speech in 2023, the government announced plans for the creation of a 'Public Advocate' to support victims and bereaved families following major incidents and disasters. This would provide just one element of what is being called for in a Hillsborough Law and even that does not go far enough.

If you are truly going to respond to the inequality in this country, then you need the full package. But, if all you want to do is to send out signals to the electorate that you are doing something, then this is probably the route that politicians would take. What they have announced will only tinker around the edges without fundamentally dealing with the issue. If something terrible like Hillsborough happened today, the families of those lost would still face many of the same hurdles that people faced more than thirty years ago, even with these changes. It is tokenistic and simply not enough. The Hillsborough families won't accept it because they know through painful experience what happens when a country gets this wrong.

I had not expected to encounter some of the issues I've mentioned here so early in my time as Mayor of Greater Manchester. Shortly after the Manchester Arena bombing, and learning from my experience with Hillsborough, I commissioned Lord Bob Kerslake to conduct an early report into what had happened with the emergency response precisely so that we do not allow a space where competing narratives could be constructed. Fortunately, around the same time, the former Bishop of Liverpool, the Rt Revd James Jones, published 'The Patronising Disposition of Unaccountable Power'. I gave a copy of it to the then Chief Constable of Greater Manchester Police and asked for the 'families first' principle to be at the heart of any response to the inquiries that would follow into what happened at the arena.

The fact that subsequently this did not happen in the way I wanted troubles me still and tells you something about how deep-rooted these defensive cultures are in some of our institutions. The Kerslake Report was not conducted on oath. Clearly, some saw that as an opportunity. At the full public inquiry, different versions of events began to emerge as did the fact that GMP had left an inaccurate version of events with Lord Kerslake for a full eleven months. I don't know how this came about but, clearly, someone at some level in the organisation was being less than truthful.

What I have learned through all these experiences is just how hard it is for people to fight for justice in this country. When public authorities pull the shutters down, people are forced to find superhuman levels of resilience and relentlessness. Some are able to tap into those reserves but others are not. The establishment game plan is to grind people down to the point where they give up.

With the Hillsborough Law Now campaign, we have tried to fight back against this by linking families in a new support network so they can find strength and advice from each other. The idea came from a visit I did to Derry with Margaret Aspinall and Jenni Hicks to meet the families of those killed in the Bloody Sunday massacre. We wanted to hear their advice on how to handle the Hillsborough truth day having gone through their own in 2010 with the publication of the Savile Inquiry report. It was humbling to be in the same room and to hear the conversation between both sets of families – divided by the Irish sea but so alike in every other way having lived through a similar experience. We learned so much from them, not least the need to bring people in the same position together more.

When I became shadow home secretary in 2016, I drew on my Derry experience to convene a number of 'justice summits' in Parliament. I know they proved helpful to a number of ongoing campaigns, in particular contaminated blood which got a breakthrough soon after with the establishment of the public inquiry. After the horrific fire at Grenfell Tower, our new way of working allowed us to move quickly to support people affected. Margaret Aspinall was good enough to go to London to meet the Grenfell families and, given the alarming echoes between both tragedies, was able to give them some good advice and encouragement. And yet, last year we went past seventy-two months since the fire without any justice for the seventy-two people lost and their families.

The year 2024 will be a decisive year in understanding the extent to which the Hillsborough families' experience is rebalancing the system in favour of victims of other tragedies. Both the Infected Blood Inquiry and the Grenfell Tower Inquiry will publish their final reports and we will be watching them closely along with the government's response.

My work with justice campaigners over the years has taken me to some of the darkest recesses of our country and revealed highly problematic cultures at the heart of the British state. But, on a more hopeful note, there are signs that the rebalancing of the system, for which Steve and I have long called, could be starting to happen.

In his speech to the Labour Conference in September 2022, Keir Starmer made a commitment to the Hillsborough Law. That was a monumental moment for us and our campaign and I sent Keir a message straight after to tell him so. More recently, in early December 2023, the government finally responded to Bishop James's report. While it doesn't deliver the Hillsborough Law in full, it would be wrong not to acknowledge that the announcement was significant. There is a commitment to a new duty of candour on police officers, if not other public servants, and some legal funding for bereaved families at inquests, if not parity.

So the campaign for a full Hillsborough Law will go on. But it is clear to me that the fight of the Hillsborough families has already changed the country. For two people whose journey into politics began on that terrible day in 1989, it is hard to put into words what it means to us to be able to say that. I don't think either of us could have imagined how far we could have come in the fifteen years since Steve whispered his invitation to the twentieth anniversary into my ear at Liverpool Cathedral. Perhaps, in the end, that says something positive about our country.

Head North is a book about changing the Westminster system from the outside and importing into it the decency and dignity represented by the Hillsborough families, the survivors and campaigners, and others like them. The fact that, when confronted with their experience, it has been able to look itself in the mirror and commit to change is something worth celebrating. Much more is needed to redistribute power, as we have so often said through the pages of this book. But maybe there are more grounds for hope now that change is coming. Maybe, just maybe, we will one day look back and say that the Hillsborough families' fight changed not only the legal system but the way the entire country is run.

15

Net Zero to a New Economy

During our lives, we have found ourselves in many bleak moments. Throughout these pages, we have tried to describe those experiences from our point of view. Our aim was to bring over to you, our reader, why we see things in the way we do. We want you to understand how people in our part of the world feel about the way things have always been. And yet, it was never our intention to make *Head North* a counsel of despair. We can't forget what has gone before, and never will, but we are genuinely optimistic about what could come next.

What is certain is that, over the next twenty-five years, Britain will have to make major changes to our economy and society as we plot a course to a net zero country. This means we could be on the brink of a period of great possibility and opportunity for the North of England and the other English regions. But only if, as a country, we choose to make it so.

Britain's energy, housing and transport systems will soon have to undergo the biggest overhaul since the privatisations of the 80s. Of course, it could be done on a business-as-usual basis, prolonging the extractive business practices that have been our reality for some time now. Or we could do things differently. We could use this moment to build a new economy and a new society.

We believe that, if we approach this mission as the rewired country we describe in this book, things could turn out very differently than might otherwise be the case. It could be a journey which gives people across the English regions higher-quality and

243

lower-cost public transport; modern homes that are cheaper to rent and cheaper to run; and a plentiful source of highly skilled, secure jobs. To put it another way, we are looking at the best chance we will ever have to reindustrialise the North of England, reduce inequality and close the North–South divide.

I'm in my sixties now and, when I was growing up, people didn't have much knowledge about the damage humans were doing to the planet. Everyone threw absolutely everything into the same rubbish bin. There was no recycling. We were burning coal and driving gas-guzzling cars. Now we know better. I have actually become much more passionate about green issues as I have aged and I am inspired by my own kids who, like so many young people, are leading and showing us oldies the way forward. My children are a huge driving force for me and it is the thought of their future and their children's future that makes this such a priority for me. I am firmly of the belief that we can all play our part, no matter how big or small, and I have tried to lead by example. I gave up my car years ago and use public transport. I am much more environmentally conscious each and every day. My passion for recycling borders on obsessive. But, while it is crucial that we all individually do what we can, Andy and I are now in positions where we can push for wide-ranging and transformational change and we wanted to close this book with a vision for how that green future could look.

The climate crisis has thrust upon us an opportunity to transform the way our economy works and we desperately want to grasp it. We believe that, here in the North West but also across the North more generally, there is scope to use the natural assets we have to drive the battle against climate change while also creating the jobs and the technology that can make the North, and the UK, rise again as a great industrial power. The benefits could be endless. As well as creating new jobs and new skills, we can improve homes and create the green technologies that we could then export to the rest of the world.

The results could be as important socially as they are economically. If you improve public transport and introduce zero emission buses, you incentivise people to give up their cars. The improvements in air quality would relieve pressure on the NHS because fewer people would suffer with respiratory diseases. If you make homes more energy efficient, you incentivise people to use less energy and they will have cheaper bills. If you transition away from fossil fuels in energy intensive industries, you reduce carbon emissions but also create new and innovative jobs. These are all areas where a green economy can drive social change and the North West can be a leader in this. With the right backing, we can do it.

'The North West is the perfect place to build the green economy.' These were the exciting words of the British green energy industrialist Dale Vince, speaking in July 2023, as he presented the findings of a report which Steve and I had asked him to do. We wanted to know the answer to a big question: could the North West become a green energy superpower in the twenty-first century?

The answer that came back from Dale's North West Green Energy Task Force was much more exciting than we could have possibly imagined. In short, due to our geography and natural assets, it concluded that the North West has the potential to produce double the amount of clean, green energy than required for our own needs. In other words, we could become a net exporter of clean energy. The value of that new industry in today's prices? No less than £50 billion per year.

Through a combination of wind (offshore and onshore), solar, green hydrogen and tidal energy production, the North West has a potential energy supply of ninety-two Terawatt-hours (TWh) per year, twice our forecast regional demand of forty-six TWh per year. It is tremendously significant and hopeful news for our region. But the next question is: how do we realise the opportunity while delivering maximum benefit for the North West and its people?

Dale is clear about this. The change to a more localised approach to the way energy is generated and distributed creates an opportunity to change the business model. It would allow new forms of ownership to be introduced into the mix, such as cooperatives and social enterprises, which would keep more of the wealth generated in the North West. Public ownership of big infrastructure, like Steve's tidal barrier, present the same opportunity to recycle the benefits through our communities in the form of lower bills and better homes.

Someone has to lead the green energy revolution in Britain so why can't it be us? After all, we've led an industrial revolution before.

A huge frustration for Andy and me is that we feel the North, a former industrial powerhouse, has not, in our lifetimes, been looked upon by those in power in London in terms of its potential. There is no vision for the North and no industrial strategy for this part of the country.

Let's take our plans for a tidal energy project on the River Mersey. Here we have a credible vision for game-changing infrastructure that could generate enough predictable, renewable energy to power up to a million homes for the next 120 years. But the government has not yet shown any appetite to back this project. Under the current orthodoxy of the Treasury, we have an almost impossible job to make the numbers stack up for a scheme of this scale. If those in the corridors of power in London had more foresight, they would see that this type of innovation could massively help to provide this country with better energy security in the future. And a big worry is that, if we as a country don't do this, then someone else will.

The Burbo Bank offshore wind farm is located in Liverpool Bay in the Irish sea. The wind farm was developed by SeaScape Energy in the early 2000s but was then bought by DONG Energy, now known as Ørsted. The majority shareholder of this company is the Danish government. When the company bought the site, some people thought they were taking a big risk and that they wouldn't be able to compete with other forms of renewable energy at the time. But now wind power is one of the most economically viable ways to generate energy. The profits made from that site, which lies off the coast of Merseyside, are all going back to Denmark. In fact, nearly half of the UK's offshore wind is owned by foreign governments, with a tiny 0.03 per cent owned by British public entities.

This speaks to the point Dale and others are making about public ownership. We have the assets and the potential here in the North West to be a leader in green energy. But it is not just about producing the energy; it is about local communities reaping the rewards from it and that is certainly not happening right now. The worry with the tidal project is that another company, backed by a national government with a more strategic and enlightened focus than ours, could just come in and do it. Our planning laws mean that there would be very little we could do to stop it. We are saying to the UK government: if you don't do this, someone else will. This is the fear we have with a government that so far has refused to provide serious backing to tidal energy.

This should be something for us to get excited about. We could be looking at thousands of skilled jobs; a clean, green future; and a more prosperous outlook for the regions of this country. But none of it works unless we have a government that has a strategic vision for places and the belief to invest in transformational, long-term projects.

There are some compelling reasons why, on the back of Dale's report, the UK government should act now to designate the North West as the UK's green energy trailblazer. We are uniquely placed to deliver. We have the most well-developed regional delivery structures of anywhere in the UK due to the fact that we have been building them together for the last seven years. We both have ambitious but credible plans to take an accelerated path to net zero: 2038 in our case and 2040 in Steve's. If the UK is to have any chance of hitting the 2050 target at a national level, it will need one or two regions to go out ahead of the pack, test the new technologies and build the skills base. Nobody is better placed than us to do that.

So, the opportunity is real – but so is the risk of not acting quickly. Other countries around us are already moving in. For instance, there is significant Danish involvement in the offshore wind projects appearing around our coast. If we dither or fudge it in typical British fashion, others will get there before us.

We simply can't let that happen. Unlike our parents, we have never lived in a time when the North West has been able to identify industries with the potential to give young people good jobs for life. For the first time in our lives, that possibility is now within our reach. We must not lose it.

There are two different routes to net zero: the traditional Whitehall way or a new Northern way. The Whitehall way is to let people pay for the cost of change in the form of requirements, bans, taxes and charges. In Greater Manchester, I resisted attempts by Whitehall to make us introduce a charging Clean Air Zone because I knew it would hit people on the lowest incomes hardest. They would struggle to find the money to upgrade their vehicles and therefore be unable to avoid the charge. If this same approach is applied to decarbonising energy and retrofitting people's homes, we may get to 2050 as a zero carbon country but we will be an even more unequal and divided one than we already are.

The Northern way to net zero is about making it a long-term, true levelling up approach. It is based on the principle of helping people to make the change and, in so doing, speeding it up. For instance, if you retrofit people's homes with clean energy systems and insulation, you can leave them with lower energy bills going forward and a higher standard of living. If you invest in public transport, and decarbonise it, you can get more people using it and that allows you to lower the fares. Crucially, if you go early on these things, you create new industry, better jobs for people and technology and services that can be exported around the world. If those new enterprises are owned locally, the wealth created can be recycled to lift up the lives of those with least.

Steve and I are ready to offer our region as the test bed to prove that the Northern way to net zero is a better way. It could take us to a UK by 2050 which is more prosperous, more equal and more contented. We are fervently hoping that this year brings in a Labour government and that it holds to its commitment to fund a green industrial revolution, investing up to £28 billion a year. We can put real meaning behind the promise to make Britain a clean energy superpower. Steve's plan for a tidal barrier on the River Mersey is hugely exciting. So is Greater Manchester's ambition around a new green hydrogen industry, with production starting later this year. If the next government backs our plan to build 30,000 new zero carbon homes for social rent, we can show how this type of investment across the UK could reduce the housing benefit bill. There is a path to decarbonising our country which at the same time improves people's jobs and homes, fixing those weaknesses exposed by the pandemic. But it requires a new national approach: a decisive move away from the damaging doctrine of the Green Book and the setting of higher ambitions for what the North of England can be in the twenty-first century.

If you have a vision, then from that you can develop the strategy. The government had previously asked combined authorities to put together local industrial strategies and lots of people put huge work into them. But, in 2021, the then business secretary Kwasi Kwarteng scrapped the industrial strategy council and everything that went with it. It would not be his last damaging decision in government.

So the real issue for all of us, not just for the North, is that they don't know what projects could be ripe for investment around the country. They don't know what the emerging and new technologies are in different areas. We have got some of those here and the government are not supporting them. There are a lot of opportunities that are being missed because of this complete lack of engagement.

If you are the first mover in a new technology, it can be very difficult. There may not be a compelling business case based

ANDY BURNHAM & STEVE ROTHERAM

on the Green Book. What we are saying to the government is: you need to take a longer-term view and trust us on this. Work with us and we can develop something important together. But they just pay lip service and nothing tangible comes from it.

One problem for the current government – and its recent incarnations – is that they are so captured by internal politics, and problems of their own making, that they just don't have the bandwidth to look ahead to the future. They just aren't that interested, perhaps because they themselves don't believe they will be in power for much longer.

The country is crying out for change and this is where Labour's plans for a new British Energy Company come in. Keir Starmer has pledged to create a new, publicly owned energy company within the first year of a Labour government, with an aim of 100 per cent clean power by 2030. When it was announced at the 2022 conference in Liverpool, there is a reason why that commitment inspired a huge standing ovation in the conference hall. This is something our country is ready to do and we hope that the North and its natural assets will be right at the heart of that plan.

By contrast, at his conference in 2023, Prime Minister Rishi Sunak performed a screeching U-turn on his government's green commitments. He confirmed the UK would push back the deadline for selling new petrol and diesel cars and the phasing out of gas boilers and promised to cancel some other green policies which didn't even exist. It was a desperate move to try to create dividing lines with Labour and make the green agenda a wedge issue for voters.

The problem with all of this is that it completely misses the big picture: temperatures are changing, the weather is fluctuating and the extremes are getting greater. We need to do something about this now but Sunak wants to kick the can down the road again. He wasn't thinking about the best thing for the country. He was thinking of the best thing for the Tories and that really sticks in my craw. It is another example of how our current political culture works against the long-term interests of the country. It also confirms how much is at stake at the coming general election.

If you look back through the North West's history, you will find an awe-inspiring record of industrial and social innovation. In the 1830s, following the Rainhill trials, our region introduced inter-city rail travel to the world, with the first-ever commuter services between Liverpool and Manchester. We invented the machinery which powered the first industrial revolution and exported that technology around the world.

But the North West way has always been to insist that economic and social progress go hand in hand. In 1819, it was people from across the old Lancashire mill towns who mobilised in support of democratic rights for working people – only to be shot down by the British army in Manchester city centre at what would become known as Peterloo. In 1862, it was Manchester's humble mill-workers who resolved that they would not handle slave-picked cotton and thereby helped bring an end to slavery and the American civil war. In 1868, the trade union movement was founded in our region. In 1918, women in the UK were finally given the right to vote – a fight which had been led from Manchester's streets by the Suffragettes.

When you think of what happened here in the past, it is hugely motivating. You could argue that our part of the world did more to secure the country's social progress than anything Westminster did voluntarily. Then, sometime in the twentieth century, the story changed. Westminster fought back. It decided that the North of England couldn't be much any more. It invited the rest of the country to think the same. It said we would have to accept decline. That has been the story of our lives so far. But that story is over. What we left Westminster to achieve is firmly established. Devolution is irreversible. The North West of England is once again setting a new progressive agenda for the country. We are on the rise again.

If you want to see where a new future for Britain is being forged, head North.

16

The Head North Plan

If *Head North* is to succeed in its aim of being a rallying cry for a more equal Britain, we always knew it would need to provide people with something substantial to rally around. There is, without any doubt, a growing mood for real change across all parts of the country and among voters of all parties. People can see Britain slipping backwards and dislike feeling powerless about it. What has not yet been established is a broad public consensus about the form that change should take. The *Head North* Plan is a serious attempt to fill that void, based on personal experience of Britain's dysfunctional political system at every level.

At the coming general election, the main political parties will doubtless propose new policy fixes for Britain's many challenges. Past experience suggests they will be less likely to focus on constitutional changes. As this book has demonstrated, the root cause of Britain's problems is that its basic wiring doesn't work in the way it should. It concentrates power in too few hands. Therefore, the change required is of a more fundamental character than that which has traditionally been on offer from our political parties.

Through our mayoral elections in May, and at the general election whenever it comes, we will be making the case for the *Head North* Plan. We will be seeking ways in which the public can show support for it too. Each of its ten points involves a transfer of power to people and places and, taken together, are intended to create the conditions for a more functional, fairer country:

1. A Written Constitution

2. A Basic Law

3. Reform of the Voting System

4. Removal of the Whip

5. A Senate of the Nations and Regions

6. Full Devolution

7. Two Equal Paths in Education

8. A Grenfell Law

9. A Hillsborough Law

10. Net Zero to Reindustrialise the North

Epilogue
To Our Grandchildren

This much we know for sure: people and places across the UK will never be equal until we change the way it is run. It's the inescapable conclusion of the story of our lives. From Hillsborough to Tier 3 and HS2, we have lived the experience of being treated as second-class citizens in our own country – looking straight into the eyes of those running it. We desperately don't want the same for you.

We decided to write this book because we wanted to pass on to you all we know. We want you to know how it felt to hear those sneering voices in the corridors of power. And we hope you will carry on what we have tried to start. By describing how the UK was governed in the second half of the last century, and the first quarter of this one, our aim is to empower you and your generation with the knowledge of what is wrong and what needs to change.

Despite everything, we love this country. We hope you will too. It is a brilliant place full of decent people. And yet, it could be so much more if all people and places were treated equally and enabled to achieve their potential.

From our experiences outside of Westminster, we have come to a much better understanding of the feeling long building in Northern Ireland, Wales and Scotland. Many years before us, people there saw a country that doesn't work for them; one that dishes out the same second-class treatment to their residents as has been given to ours; and one that is quick to divide and rule to maintain power at the centre. But, unlike some in those places, we would never advocate for the break-up of the UK. If we believe in anything, it is in unions: unions of people and unions of nations. It would make us proud if you did too. Human progress only comes when people work together and reach out across divides.

We hope that the union that is the United Kingdom survives this century and many after. We also hope that your generation will take us back into the European Union. We also know, though, that both of those things are only likely to happen if Britain becomes a true union where the benefits of working together are more equally shared and there is a greater sense of social contentment across all of its regions and nations. If there is ever to be another Scottish independence referendum, one thing is clear: it must be a choice between independence and a rewired Britain, not independence and the status quo. If it is the latter, it may well signal the end of the UK. Don't let that happen.

In the end, Head North is about a mindset. It is an invitation to our readers to do what we did: to take their heads out of the restricted confines of the current political system and to start imagining a new one, with Northern values at its heart, that would work better for everywhere. We know the big changes we have put forward will take time. They can't be achieved in any one Parliament. This is a big part of the problem: the political parties will always say constitutional changes are not a priority and that is what keeps power in a small number of hands.

But, as we write, we sense things are changing. People are getting ahead of the politicians. The Covid public inquiry has laid bare the dysfunctional nature of the governance of Britain. Everyone can now see how dangerous it was to have so many lives in the hands of so few incompetent and venal politicians.

Our hope is that this book takes that anger and turns it towards solutions. We hope Head North will help build a movement of people over the next twenty-five years which will eventually change Westminster from the outside. By the time we reach the middle of this century – the end of our lives and the start of yours – that movement could have grown so big that real change could then be imminent.

This is why we write this letter to you: your generation could be the one that achieves the rewiring of Britain.

You could be the ones who create a country where another Hillsborough or Grenfell could never happen.

You could make the North of England everything we wanted it to be but never had time to see.

You could create a Britain where people have equal treatment and equal living standards right across its regions and nations.

If you stand for any of that, you will make two old Scousers (and one adopted Manc) immensely proud.

Acknowledgements

Throughout my journey to this point, I have been lucky to work with exceptional people in so many different walks of life, particularly politics, the wider Labour movement, public services, the civil service and the media. To the extent that I have made criticisms in this book, it is almost always of the systems and structures within which people are made to work and not of any of you. You may well recall some of the incidents I describe and your involvement in them. I certainly do. I wish I could mention you all, but I like to think you know who you are. Thank you for helping me along the way. There are stand-out people and institutions to whom I owe a particular debt of thanks for changing the course of my life:

To my English teacher Stephen Harrington and everyone at St Aelred's in the 80s – for putting me on a path to all of this and pointing me in the right direction.

To the great Tony Harrison – for showing me poetry could have a Northern voice.

To everyone at Fitzwilliam College – for giving me a second chance and opening Cambridge University up to the likes of me.

To the people in the unseen roles in the House of Commons – for your warmth, friendship and always making me feel so welcome.

To James Purnell – for believing in me and seeing things others didn't.

To Sally Morgan – for my big break.

To the original Northern Powerhouse David Blunkett – for giving me the best apprenticeship scheme it is possible to imagine.

To Tony Blair – for allowing me to play a part in the positive changes you brought to the country.

To Gordon Brown – for backing me when I needed it most and when my whole world depended upon it.

To Bev Hughes – for being with me every step of the way when we started something new in Greater Manchester, particularly in May 2017, and helping to establish something that is changing the country for the better.

To Kate Green – for joining me on the next stage.

To everyone who has worked for me over the years in Leigh, Westminster and Greater Manchester – for putting up with all of my many flaws and making me look better than I am!

To Tom Whitney – for outstanding advice, support and for sticking with me.

To Kevin Lee – for being there at the beginning and ever since.

To the Hillsborough families – for showing me what true dignity looks like.

To the wonderful people of Leigh – for giving me the privilege of representing you.

HEAD NORTH

To the great people of Greater Manchester – for being the best people you could meet anywhere in the world.

And in loving memory of Tessa Jowell and Paul Goggins – for setting the standard and proving to the rest of us that it is possible to be both a serving politician and a wonderful human being.

I have been particularly lucky in life. I was brought up in a loving home with a loving family who provided the bedrock for the values and principles I have always tried to follow. Although I didn't do well at school, I made up the educational deficit in later life and, like my beautiful mum, am a huge advocate of lifelong learning. Never give up. Education can be wonderful. To the institutions that assisted me I am forever grateful.

There are too many people who have helped me in my career/s. Although some have made it into this book, many have not, and I would like to apologise to anyone left out as you will know how I feel about you. So, thanks for being there.

Along my journey, I have faced many crossroads and have been privileged to meet people who steered me in the right direction. I am fortunate to have been born and have lived most of my life in a place I am immensely proud of and a city with an indomitable spirit. To the people I have represented: as a Councillor in Fazakerley (2002–2011); the Lord Mayor of Liverpool (2008); the MP for Liverpool Walton (2010–2017); and as the Liverpool City Region Metro Mayor (2017–present), thanks for your votes and your trust.

Likewise, there are stand-out people and institutions to whom I am eternally grateful:

To my wider family and friends, some taken far too soon, your support has meant everything to me.

To the football teams, managers and teammates I played with, and for, who I never gave less than 100 per cent to. You are uniquely positioned to understand they were some of the best days in anyone's life.

To all the political staff who have supported my efforts over the years. Thank you for your sage advice and comradeship.

To the Labour Party over many decades. I may not always agree with you, but I will never stop supporting you.

To the volunteers who have helped in my campaigns. You are the unsung heroes.

To health and happiness, save our NHS.

To Jürgen Klopp and the giants that went before him, like the great Bill Shankly who was our manager when I first fell in love with the beautiful game, for unbridled moments of sheer ecstasy (too many to list!).

To Paul Weller, four lads that shook the earth and the bands who made and continue to make the music that is the soundtrack of my life. If music be the food of love, play on...

To Tierney Witty and Liam Thorp for all your considerable efforts (on behalf of us both).

Finally, to the Hillsborough families, campaigners and supporters. You have been an inspiration. I am lucky to have met many of you, but wish it had been in much happier circumstances.

JFT 97

References

Chapter Two

'Mod father of the city':
https://www.liverpoolecho.co.uk/news/liverpool-news/mod-father-of-the-city-3480708

Chapter Three

'Breastfeeding baby upstages lazy Tory favourite':
https://www.theguardian.com/politics/2005/may/24/houseofcommons.politicalcolumnists

'Hillsborough: how stories of disaster police were altered':
https://www.theguardian.com/football/2009/apr/13/hillsborough-disaster-police-south-yorkshire-liverpool

Chapter Four

'Peter Hain resigns after donations now referred to police':
https://www.theguardian.com/politics/2008/jan/24/partyfunding.uk

'Andy Burnham: Stuart-Smith's Hillsborough inquiry had feel of Establishment cover-up':
https://www.liverpoolecho.co.uk/news/nostalgia/andy-burnham-stuart-smiths-hillsborough-inquiry-3334540

'Hillsborough disaster: deadly mistakes and lies that lasted decades':
https://www.theguardian.com/football/2016/apr/26/hillsborough-disaster-deadly-mistakes-and-lies-that-lasted-decades

'Hillsborough: how stories of disaster police were altered':
https://www.theguardian.com/football/2009/apr/13/hillsborough-disaster-police-south-yorkshire-liverpool

Chapter Five

'Andy Burnham gives EU referendum speech':
https://www.ljmu.ac.uk/about-us/news/articles/2016/3/17/andy-
burnham-roscoe-lecture

Chapter Six

'Tensions rising between Liverpool Mayor and Metro Mayor':
https://www.liverpoolecho.co.uk/news/liverpool-news/tensions-rising-
between-liverpool-mayor-13224506

'Two mayors at war over claims Joe Anderson tried to arrange
secret meeting':
https://www.liverpoolecho.co.uk/news/liverpool-news/two-mayors-
war-over-claims-13246519

'Rotheram "excited" as former New York Mayor Michael
Bloomberg offers help for Metro Mayors':
https://lbndaily.co.uk/rotheram-excited-former-new-york-mayor-
michael-bloomberg-offers-help-metro-mayors/

'Thatcher urged "let Liverpool decline" after 1981 riots':
https://www.bbc.co.uk/news/uk-16361170

'Mum whose son was killed in crash wins 8-year fight in his
memory':
https://www.liverpoolecho.co.uk/news/liverpool-news/victory-mum-
whose-son-killed-18600453

'Manchester Arena attack: Key failings of emergency response':
https://www.bbc.co.uk/news/uk-england-manchester-63472531

'An independent public inquiry to investigate the deaths of the
victims of the 2017 Manchester Arena terror attack':
https://manchesterarenainquiry.org.uk/

'"Mancunians forever": Tony Walsh reads out emotional poem at
vigil':
https://www.theguardian.com/global/video/2017/may/23/mancunians-
forever-tony-walsh-reads-poem-manchester-vigil-video

Chapter Seven

Liverpool vs Atlético Madrid:
https://www.liverpoolecho.co.uk/news/liverpool-news/damning-
report-suggests-liverpool-atletico-21836697

'Bigley's fate':
https://www.spectator.co.uk/article/bigley-s-fate/

Chapter Ten

'The contaminated blood scandal':
https://haemophilia.org.uk/public-inquiry/the-infected-blood-inquiry/
the-contaminated-blood-scandal/

'Whips':
https://www.parliament.uk/about/mps-and-lords/principal/whips/

'The Brown commission's proposals on reform of the House of
Lords':
https://constitution-unit.com/2023/03/01/the-brown-commissions-
proposals-on-reform-of-the-house-of-lords/

'How long have we used first past the post?':
https://www.electoral-reform.org.uk/how-long-have-we-used-first-
past-the-post/

'Voters Left Voiceless – The 2019 General Election':
https://www.electoral-reform.org.uk/voters-left-voiceless-the-2019-
general-election/

'How MSPs are elected':
https://www.parliament.scot/msps/about-msps/how-msps-are-elected

Chapter Eleven

'More than 3,000 bus routes cut in past decade':
https://www.bbc.co.uk/news/business-50166423

'UK bus privatisation breached basic rights, says ex-UN rapporteur':
https://www.theguardian.com/politics/2021/jul/19/uk-bus-
privatisation-has-caused-poverty-and-job-losses-says-un

'Ugly concrete stilts could soon tower over Manchester, kill 14,000
jobs and wreck city's "once-in-a-lifetime" chance':
https://www.manchestereveningnews.co.uk/news/greater-manchester-
news/manchester-hs2-crewe-bill-railways-24249977

'Nobody believes me when I tell them how bad TransPennine
Express is':
https://www.theguardian.com/world/2023/may/11/nobody-believes-
me-when-i-tell-them-how-bad-transpennine-express-is

'Revealed: north of England train line vastly under-reports
cancellations':
https://www.theguardian.com/uk-news/2022/nov/27/revealed-north-
of-england-train-line-vastly-under-reports-cancellations

Chapter Thirteen

'Privatising the UK's nationalised industries in the1980s':
https://www.centreforpublicimpact.org/case-study/privatisation-uk-companies-1970s

'The Damaging Legacy of Right to Buy':
https://neweconomics.org/2022/05/the-damaging-legacy-of-right-to-buy

'From Thatcher to Johnson: how right to buy has fuelled a 40-year housing crisis':
https://www.theguardian.com/society/2022/jun/29/how-right-to-buy-ruined-british-housing

'14,000 social homes lost last year, as over a million households sit on waiting lists':
https://england.shelter.org.uk/media/press_release/14000_social_homes_lost_last_year_as_over_a_million_households_sit_on_waiting_lists

'Housing association throws councillors off panel over criticism of plans to demolish landmark flats':
https://www.manchestereveningnews.co.uk/news/greater-manchester-news/housing-association-throws-councillors-panel-23681741

'Grenfell inquiry told government had ideological aversion to red tape':
https://www.theguardian.com/uk-news/2022/mar/30/grenfell-inquiry-told-government-had-ideological-aversion-to-red-tape

'Homelessness in Finland 2020':
https://www.ara.fi/en-US/Materials/Homelessness_reports/Report_2021_Homelessness_in_Finland_2020

'Over a million more health and care staff needed in the next decade to meet growing demand for care':
https://www.health.org.uk/news-and-comment/news/over-a-million-more-health-and-care-staff-needed-in-the-next-decade

Chapter Fifteen

'Can the North West be a green energy superpower':
https://downloads.ctfassets.net/twnesw7vrvq9/5rqSXouPLwLxlqfPGMHl5O/29e128e31650d8d82c476d7dcc41689f/GBF-Report-GreenEnergyTaskForce.pdf